THE NATURE AND DESTINY OF MAN

Volume I: Human Nature

THE NATURE
AND DESTINY OF MAN

A Christian Interpretation

Volume I: Human Nature

Reinhold Niebuhr

Introduction by
Robin W. Lovin

Westminster John Knox Press
LOUISVILLE • LONDON

First edition

Published by Westminster John Knox Press
Louisville, Kentucky

This book is printed on acid-free paper that meets the American National Standards Institute Z39.48 standard. ♾

PRINTED IN THE UNITED STATES OF AMERICA

03 04 05 — 10 9 8 7 6 5 4

Library of Congress Cataloging-in-Publication Data

Niebuhr, Reinhold, 1892–1971.
    The nature and destiny of man : a Christian interpretation /
Reinhold Niebuhr ; introduction by Robin W. Lovin.
        p.   cm. — (Library of theological ethics)
    Originally published as two volumes: New York : C. Scribner's
Sons, 1941–1943.
    Includes index.
    Contents: v. 1. Human nature — v. 2. Human destiny.
    ISBN 0-664-25709-7 (set : alk. paper)

    1. Man (Christian theology)   I. Title.   II. Series.
BT701.N5213 1996
233—dc20   96-32259

To my wife

URSULA

who helped, and

To my children

CHRISTOPHER *and* ELIZABETH

*who frequently interrupted me
in the writing of these pages*

CONTENTS

Library of Theological Ethics
General Editors' Introduction ix

Introduction by Robin W. Lovin xi

Preface to the 1964 Edition xxv

I. MAN AS A PROBLEM TO HIMSELF 1

The Classical View of Man 4
The Christian View of Man 12
The Modern View of Man 18

II. THE PROBLEM OF VITALITY AND FORM
IN HUMAN NATURE 26

The Rationalistic View of Human Nature 30
The Romantic Protest Against Rationalism 33
The Errors of Romanticism 39

III. INDIVIDUALITY IN MODERN CULTURE 54

The Christian Sense of Individuality 57
The Idea of Individuality in the Renaissance 61
Bourgeois Civilization and Individuality 65
The Destruction of Individuality in Naturalism 68
The Loss of the Self in Idealism 74
The Loss of the Self in Romanticism 81

IV. THE EASY CONSCIENCE OF MODERN MAN 93

The Effort to Derive Evil from Specific Historical Sources 96
Nature as a Source of Virtue 104
The Optimism of Idealism 112

V. THE RELEVANCE OF THE CHRISTIAN VIEW OF MAN   123

Individual and General Revelation   125
Creation as Revelation   131
Historical and Special Revelation   136

VI. MAN AS IMAGE OF GOD AND AS CREATURE   150

Biblical Basis of the Doctrines   151
The Doctrine of Man as Creature   167

VII. MAN AS SINNER   178

Temptation and Sin   179
The Sin of Pride   186
The Relation of Dishonesty to Pride   203

VIII. MAN AS SINNER (CONTINUED)   208

The Equality of Sin and the Inequality of Guilt   219
Sin as Sensuality   228

IX. ORIGINAL SIN AND MAN'S RESPONSIBILITY   241

Pelagian Doctrines   245
Augustinian Doctrines   248
Temptation and Inevitability of Sin   251
Responsibility Despite Inevitability   255
Literalistic Errors   260

X. JUSTITIA ORIGINALIS   265

Essential Nature and Original Righteousness   269
The Locus of Original Righteousness   276
The Content of Justitia Originalis as Law   280
The Transcendent Character of Justitia Originalis   296

Index of Scriptural Passages   303
Index of Proper Names   303
Index of Subjects   304

LIBRARY OF THEOLOGICAL ETHICS

General Editors' Introduction

The field of theological ethics possesses in its literature an abundant inheritance concerning religious convictions and the moral life, critical issues, methods, and moral problems. The Library of Theological Ethics is designed to present a selection of important texts that would otherwise be unavailable for scholarly purposes and classroom use. The series will engage the question of what it means to think theologically and ethically. It is offered in the conviction that sustained dialogue with our predecessors serves the interests of responsible contemporary reflection. Our more immediate aim in offering it, however, is to enable scholars and teachers to make more extensive use of classic texts as they train new generations of theologians, ethicists, and ministers.

The volumes included in the Library will comprise a variety of types. Some will make available English-language texts and translations that have fallen out of print; others will present new translations of texts previously unavailable in English. Still others will offer anthologies or collections of significant statements about problems and themes of special importance. We hope that each volume will encourage contemporary theological ethicists to remain in conversation with the rich and diverse heritage of their discipline.

ROBIN W. LOVIN
DOUGLAS F. OTTATI
WILLIAM SCHWEIKER

INTRODUCTION

[A] free society prospers best in a cultural, religious, and moral atmosphere which encourages neither a too pessimistic nor a too optimistic view of human nature.[1]

—Reinhold Niebuhr (1959)

The Nature and Destiny of Man offers a sweeping review of philosophy, religion, and politics. Hebrew and Christian scriptures, classical and contemporary philosophy, the Romanticism of nineteenth-century idealism, Marxist materialism, and more are drawn together in an account of "Human Nature" and "Human Destiny." Like all of Reinhold Niebuhr's works, the scope of *The Nature and Destiny of Man* reflects the author's genius, but its power comes from the specificity of its message. The work we have today began as Niebuhr's Gifford Lectures, delivered at the University of Edinburgh in 1939. As another war with Germany began to seem inevitable, Niebuhr's British audience drew strength from his summary of the contributions Western thought had made to human self-understanding, and from his spirited defense of the Christian interpretation of the human condition. It was a time when people needed to see historic choices in large terms, not in order to inhabit the whole range of human possibilities, but so that they might know exactly where they stood in the present.

Reinhold Niebuhr was well prepared to give that orientation, first to the audience in Edinburgh, and then to the wider readership of the published lectures.[2] Born in 1892 in Missouri, he had grown to maturity in Lincoln, Illinois, and studied at Elmhurst College and Yale Divinity School. In 1915, he became pastor of Bethel Evangelical Church in Detroit, where he learned firsthand about the racial conflicts and labor unrest that strained America's growing cities in the years after World War I. By the late 1920s, he had a growing reputation as a preacher, writer, and political activist. In 1928, he joined the faculty of Union Theological Seminary in the City of New York. The publication of *Moral Man and Immoral Society*[3] in 1932 made him a dominant voice in Protestant social ethics.

Niebuhr's work reflected the emerging shape of his discipline in the theological schools of North America. Niebuhr and his colleagues were more engaged with contemporary social problems than their European counterparts, and they were as much committed to the emerging methods of the social sciences as to the traditions of moral theology.

Yet Reinhold Niebuhr also maintained strong ties with European theologians, and he traveled extensively in Germany during the 1920s. Better than most North Americans, Niebuhr understood that the communist revolutions and nationalistic dictatorships that had changed the political landscape of Europe were not simply the results of events since 1914. Communism and fascism were both deeply rooted in the hopes and dreams of European Romantics early in the nineteenth century, and each movement in its way illustrated the tragic failure of human beings to grasp the complexity of their own situation. Niebuhr began to think that those who might in the future have to contend against Marxism and fascism in a decisive conflict would do well to attend to the complexities of social and historical reality, rather than relying on an overly simple vilification of their enemies and an exaggerated confidence in their own virtue.

CHRISTIAN REALISM

Attentiveness to the powers and interests that shape events was central to the "realism" that Niebuhr and other social ethicists proposed in the years of economic dislocation and political disillusionment that followed World War I. The call for "religious realism" or a "realistic theology" originated with a small group that had ties to Yale Divinity School and included Reinhold Niebuhr, his brother H. Richard Niebuhr, their teacher at Yale, D. C. Macintosh, Walter Marshall Horton, and others. To these younger theologians, the Social Gospel movement, which had sometimes believed too easily that moral exhortation would lead people to work for justice, now seemed hopelessly sentimental. *Moral Man and Immoral Society* examined the cherished beliefs of middle-class morality and exposed the self-interest behind it moral commitments to law and to the protection of property rights. But he took an equally skeptical view of the revolutionary ethics of the poor and powerless. "The conflict between proletarian and middle-class morality is thus a contest between hypocrisy and brutality, and between sentimentality and cynicism."[4]

Realism as Niebuhr understood it, however, included more than this frank acknowledgment of the pervasive rule of self-interest, although that was the most obvious and most controversial part of his analysis in *Moral Man and Immoral Society*. A realist would never expect moral commands to love one's neighbor to overcome the forces of self-interest and power all by themselves, but a realist like Reinhold Niebuhr would never forget that moral ideas and faith commitments are also real and exert their own pressures on the course of events.

Niebuhr came to use the name "Christian Realism" for this attentiveness *all* of the realities at work in social change and conflict. The Christian Realist begins, as *Moral Man and Immoral Society* suggests, with *political realism*, identifying the forms of economic and political power at work in history: The majority use the power of numbers to press their claims for a more egalitarian justice against those whose privileged positions rest on the power of wealth. The wealthy respond with their own claims to a just reward for the resources they make available to the whole society. In this, they always claim more reward than strict justice requires, but their adversaries concede them less than they deserve. A realist expects no final resolution to these conflicts, but a stable society must establish a work equilibrium between the claims of liberty and equality, freedom and order, or need and merit.

Niebuhr developed a great knowledge of politics, and he could trace these themes through Western history with considerable erudition.[5] Political insight alone, however, does not explain the widespread interest in his work or the esteem in which he was held by scholars and political leaders whose knowledge and experience clearly exceeded his own. Niebuhr's great achievement was what we might call a *moral realism*, which connects the shifting forces in political conflict to deeper, more lasting currents in human nature. Many other commentators could draw connections between individual motivation and actions, or account for events in terms of the character of a nation and its people. The crisis in Europe, for example, could be explained by Adolf Hitler's limitless ambition, or by the inflexiblity of German national pride. Niebuhr gave such interpretations a more nuanced and universal form, so that motives and actions were never pure manifestations of good or evil, and every fault of the evil or the enemy could be related to some more basic form of pride or will to power that all people share.

Mapping the complex moral realities that shape our politics and our history is the primary task of the first part of *The Nature and Destiny of Man*, ten chapters on human nature that formulate the tensions and balances necessary to a full description of human life. Human beings require both vitality and form. Life asserts itself against all imposed limits, yet quickly dies when deprived of structure. Human beings are characterized by both freedom and finitude. They have an imaginative grasp of possibilities that can never be confined to the given conditions of their lives, and yet their creativity always reflects the place where they begin, and their capacity for change is profoundly limited. "Man knows more than the immediate natural situation in which he stands, and he constantly seeks to understand his immediate situation in terms of a total situation. Yet he is unable to define the total human situation without colouring his definition with finite perspectives drawn from his immediate situation."[6]

The motives that shape the action of leaders and peoples alike are drawn from the complexity of this human situation, and the tragedies of history arise when we oversimplify our situation to conceal these ambiguities from others or to convince ourselves that we have somehow escaped them. "[M]an is tempted to deny the limited character of his knowledge, and the finiteness of his perspectives. He pretends to have achieved a degree of knowledge which is beyond the limit of finite life. This is the 'ideological taint' in which all human knowledge is involved, and which is always something more than mere human ignorance. It is always partly an effort to hide that ignorance by pretension."[7]

Niebuhr's moral realism thus provides the starting point for the analysis of ideas and movements in his political realism. But the moral realism, in turn, rests on a *theological realism*. That is, we can truly understand the characteristic possibilities and limits that must guide our lives and the life of society only if we also know the limits of that understanding. Awareness of human nature must grow in ways that point us to a source of understanding that lies beyond ourselves:

> This ability to stand outside and beyond the world, tempts man to megalomania and persuades him to regard himself as the god around and about whom the universe centres. Yet he is too obviously involved in the flux and finiteness of nature to make such pretensions plausibly. The real situation is that he has an environment of eternity which he cannot know through the mere logical ordering of his experience. . . . The only principle for the comprehension of the whole (the whole which includes both himself and his world) is therefore inevitably beyond his comprehension. Man is thus in the position of being unable to comprehend himself in his full stature of freedom without a principle of comprehension which is beyond his comprehension.[8]

Many things will answer to this need for a "principle of comprehension beyond our comprehension." The identification of this principle with biblical faith is established by a rather specific sort of extended argument. (Just what sort of argument it is we will consider more fully in the next section of this Introduction.) The important thing to note for the present is that for Niebuhr, political and moral insight are bound up inseparably with the reality of God, who both calls us to freedom and sets limits on it. The political scientists of Niebuhr's day who jocularly proclaimed themselves "Atheists for Niebuhr"[9] because they admired his political analysis and were baffled by his theology perhaps did not understand how closely the politics and the theology were connected in his own thinking. A large part of *The Nature and Destiny of Man* is devoted to tracing those connections and making them explicit. In this work, perhaps more than in any other Niebuhr wrote, it become clear that "Christian Realism" is more than a set of opinions on the issues of the day. It is a synthesis of political, moral, and theological reflection, in which the undeniability of human freedom and the inescapability of its limits are the twin realities that together form a framework for understanding both the multiplicity of our specific choices and the ultimate unity of the environment in which they all take place.

"A CHRISTIAN INTERPRETATION"

Niebuhr gives *The Nature and Destiny of Man* the subtitle "A Christian Interpretation," and he begins the work with a statement that shows how difficult any comprehensive interpretation of our human nature must be: "Man has always been his own most vexing problem. How shall he think of himself? Every affirmation which he may make about his stature, virtue, or place in the cosmos becomes involved in contradictions when fully analyzed. The analysis reveals some presupposition or implication that seems to deny what the proposition intended to affirm."[10]

Much is suggested in this opening passage about the twenty chapters that follow. The problem of the study is not framed in theological terms: "Is there a God?" "What is the nature of God?" The problem is human self-understanding, but concealed within that problem, Niebuhr suggests, are all the other problems we create for ourselves—violence and domination, creativity and tragedy, morality, self-centeredness, cynicism, foolishness, and hope. What we do as individuals and as a society is an expression of the self as we understand it, or, more often, the product of a characteristic *mis*-understanding that distorts the self that is seeking to understand itself.

The Nature and Destiny of Man explores the Christian Realist's way of dealing with these issues, but it also makes a case for this understanding of the Christian faith. We not only learn the Christian Realist's answer to this "most vexing problem." We get reasons for accepting that this is the right answer.

It is important to understand how Niebuhr makes that case in order to understand the structure he has given to the book, which moves from the first part, "Human Nature," to a second part, also composed of ten chapters, titled "Human Destiny." The progression is from a detailed account of human life that contrasts the Christian interpretation with the alternatives offered by ancient and modern cultures (Part I) to an interpretation of Christian eschatology that points to the limits of even our most successful attempts to understand history as a whole (Part II). In the process, we see how Niebuhr makes the case for Christian Realism.

Although the endowment of the Gifford Lectures originated in a provision in Lord Gifford's will that they should deal with the problems of natural theology, Niebuhr does not make an argument that attempts to prove points about the existence, nature, and purposes of God by means of logical argument. The Christian account of our experience of freedom and finitude is not dictated by logic alone. Niebuhr's conclusions rarely follow from his evidence with the force of logical necessity, as his critics among the philosophers were quick to point out.

Niebuhr's link between Christian faith and ordinary experience is rather, as his subtitle alerts us, an interpretation. He resolves the problem of freedom and finitude by interpreting it through the Christian idea of sin. The anxiety that we all feel upon recognizing our own finitude provokes us to deny that finitude and magnify our freedom. That attempt to become the source of our own security epitomizes what Christians have called "sin," turning away from the true God to other gods of our own making. The only resolution to this tension in which one element of our nature—our freedom—is at war with another—our finitude—is a complete trust in God which alleviates all anxiety and thus relieves us of the need to make ourselves the object of our trust.[11]

This is not the only interpretation of the problem of finitude and freedom, nor is it the simplest. A Romantic idealist or a cynical materialist would offer other interpretations, quite different from the one that Niebuhr proposes. When he concedes that the Christian interpretation cannot be established with logical necessity, he does not mean for us to think that all interpretations are equal, or that the choice between them is arbitrary. Conclusive proof is not available, but we are not left simply to choose blindly between the competing interpretations of our human situation. Writing some years after *The Nature and Destiny of Man*, Niebuhr explained the sense in which we can establish an argument for the Christian understanding:

> Nevertheless, a limited rational validation of the truth of the Gospel is possible. It consists of a negative and a positive approach to the relation of the truth of the Gospel to other forms of truth, and of the goodness of perfect love to historic forms of virtue. Negatively, the Gospel must and can be validated by exploring the limits of historic forms of wisdom and virtue. Positively, it is validated when the truth of faith is correlated with all truths which may be known by scientific and philosophical disciplines and proves itself a resource for coordinating them into a deeper and wider system of coherence.[12]

Niebuhr adheres to the Christian interpretation because he finds it superior to the other interpretations that are available, and he thinks he can explain that preference in terms that will make sense to others. To do so requires, however, a complex system of interpretations, taking up both the central meaning of the Christian faith and alternative ways of understanding the human situation, always with a view to that "vexing problem" that human beings put to themselves. Toward the beginning of *The Nature and Destiny of Man*, Niebuhr explains this method succinctly: "[We] shall seek, on the one hand, to trace the various efforts within the Christian faith, to state the logic of this Biblical doctrine clearly against the constant perils of confusing admixtures from other, partially contradictory, views of man. On the other hand, we must seek to validate the Christian view by measuring the adequacy of its answer for human problems which other views have ignored or confused."[13]

In this complex interpretation, there is no one fixed point from which all the rest may be determined. Each step in the interpretation calls for critical judgment. The biblical understanding of human nature centers on the paradoxical relationship between the self-transcending freedom which human beings have because they are "made in the image of God" and the inescapable limitations which they encounter because they are finite creatures and not God.[14] Each attempt to state the "logic" of this biblical understanding involves separating what is integral to the biblical view from the other viewpoints that are commingled with it, sometimes quite appealingly.[15] The formulation of the biblical understanding is also influenced by the specific alternative views to which it is juxtaposed. The Christian Realist will formulate Christian doctrine differently to deal with a sentimental idealist's belief in the inevitability of human progress or to answer a cynical political realist's reduction of everything to a question of power. In that sense, there is a "logic" that governs Christian interpretations of events, but there is no definitive formulation of the Christian understanding of human nature against which all other interpretations might be judged. The standard is one of relative adequacy to the human needs that we bring to the situation, and relative coherence with all the other things that we think we know by means of other scientific and philosophical methods.

THE CHRISTIAN REALIST
AND THE CHRISTIAN FAITH

The relationship which Niebuhr sets up between the Christian Realist who interprets Christian doctrine and the doctrine which is interpreted is distinctive, and it requires further exploration if we are to understand the argument of *The Nature and Destiny of Man*. Reinhold Niebuhr sometimes found it important to his own identity to deny that he was a theologian, preferring to call himself a "teacher of social ethics."[16] He meant by that perhaps to be modest in his claims to understand the theological debates that preoccupied some of his colleagues, but his statement also points to the diversity of sources and perspectives that were important to his interpretive task. He drew heavily on theology, church history, and biblical studies in *The Nature and Destiny of Man*, but he also relied on political theory, philosophy, social science, and law, and in many of his shorter works, explicit theological questions were eclipsed by political and economic issues.[17]

During the years after World War I, Protestant theologians both in Europe and in North America sought to disentangle core Christian beliefs from the ideas about national destiny, racial superiority, or the inevitability of human progress with which Christian faith had often been fused during the nineteenth century. Niebuhr's effort "to state the logic of this Biblical doctrine clearly against the constant perils of confusing admixtures from other, partially contradictory, views of man" reflects this more general concern among his contemporaries, but Niebuhr's way of approaching this goal was often quite different from theirs.

Karl Barth insisted that theology must become a "science of faith," proceeding like other systems of knowledge from its own first premises and refusing judgment on any issues which cannot be addressed from that starting point.[18] The theologian must rely only on the Word of God. Outside of that, theology has nothing to say.

Subsequent theologians have put less emphasis than Barth did on the positive content of theology, but they have also suggested that theologians do their proper work within a framework of discourse that is distinctive to the community of Christian faith. George Lindbeck speaks of a "grammar" of Christian doctrine that determines how language about God is properly used within the Christian community.[19] Apart from that grammar, we have no way to know whether a theological assertion makes sense or not. To do social ethics in that context is primarily a matter of understanding the Christian community as the embodiment of social ethics in itself. The Christian narrative which the community shares gives rise to distinctive virtues which fit its members for its own life.[20] That shared life bears witness to a possibility that sets the Christian community apart from others, but the beliefs which sustain it cannot really be weighed and tested against alternatives. To understand Christian doctrine, one must know how to use the "grammar" on which it is constructed. It is pointless to ask how some other system of beliefs would fare if we tried to apply the same set of rules to it. One might as well ask whether a sentence of English words ordered by Hebrew grammar is true. Neither the question nor the sentence makes any sense.

Niebuhr's interpretative method sets up a very different relationship between the interpreter and the Christian faith. The "logic"of the biblical doctrine, or its "grammar," if you prefer (both Niebuhr's term and Lindbeck's are metaphors for the implicit rules by which we distinguish sense from nonsense in statements of the Christian faith) is not the only language that the believer knows. That is why we so often confuse the biblical understanding of human nature with other ideas that are widely shared in the culture. The fact that we know more than one "logic" or "grammar," however, also makes it possible to interpret the biblical doctrine to others (and sometimes to ourselves) by recasting its insights in terms drawn from psychology, or to understand the analogies between the slavery of the Hebrew people in Egypt and the slavery of African Americans before the Civil War, or to connect the care for the widow and the orphan that the biblical prophets enjoin with a societal responsibility for people who are economically vulnerable today. The very possibility of the "limited rational validation of the truth of the Gospel" which Niebuhr undertakes depends on a framework of discourse that is broader than the "logic" of Christian doctrine. Without that, we can explain neither the problems Christians have understanding what their faith means, nor the fact that they *do* understand it well enough to distinguish it from the alternatives.

Those who undertake to explain biblical faith and draw out its implications for contemporary life do this precisely by understanding the alternatives. Their confidence grows with experience, as the alternatives they explore consistently fail to guide actions and explain situations as well as the Christian interpretation does. At first, their intellectual commitment may be tentative and their ability to distinguish between biblical faith and other beliefs and values may be limited. Over time, the content of Christian teaching and its specific points of difference with other systems become better defined, and the intellectual identification between the believer and the beliefs grows closer. But it is important for Niebuhr that this identification is never complete. The interpretative task continues indefinitely, and Christian Realism's conviction of the "adequacy of its answer for human problems" depends on at least a measure of sympathy for the experiences that make other beliefs plausible to other people.

HUMAN DESTINY

In Niebuhr's theology, the final argument that would prove the case for Christian Realism and close the books on the alternatives always eludes us. This is not because the Christian Realist is weak in faith or a weak advocate for what faith today requires. Niebuhr himself gave tremendous energy to political causes and the audience for his Gifford Lectures did not hear a doubtful or ambiguous message. The lectures on "Human Destiny" began on October 11, 1939, a little over a month after the outbreak of World War II. Richard Fox recounts the effect they had on the listeners:

> [D]espite the war the audience remained faithful—even after Edinburgh itself was bombed in the middle of his third lecture. . . . Niebuhr was so wrapped up in his message that he heard nothing; he thought [the audience] were squirming about something he had said. [John] Baillie was surprised they came back for the rest of the lectures. But they probably stuck it out precisely because these were not standard Gifford lectures; they were inspirational if sometimes dense sermons on the Christian view of human destiny. If bombs were going to fall it made sense to make time three afternoons a week for some stirring reflections that went beyond tragedy.[21]

The incomplete case for Christianity that *The Nature and Destiny of Man* provides does not reflect any lack of conviction on Niebuhr's part. Rather, he believed that the biblical doctrine itself requires the incompleteness.

The chapters on "Human Destiny" point to a fulfillment of history that must lie outside of history. We can give some meaning to events by understanding the forces deep within human nature that drive these events. We can rise above tragedy by finding larger meanings that survive the loss of life and the destruction of things that we deeply value. But nothing that happens within history can clear up all of its ambiguities or turn its tragedies to triumphs. In cultures and religions where expectations of history are bounded by history, Niebuhr suggests, the inevitable conclusion is that history is meaningless. Mysticism and materialism offer relief by facing this meaninglessness frankly. Beliefs that hope for more than the consolation of an ultimate escape from history must, however, find a point beyond history on which to pin their hopes.

The paradigm case of this hope is the Messianic hope of biblical religion. But the specific way in which Christianity finds this Messianic hope fulfilled shows why the ultimate fulfillment must lie beyond history.

> [Christ] may be a stumblingblock because, though expected, he proves not to be the kind of a Messiah who was expected. In fact one can assert dogmatically that the true Christ *must* be a stumblingblock in the sense that he must disappoint, as well as fulfill, expectations. He must disappoint some expectations because Messianic expectations inevitably contain egoistic elements, which could

not be fulfilled without falsifying the meaning of history. Every Messianic expectation contains an explicit or implicit assumption that history will be fulfilled from the particular locus of the civilization and culture which has the expectation.[22]

In other words, the very embeddedness of faith in history which makes interpretation necessary also ensures that no interpretation can achieve its implicit goal of making history meaningful from every perspective. The central claim of Christianity, that Jesus fulfilled the Messianic expectations of biblical faith precisely by disappointing them, decisively sets aside all claims to complete the project of giving meaning to history from within history. Neither our interpretations nor our actions can aspire to finality. Once this is clearly understood, the Christian Realist will try to disabuse those who think they have achieved a final answer of their illusions, and will join in efforts to liberate those who have been exploited by the people who hold these illusions.

Niebuhr opposes the shrill certainty of theologies that claim to have the last word, of course, but the most important problem in his writing is not Messianic certainty in religion, but the forms which that certainty takes in politics. Increasingly, after the publication of *The Nature and Destiny of Man*, his writing is directed against Hitler's claims to have fulfilled the historical destiny of the German people, and against Marxist claims to have achieved the final political revolution that will make further political change impossible.

For that reason, too, Niebuhr turns his attention to political questions of tolerance and justice toward the close of his chapters on "Human Destiny."[23] If no form of government can overcome the ambiguities of history, then the task of Christian Realists must be to craft a way of living with those uncertainties and ambiguities in a political community. The demand that every political problem yield to a specific Christian solution betrays a lack of faith, because it insists that God's sovereignty over all of history must take a determinate cultural form within history. Christian Realism, by contrast, supports the checks and balances of constitutional democracy as the most appropriate form of government for human beings whose self-transcending freedom enables them to anticipate a meaningful history, even though their finitude ensures that they will never achieve it.

The measured affirmation of democracy in *The Nature and Destiny of Man* spoke to the needs of wartime political leaders who believed that their struggle against Nazism had moral and even religious dimensions, but who wanted to avoid the promise of a final conflict to "make the world safe for democracy" that led to so much disillusionment after the previous war. Niebuhr's realistic assessment of democracy as a system of government that can accommodate the moral uncertainty of history offered a plausible interpretation of events to those who faced the discipline and sacrifices of years of global warfare. It allowed them to believe in what they were doing without having to believe too much in their own virtue or to expect too much from their eventual victory.

CHRISTIAN REALISM AFTER "NATURE AND DESTINY"

Niebuhr drew out further implications of his interpretation of human nature for democratic politics in *The Children of Light and the Children of Darkness,* which was first published in 1944, and he wrote many essays on politics during the transition from World War II to the Cold War conflict with Soviet Communism.[24] By the end of the 1940s, he was internationally known not only as a theologian but as a political analyst whose interpretations pointed the way to a form of democracy that could deal with the real evils that threatened it and that did not rest its future on exaggerated hopes for human progress.

Because of Niebuhr's repeated warnings against expecting too much from our efforts to secure freedom and justice, Christian Realism was seen by many as a pessimistic way of looking at human nature and society. When *Time* magazine featured Reinhold Niebuhr on the cover of its twenty-fifth anniversary issue in 1948, it included along with the portrait a caption that read, "Man's story is not a success story."[25]

Niebuhr would certainly reject an interpretation of human history as a "success," a simple story of human progress. Christian Realism, however, is neither optimistic nor pessimistic. It accepts the ambiguity in human possibilities that follows inevitably from the tension between freedom and finitude in human nature. At the end of the twentieth century, there are few theologians who could share the conviction of the Social Gospel that humanity is on the verge of a social transformation that will realize the ancient promise of the Kingdom of God, nor would many political analysts any longer chart a future based on the inevitable progress of Western democracy and modern science. The alternative understandings of human nature against which Niebuhr had shaped his interpretation of the logic of the biblical doctrine have faded from the scene, swept away by the tide of events, but also in part by the very success of Niebuhr's argument that a human "success story" is impossible.

The logic of *The Nature and Destiny of Man* might seem to require at this point a new interpretation of Christian Realism which would remind a more pessimistic generation that "Man's freedom over the limits of nature in indeterminate regression means that no fixed limits can be placed on either the purity or the breadth of the brotherhood for which men strive in history."[26] For a variety of reasons, however, Christian Realism has remained associated in the minds of many readers with the limitations on social progress and institutional virtue which Niebuhr sought to impress on our consciousness at mid-century.

One reason for the persistence of these Niebuhrian formulations is that Niebuhr himself was not able to provide the necessary reassessment. His prodigious activity and literary output slackened after an illness in 1952 left him partly paralyzed, and although he continued to teach until his retirement from Union Theological Seminary in 1960, there would be no more works with the scope and system of *The Nature and Destiny of Man.*

By the time of his death in 1971, Niebuhr's work so dominated the memory of his time that for most scholars in social ethics, Christian Realism simply meant the judgments and opinions that Reinhold Niebuhr had held on the issues of the day. Once Niebuhr had passed from the scene, these opinions became a benchmark against which subsequent writers measured their progress. Niebuhr had worked for racial justice since his early days as a pastor in Detroit, but from the perspective of the 1970s, his cautious warnings in the 1950s against expecting too much too soon from the Supreme Court's school desegregation decisions seemed to confirm the impression of some African American ethicists that Christian Realism was inherently conservative, unable to sympathize with the urgency and anger in their community.[27] Similarly, Niebuhr could hardly have guessed, even in 1971, how soon the very terminology of *The Nature and Destiny of Man* would become a signal for critical reassessment by feminist theologians and ethicists. The noninclusive language of the quotations from Niebuhr used in this Introduction calls attention to itself sharply when we read it today, and whatever we may think that Niebuhr would write if he were alive now, the discrepancy between his language and ours reminds us that twenty-five years after his death, Reinhold Niebuhr is no longer our contemporary.

As that distance in time increases, however, new possibilities emerge. Instead of treating *The Nature and Destiny of Man* as the definitive statement of Christian Realism, we can begin to read it by the method that Niebuhr himself proposed in its pages. We must state the "logic" of the Christian Realist understanding of human nature clearly, and separate out the "confusing admixtures from other, partially contradictory" views that Niebuhr himself may have held. Then, we must again for our time measure "the adequacy of its answer for human problems which other views have ignored or confused."

The array of problems will be different from those which Reinhold Niebuhr faced. The end of the Cold War and the collapse of the bipolar superpower confrontation have changed beyond recognition the global landscape Niebuhr knew. New problems of environmental degradation and new economic relationships on a global scale have altered the balances he described, and new voices he could not have anticipated now cry for attention.

Yet beyond these limitations in Niebuhr's work which we can now see, his lasting contribution to Christian thought also becomes more clear. His realistic insistence that we attend both to human freedom and to human finitude may serve the future as well as his own writing served the past. His emphasis on the realities of power served to correct the optimistic assumptions of our culture at the beginning of the century. Now, in a time that seems dominated by the failures of technology and a fear of human limits, Christian Realism may require more emphasis on human possibility than Niebuhr's own writings usually allow. His insistence that we understand ourselves both as finite creatures of God and as created in God's own image will, however, continue to provide directions for Christian social ethics.

ROBIN W. LOVIN

NOTES

1. Reinhold Niebuhr, *The Children of Light and the Children of Darkness* (New York: Charles Scribner's Sons, 1972), viii.

2. *The Nature and Destiny of Man* was first published in two volumes, in 1941 and 1943, by Charles Scribner's Sons, New York. A paperback edition, with a new preface by Niebuhr, was published in 1964.

3. Reinhold Niebuhr, *Moral Man and Immoral Society* (New York: Charles Scribner's Sons, 1932).

4. *Moral Man and Immoral Society*, 177.

5. See, for example, the essay "Liberty and Equality," in Reinhold Niebuhr, *Pious and Secular America* (New York: Charles Scribner's Sons, 1958), 185–98.

6. *The Nature and Destiny of Man*, I, 182.

7. Ibid.

8. *The Nature and Destiny of Man*, I, 124–25.

9. See Daniel F. Rice, *Reinhold Niebuhr and John Dewey: An American Odyssey* (Albany, N.Y.: SUNY Press, 1993), 217.

10. *The Nature and Destiny of Man*, I, 1.

11. *The Nature and Destiny of Man*, I, 287–95.

12. Reinhold Niebuhr, *Faith and History: A Comparison of Christian and Modern Views of History* (New York: Charles Scribner's Sons, 1949), 152.

13. *The Nature and Destiny of Man*, I, 150–51.

14. *The Nature and Destiny of Man*, I, 150–77.

15. This interpretative distinction must begin with the interpretation of the biblical text itself, where elements of other systems of belief can be found in tension with the Bible's core understanding of the human being as both image of God and finite creature.

16. Reinhold Niebuhr, "Intellectual Autobiography," in Charles W. Kegley and Robert W. Bretall, eds., *Reinhold Niebuhr: His Religious, Social, and Political Thought* (New York: Macmillan Co., 1956), 3.

17. See the essays collected in D. B. Robertson, ed., *Love and Justice: Selections from the Shorter Writings of Reinhold Niebuhr* (Louisville, Ky.: Westminster/John Knox Press, 1992).

18. Karl Barth, *Anselm: Fides Quarens Intellectum* (London: SCM Press, 1960), 26–30.

19. George Lindbeck, *The Nature of Doctrine* (Philadelphia: Westminster Press, 1984).

20. See, for example, Stanley Hauerwas, *Against the Nations: War and Survival in a Liberal Society* (Minneapolis: Winston Press, 1985), 11–12.

21. Richard Fox, *Reinhold Niebuhr: A Biography* (New York: Pantheon Books, 1985), 191.

22. *The Nature and Destiny of Man*, II, 16.

23. *The Nature and Destiny of Man*, II, 247–84.

24. See, for example, Reinhold Niebuhr, *Christian Realism and Political Problems* (New York: Charles Scribner's Sons, 1953).

25. See Fox, *Reinhold Niebuhr*, 233.

26. Niebuhr, *The Nature and Destiny of Man*, II, 244.

27. Herbert O. Edwards, "Racism and Christian Ethics in America," *Katallagete* (winter 1971), 15–24.

PREFACE TO THE 1964 EDITION

The Gifford Lectures, delivered in Edinburgh about a quarter century ago and embodied in the two volumes entitled "Human Nature" and "Human Destiny," were devoted to the thesis that the two main emphases of Western culture, namely the sense of individuality and the sense of a meaningful history, were rooted in the faith of the Bible and had primarily Hebraic roots. It was my purpose to trace the growth, corruption and purification of these two concepts in the ages of Western history in order to create a better understanding between the historic roots and the several disciplines of our modern culture which were concerned with the human situation.

In regard to the Western emphasis on the individual, my thesis, which I still hold, was that individual selfhood is expressed in the self's capacity for self-transcendence and not in its rational capacity for conceptual and analytic procedures. Thus a consistent idealism and a consistent naturalism both obscure the dimension of selfhood, the former by equating the self with universal reason (as in Plato and Hegel) and the latter by reducing the self to an unfree nature not capable of viewing itself and the world from the position transcending the flow of events, causes and sequences.

The second Biblical-Hebraic emphasis about human selfhood was the unity of the self in its body, mind and spirit, in its freedom from natural necessity and in its involvement as creature in all these necessities. This unity was obscured in all forms of dualism, of which that of Descartes is a convenient example, which cut the self into two entities, body and mind, or body and spirit. The unity of the self can only be expressed in poetic, religious and metaphorical symbols.

Since the delivery of these lectures modern "ego-psychology," particularly as elaborated by my friend Erik Erikson, has developed this paradoxical position of the self scientifically. I agree with this position, but it would have prompted some changes in my statement of the reality.

The third problem about human selfhood has to do with its moral stature. I believed and still believe that human evil, primarily expressed in undue self-concern, is a corruption of its essential freedom and grows with its freedom. Therefore, every effort to equate evil purely with the ignorance of the mind and with the passions of the body is confusing and erroneous. I used the traditional religious symbols of the "Fall" and of "original sin" to counter these conceptions. My only regret is that I did not realize that the legendary character of the one and the dubious connotations of the other would prove so offensive to the modern mind, that my use of them obscured my essential thesis and my "realistic" rather than "idealistic" interpretation of human nature.

The second main emphasis of Biblical and Hebraic faith consists in the hazardous assertion of a meaningful history. The effort to discern meaning in all the confusions and cross purposes of history distinguishes Western culture and imparts historical dynamic to its striving. It must be distinguished from all religions, mystical or rationalistic, which equate "salvation" with flight from the confusions and responsiblities of man's historic dynamic with two evils inhering in the historical emphasis. One is the evil of fanaticism, the consequence of giving ultimate significance to historically contingent goals and values. The other is the creative, but also confusing, Messianism, the hope for a heaven on earth, for a kingdom of universal peace and righteousness. I have sought to interpret modern Communism as a secularized version of the persistent Messianism characteristic of both Hebraic and Christian thought. I still think that this is the context in which we must understand modern Communism.

I placed a special emphasis on the eschatology of the New Testament with its special symbols of the Christ and anti-Christ, taking them as symbols of the fact that both good and evil grow in history, and that evil has no separate history, but that a greater evil is always a corruption of a greater good. I believe that the perils of a nuclear age substantiate this interpretation much more vividly than I expected when I presented the thesis. But I am not now so sure that the historic symbols will contribute much to the understanding by modern man of his tragic and ironic history with its refutation of the messianic and utopian hopes of the Renaissance and Enlightenment.

Thus it is apparent that old men are incapable of changing their essential emphases and must in any case stand by the record, hoping that the moving drama of history may validate a part of the truth they sought to discern. We will say nothing about the insights which have been refuted and cast into the dustpan of history.

REINHOLD NIEBUHR

1963

THE NATURE AND DESTINY OF MAN
Volume I: Human Nature

CHAPTER I

MAN AS A PROBLEM TO HIMSELF

MAN has always been his own most vexing problem. How shall he think of himself? Every affirmation which he may make about his stature, virtue, or place in the cosmos becomes involved in contradictions when fully analysed. The analysis reveals some presupposition or implication which seems to deny what the proposition intended to affirm.

If man insists that he is a child of nature and that he ought not to pretend to be more than the animal, which he obviously is, he tacitly admits that he is, at any rate, a curious kind of animal who has both the inclination and the capacity to make such pretensions. If on the other hand he insists upon his unique and distinctive place in nature and points to his rational faculties as proof of his special eminence, there is usually an anxious note in his avowals of uniqueness which betrays his unconscious sense of kinship with the brutes. This note of anxiety gives poignant significance to the heat and animus in which the Darwinian controversy was conducted and the Darwinian thesis was resisted by the traditionalists. Furthermore the very effort to estimate the significance of his rational faculties implies a degree of transcendence over himself which is not fully defined or explained in what is usually connoted by "reason." For the man who weighs the importance of his rational faculties is in some sense

more than "reason" and has capacities which transcend the ability
to form general concepts.

If man takes his uniqueness for granted he is immediately involved
in questions and contradictions on the problem of his virtue. If he
believes himself to be essentially good and attributes the admitted
evils of human history to specific social and historical causes he involves himself in begging the question; for all these specific historical
causes of evil are revealed, upon close analysis, to be no more than
particular consequences and historical configurations of evil tendencies in man himself. They cannot be understood at all if a capacity for, and inclination toward, evil in man himself is not presupposed. If, on the other hand, man comes to pessimistic conclusions
about himself, his capacity for such judgments would seem to negate
the content of the judgments. How can man be "essentially" evil if
he knows himself to be so? What is the character of the ultimate
subject, the quintessential "I," which passes such devastating judgments upon itself as object?

If one turns to the question of the value of human life and asks
whether life is worth living, the very character of the question reveals that the questioner must in some sense be able to stand outside
of, and to transcend the life which is thus judged and estimated. Man
can reveal this transcendence more explicitly not only by actually
committing suicide but by elaborating religions and philosophies
which negate life and regard a "lifeless" eternity, such as Nirvana,
as the only possible end of life.

Have those who inveigh so violently against otherworldliness in
religion, justified as their criticisms may be, ever fully realized what
the error of denying life implies in regard to the stature of man? The
man who can negate "life" must be something other than mere
vitality. Every effort to dissuade him from the neglect of natural
vitality and historic existence implies a vantage point in him above
natural vitality and history; otherwise he could not be tempted to
the error from which he is to be dissuaded.

Man's place in the universe is subject to the same antinomies. Men

have been assailed periodically by qualms of conscience and fits of dizziness for pretending to occupy the centre of the universe. Every philosophy of life is touched with anthropocentric tendencies. Even theocentric religions believe that the Creator of the world is interested in saving man from his unique predicament. But periodically man is advised and advises himself to moderate his pretensions and admit that he is only a little animal living a precarious existence on a second-rate planet, attached to a second-rate sun. There are moderns who believe that this modesty is the characteristic genius of modern man and the fruit of his discovery of the vastness of interstellar spaces; but it was no modern astronomer who confessed, "When I consider thy heavens, the work of thy fingers, the moon and the stars, which thou hast ordained; What is man that thou art mindful of him?" (Ps. 8:4). Yet the vantage point from which man judges his insignificance is a rather significant vantage point. This fact has not been lost on the moderns whose modesty before the cosmic immensity was modified considerably by pride in their discovery of this immensity. It was a modern, the poet Swinburne, who sang triumphantly:

The seal of his knowledge is sure, the truth and his spirit are wed; . . .
Glory to Man in the highest! for man is the master of things,

thereby proving that the advance of human knowledge about the world does not abate the pride of man.

While these paradoxes of human self-knowledge are not easily reduced to simpler formulæ, they all point to two facts about man: one of them obvious and the other not quite so obvious. The two are not usually appreciated with equal sympathy. The obvious fact is that man is a child of nature, subject to its vicissitudes, compelled by its necessities, driven by its impulses, and confined within the brevity of the years which nature permits its varied organic form, allowing them some, but not too much, latitude. The other less obvious fact is that man is a spirit who stands outside of nature, life, himself, his reason and the world. This latter fact is appreciated in one or the other of its aspects by various philosophies. But it is not frequently appreciated in its total import. That man stands outside of nature in some sense is admitted even by naturalists who are intent upon keeping him as close to nature as possible. They must at least admit that he is *homo faber,* a tool-making animal. That man stands outside the world is admitted by rationalists who, with Aristotle, define man as a rational animal and interpret reason as the capacity for making general concepts. But the rationalists do not always understand that man's rational capacity involves a further ability to stand outside himself, a capacity for self-transcendence, the ability to make himself his own object, a quality of spirit which is usually not fully comprehended or connoted in *"ratio"* or *"νοῦς"* or "reason" or any of the concepts which philosophers usually use to describe the uniqueness of man.

How difficult it is to do justice to both the uniqueness of man and his affinities with the world of nature below him is proved by the almost unvarying tendency of those philosophies, which describe and emphasize the rational faculties of man or his capacity for self-transcendence to forget his relation to nature and to identify him, prematurely and unqualifiedly, with the divine and the eternal; and of naturalistic philosophies to obscure the uniqueness of man.

II

THE CLASSICAL VIEW OF MAN

Though man has always been a problem to himself, modern man has aggravated that problem by his too simple and premature solutions. Modern man, whether idealist or naturalist, whether rationalist or romantic, is characterized by his simple certainties about himself. He has aggravated the problem of understanding himself because these certainties are either in contradiction with each other or in contradiction with the obvious facts of history, more particularly of contemporary history; and either they have been controverted by that history or they are held in defiance of its known facts. It is not unfair to affirm that modern culture, that is, our culture since the Renaissance, is to be credited with the greatest advances in the understanding of nature and with the greatest confusion in the understanding of man. Perhaps this credit and debit are logically related to each other.

Fully to appreciate the modern conflicts in regard to human nature, it is necessary to place the characteristically modern doctrines of man in their historic relation to the traditional views of human nature which have informed western culture. All modern views of human nature are adaptations, transformations and varying compounds of primarily two distinctive views of man: (*a*) The view of classical antiquity, that is of the Græco-Roman world, and (*b*) the Biblical view. It is important to remember that while these two views are distinct and partly incompatible, they were actually merged in the thought of medieval Catholicism. (The perfect expression of this union is to be found in the Thomistic synthesis of Augustinian and Aristotelian thought.) The history of modern culture really begins with the destruction of this synthesis, foreshadowed in nominalism, and completed in the Renaissance and Reformation. In the dissolution of the synthesis, the Renaissance distilled the classical elements out of the synthesis and the Reformation sought to free the Biblical from the classical elements. Liberal Protestantism is an effort (on the whole an abortive one) to reunite the two elements. There is, in fact, little that is common between them. What was common in the two views was almost completely lost after modern thought had reinterpreted and transmuted the classical view of man in the direction of a greater naturalism. Modern culture has thus been a battleground of two opposing views of human nature. This conflict could not be resolved. It ended in the more or less complete triumph of the modernized classical view of man, a triumph which in this latter day is imperilled not by any external foe but by confusion within its own household. To validate this analysis of the matter requires at least a brief preliminary analysis of the classical and the Christian views of human nature.

The classical view of man, comprised primarily of Platonic, Aristotelian and Stoic conceptions of human nature, contains, of course, varying emphases but it may be regarded as one in its common conviction that man is to be understood primarily from the standpoint of the uniqueness of his rational faculties. What is unique in man is his *voῦs*. Noῦs may be translated as "spirit" but the primary emphasis lies upon the capacity for thought and reason. In Aristotle the *nous* is the vehicle of purely intellectual activity and is a universal and immortal principle which enters man from without. Only one element in it, the "passive" in distinction to the "active" *nous* becomes involved in, and subject to, the individuality of a particular physical organism. How completely the Aristotelian *nous* is intellectual may best be understood by Aristotle's explicit denial of its capacity for self-consciousness. It does not make itself its own object except in making things known the object of consciousness: "No mind knows itself by participation in the known; it becomes known by touching and knowing, so that the same thing is mind and object of mind."[1] This definition is the more significant when contrasted with Aristotle's conception of divine consciousness which expresses itself only in terms of self-knowledge.

In Plato the *nous* or *logistikon* is not as sharply distinguished from the soul as in Aristotle. It is, rather, the highest element in the soul, the other two being the spirited element (θυμοειδές) and the appetitive element (ἐπιθυμητικόν). In both Plato and Aristotle "mind" is sharply distinguished from the body. It is the unifying and ordering principle, the organ of *logos*, which brings harmony into the life of the soul, as *logos* is the creative and forming principle of the world. Greek metaphysical presuppositions are naturally determinative for the doctrine of man; and since Parmenides Greek philosophy had assumed an identity between being and reason on the one hand and on the other had presupposed that reason works upon some formless or unformed stuff which is never completely tractable. In the thought of Aristotle matter is "a remnant, the

[1]*Physics,* 20.

non-existent in itself unknowable and alien to reason, that remains after the process of clarifying the thing into form and conception. This non-existent neither is nor is not; it is 'not yet,' that is to say it attains reality only insofar as it becomes the vehicle of some conceptual determination."[2]

Plato and Aristotle thus share a common rationalism; and also a common dualism which is explicit in the case of Plato and implicit and covert in the case of Aristotle.[3] The effect of this rationalism and dualism has been determinative for the classical doctrine of man and for all modern doctrines which are borrowed from it. The consequences are: (*a*) The rationalism practically identifies rational man (who is essential man) with the divine; for reason is, as the creative principle, identical with God. Individuality is no significant concept, for it rests only upon the particularity of the body. In the thought of Aristotle only the active *nous,* precisely the mind which is not involved in the soul, is immortal; and for Plato the immutability of ideas is regarded as a proof of the immortality of the spirit. (*b*) The dualism has the consequence for the doctrine of man of identifying the body with evil and of assuming the essential goodness of mind or spirit. This body-mind dualism and the value judgments passed upon both body and mind stand in sharpest contrast to the Biblical view of man and achieve a fateful influence in all subsequent theories of human nature. The Bible knows nothing of a good mind and an evil body.

While Stoicism, as a monistic and pantheistic philosophy, sharply diverges from the Aristotelian and Platonic concepts in many respects, its view of human nature betrays more similarities than differences. The similarities are great enough, at any rate, to constitute it a part of the general "classical" picture of man. The Stoic reason is

[2]*Cf.* Werner Jaeger, *Aristotle,* Ch. VIII.
[3]Despite Aristotle's naturalism, his psychology is dependent upon Plato's and it may be wrong to speak of his dualism as covert. It was fairly explicit. He believed that life without the body was the soul's normal state and that its sojourn in the body was a severe illness. *Cf.* Jaeger, *ibid.,* p. 51.

more immanent in both the world process and in the soul and body of man than in Platonism; yet man is essentially reason. Even the dualism is not completely lacking. For while Stoicism is not always certain whether the reason which governs man must persuade him to emulate nature as he finds it outside of his reason or whether it, being a special spark of the divine reason, must set him against the impulses of nature, it arrives on the whole at convictions which do not qualify the classical concepts essentially.[4] The emphasis upon human freedom in its psychology overcomes the pantheistic naturalism of its metaphysics; and its completely negative attitude toward the passions and the whole impulsive life of man set reason in contrast to the impulses of the body, however much it conceives reason as basically the principle of harmony within the body.

Obviously, the Platonic, Aristotelian and Stoic conceptions which define the "classical" view of man do not exhaust Greek speculations about human nature. Modern vitalism and romanticism have their antecedents in the earlier Dionysian religion, in Heraclitus' conception of ultimate reality as Flux and Fire and more particularly in the development of the Dionysian theme in Greek tragedy.[5] Subsequent mysticism is anticipated in Orphism and Pythagoreanism.

[4] The confusion in Stoic thought between the reason in man and the reason in nature, a confusion which was perpetuated constantly in eighteenth-century borrowings from Stoicism, is clearly revealed in Diogenes Laërtius' account of Zeno's thought. He writes: "When rational animals are endowed with reason in token of a more complete superiority, life in them in accordance with nature is rightly understood to mean life in accordance with reason. For reason is like a craftsman, shaping impulses and desires. Hence Zeno's definition of the end is to live in conformity with nature, which means to live a life of virtue; for it is virtue to which nature leads. On the other hand a virtuous life is one which conforms to our experience of the course of nature, our human natures being parts of universal nature." Diogenes Laërtius VII, 85.

[5] Nietzsche in his *Birth of Tragedy* claims the Greek dramatists too unreservedly for his vitalistic philosophy. The significance of the tragedies lies in the unresolved conflict between the Olympian and Dionysian, the rational and the vitalistic, principles in Greek thought. Significantly Zeus, the god of order and measure, remains the ultimate arbiter in the Greek tragedies.

Even more significant for developments in contemporary culture, Democritus and Epicurus interpreted man, in accordance with their naturalism and materialism, not as standing outside of nature by the quality of his unique reason, but as wholly a part of nature. This Greek materialism was no less rationalistic than Platonism or Aristotelianism but it reduced the immanental reason in the world to mechanical necessity and sought to understand man in terms of this mechanism. It was by combining Stoic with Democritan and Epicurean naturalism that modern culture arrived at concepts which were to express some of its most characteristic interpretations of man, as primarily a child of nature.

It must be observed that while the classical view of human virtue is optimistic when compared with the Christian view (for it finds no defect in the centre of human personality) and while it has perfect confidence in the virtue of the rational man, it does not share the confidence of the moderns in the ability of all men to be either virtuous or happy. Thus an air of melancholy hangs over Greek life which stands in sharpest contrast to the all-pervasive optimism of the now dying bourgeois culture, despite the assumption of the latter that it had merely restored the classical world view and the Greek view of man. "There is nothing, methinks, more piteous than a man, of all things that creep and breathe upon the earth," declares Zeus in the *Iliad,* and that note runs as a consistent strain through Greek thought from Homer to the Hellenistic age. Primarily it was the brevity of life and the mortality of man which tempted the Greeks to melancholy. They were not dissuaded from this mood either by Plato's assurance of immortality nor yet by Epicurus' counsel that death need not be feared, since there was nothing on the other side of the grave.

Aristotle confessed that "not to be born is the best thing and death is better than life," and gave it as his opinion that melancholy was a concomitant of genius. The philosophers were optimistic in their confidence that the wise man would be virtuous; but, alas, they had no confidence that the many could be wise. The Stoic Chryssipus could conceive happiness only for the wise and was certain that most men were fools. The Stoics tended on the one hand to include all men in the brotherhood of man on the ground that they all had the spark of divine reason; but on the other hand they pitied the multitude for having no obvious graces of rationality. Thus their equalitarianism rapidly degenerated into an aristocratic condescension not very different from Aristotle's contempt for the slave as a "living tool." Seneca, despite his pious universalism, prays "forgive the world: they are all fools."

Neither Greek nor Roman classicists had any conception of a meaning in human history. History was a series of cycles, a realm of endless recurrences. Aristotle maintained that the arts and sciences were lost and found again not once but an infinite number of times.[6] Zeno envisaged the end of the world as a huge conflagration which would destroy the world's body. This pessimism about both man and his history is the natural consequence of the mind-body dualism which characterizes Greek thought far beyond the limits of Platonism. It culminated invariably in the conviction that the body is a tomb (σῶμα_σῆμα)[7] a conviction which makes neo-Platonism the logical consummation of Greek thought.

The pessimism of Greek tragedy is somewhat different from that of the philosophers and most nearly approaches the Christian interpretation of life. But, unlike Christian thought, it has no answer for the problem it presents. In Æschylus and Sophocles the capricious jealousy of Zeus against mortal men of Homeric legend had been transmuted into the justified jealousy of the ultimate principle of law and order against the lawlessness of human passions. But, unlike the philosophers, the dramatists see human passions as something more than mere impulses of the body. The principle of order and measure, represented by Zeus, is constantly defied by vitalities in human life which are creative as well as destructive. The tragedy

---

[6]*Cf.* S. H. Butcher on "The Melancholy of the Greeks," in *Some Aspects of the Greek Genius*.

[7]*Cf.* E. Bevan, *Stoics and Sceptics*, p. 100.

of human history consists precisely in the fact that human life cannot be creative without being destructive, that biological urges are enhanced and sublimated by dæmonic spirit and that this spirit cannot express itself without committing the sin of pride. The heroes of Greek tragedy are always being counselled to remember their mortality and to escape νέμεσις by observing a proper restraint. But the ὕβρις which offends Zeus is an inevitable concomitant of their creative action in history. The tragic heroes are heroes precisely because they disregard this prudent advice of moderation. In that sense Greek tragedy is an explication of Nietzsche's observation: "Every doer loves his deed much more than it deserves to be loved; and the best deeds are born out of such an excess of love that they could not be worthy of it, even though their worth be very great."[8] The various vitalities of human history are moreover not only in conflict with Zeus but in conflict with each other. There is no simple resolution of the conflict between the state and the family, usually symbolized as a conflict between man and woman, the latter representing the community of blood and family in contrast to the political community (as in *Iphigenia at Aulis* and in *Antigone*). The conflict in Greek tragedy is, in short, between Gods, between Zeus and Dionysus; and not between God and the devil, nor between spirit and matter. The spirit of man expresses itself in his vital energies as well as in the harmonizing force of mind; and while the latter, as the rational principle of order, is the more ultimate (here the dramatists remain typically Greek) there can be creativity in human affairs only at the price of disturbing this order.

Thus life is at war with itself, according to Greek tragedy. There is no solution, or only a tragic solution for the conflict between the vitalities of life and the principle of measure. Zeus remains God. But one is prompted to both admiration and pity toward those who defy him. It is significant that this profound problem, posed by Greek tragedy, was never sensed by the moderns who revived classicism and ostensibly built their view of man upon Greek thought.

[8] *Kritik und Zukunft der Kultur,* Ch. IV, Par. 13.

They may have understood or misunderstood Plato and Aristotle: but the message of Æschylus and Sophocles was neither understood nor misunderstood. It was simply neglected, except as the minor romantic note in modern culture appreciated and partly misunderstood it.

III

THE CHRISTIAN VIEW OF MAN

The Christian view of man, which modern culture ostensibly rejects in its entirety but by which its estimate of human nature is influenced more than it realizes, will be more fully analysed in this book. At this point we must anticipate subsequent elaborations briefly by distinguishing the Christian view from the classical doctrine of man. As the classical view is determined by Greek metaphysical presuppositions, so the Christian view is determined by the ultimate presuppositions of Christian faith. The Christian faith in God as Creator of the world transcends the canons and antinomies of rationality, particularly the antinomy between mind and matter, between consciousness and extension. God is not merely mind who forms a previously given formless stuff. God is both vitality and form and the source of all existence. He creates the world. This world is not God; but it is not evil because it is not God. Being God's creation, it is good.

The consequence of this conception of the world upon the view of human nature in Christian thought is to allow an appreciation of the unity of body and soul in human personality which idealists and naturalists have sought in vain. Furthermore it prevents the idealistic error of regarding the mind as essentially good or essentially eternal and the body as essentially evil. But it also obviates the romantic error of seeking for the good in man-as-nature and for evil in man-as-spirit or as reason. Man is, according to the Biblical view, a created and finite existence in both body and spirit. Obviously a view which depends upon an ultra-rational presupposition is immediately en-

myth: lang that takes into acc't both of self-evident facts of human Nature

dangered when rationally explicated; for reason which seeks to b
all things into terms of rational coherence is tempted to make one
known thing the principle of explanation and to derive all other
things from it. Its most natural inclination is to make itself that
ultimate principle, and thus in effect to declare itself God. Christian
psychology and philosophy have never completely freed themselves
from this fault, which explains why naturalists plausibly though
erroneously regard Christian faith as the very fountain source of
idealism.

This is also the reason why the Biblical view of the unity of man
as body and soul has often seemed to be no more than the consequence of primitive Hebraic psychology. In Hebrew thought the
soul of man resides in his blood and the concept of an immortal
mind in a mortal body remains unknown to the end. It is true that
certain distinctions are gradually made. At first both *ruach* and
nephesh mean little more than "breath"; but they are gradually distinguished and *ruach* becomes roughly synonymous with spirit or
nous and *nephesh* with soul or *psyche*. But, unlike Greek thought,
this distinction does not lead to dualistic consequences. The monism
of the Biblical view is something other than the failure to differentiate *physis, psyche* and *nous,* which characterized Greek thought
before Anaxagoras; nor is it merely the consequence of an un-
developed psychology. It is ultimately derived from the Biblical view
of God as the Creator and of the Biblical faith in the goodness of
creation.

The second important characteristic of the Christian view of man
is that he is understood primarily from the standpoint of God, rather
than the uniqueness of his rational faculties or his relation to nature.
He is made in the "image of God." It has been the mistake of many
Christian rationalists to assume that this term is no more than a
religious-pictorial expression of what philosophy intends when it
defines man as a rational animal. We have previously alluded to
the fact that the human spirit has the special capacity of standing
continually outside itself in terms of indefinite regression. Conscious-

ness is a capacity for surveying the world and determining action from a governing centre. Self-consciousness represents a further degree of transcendence in which the self makes itself its own object in such a way that the ego is finally always subject and not object. The rational capacity of surveying the world, of forming general concepts and analysing the order of the world is thus but one aspect of what Christianity knows as "spirit." The self knows the world, insofar as it knows the world, because it stands outside both itself and the world, which means that it cannot understand itself except as it is understood from beyond itself and the world.

This essential homelessness of the human spirit is the ground of all religion; for the self which stands outside itself and the world cannot find the meaning of life in itself or the world. It cannot identify meaning with causality in nature; for its freedom is obviously something different from the necessary causal links of nature. Nor can it identify the principle of meaning with rationality, since it transcends its own rational processes, so that it may, for instance, ask the question whether there is a relevance between its rational forms and the recurrences and forms of nature. It is this capacity of freedom which finally prompts great cultures and philosophies to transcend rationalism and to seek for the meaning of life in an unconditioned ground of existence. But from the standpoint of human thought this unconditioned ground of existence, this God, can be defined only negatively. This is why mystic religions in general, and particularly the neo-Platonic tradition in western culture, have one interesting similarity with Christianity and one important difference in their estimate of human nature. In common with Christianity they measure the depth of the human spirit in terms of its capacity of self-transcendence. Thus Plotinus defines *nous* not as Aristotle defines it. For him it is primarily the capacity for self-knowledge and it has no limit short of the eternal. Mysticism and Christianity agree in understanding man from the standpoint of the eternal. But since mysticism leads to an undifferentiated ultimate reality, it is bound to regard particularity, including individuality, as essentially evil. All mystic religions therefore have the characteristic of accentuating individuality inasfar as individuality is inherent in the capacity for self-consciousness emphasized in mysticism and is something more than mere bodily particularity; but all mystic philosophies ultimately lose the very individuality which they first emphasize, because they sink finite particularity in a distinctionless divine ground of existence.

God as will and personality, in concepts of Christian faith, is thus the only possible ground of real individuality, though not the only possible presupposition of self-consciousness. But faith in God as will and personality depends upon faith in His power to reveal Himself. The Christian faith in God's self-disclosure, culminating in the revelation of Christ, is thus the basis of the Christian concept of personality and individuality. In terms of this faith man can understand himself as a unity of will which finds its end in the will of God. We thus have in the problem of human nature one of the many indications of the relation of general and special revelation, which concerns theology so perennially. The conviction that man stands too completely outside of both nature and reason to understand himself in terms of either without misunderstanding himself, belongs to general revelation in the sense that any astute analysis of the human situation must lead to it. But if man lacks a further revelation of the divine he will also misunderstand himself when he seeks to escape the conditions of nature and reason. He will end by seeking absorption in a divine reality which is at once all and nothing. To understand himself truly means to begin with a faith that he is understood from beyond himself, that he is known and loved of God and must find himself in terms of obedience to the divine will. This relation of the divine to the human will makes it possible for man to relate himself to God without pretending to be God; and to accept his distance from God as a created thing, without believing that the evil of his nature is caused by this finiteness. Man's finite existence in the body and in history can be essentially affirmed, as naturalism wants to affirm it. Yet the uniqueness of man's spirit can be appreciated even more than idealism appreciates it, though always preserving a proper distinction between the human and divine. Also the unity of spirit and body can be emphasized in terms of its relation to a Creator and Redeemer who created both mind and body. These are the ultra-rational foundations and presuppositions of Christian wisdom about man.

This conception of man's stature is not, however, the complete Christian picture of man. The high estimate of the human stature implied in the concept of "image of God" stands in paradoxical juxtaposition to the low estimate of human virtue in Christian thought. Man is a sinner. His sin is defined as rebellion against God. The Christian estimate of human evil is so serious precisely because it places evil at the very centre of human personality: in the will. This evil cannot be regarded complacently as the inevitable consequence of his finiteness or the fruit of his involvement in the contingencies and necessities of nature. Sin is occasioned precisely by the fact that man refuses to admit his "creatureliness" and to acknowledge himself as merely a member of a total unity of life. He pretends to be more than he is. Nor can he, as in both rationalistic and mystic dualism, dismiss his sins as residing in that part of himself which is not his true self, that is, that part of himself which is involved in physical necessity. In Christianity it is not the eternal man who judges the finite man; but the eternal and holy God who judges sinful man. Nor is redemption in the power of the eternal man who gradually sloughs off finite man. Man is not divided against himself so that the essential man can be extricated from the nonessential. Man contradicts himself within the terms of his true essence. His essence is free self-determination. His sin is the wrong use of his freedom and its consequent destruction.

Man is an individual but he is not self-sufficing. The law of his nature is love, a harmonious relation of life to life in obedience to the divine centre and source of his life. This law is violated when man seeks to make himself the centre and source of his own life. His sin is therefore spiritual and not carnal, though the infection of rebellion spreads from the spirit to the body and disturbs its harmonies also. Man, in other words, is a sinner not because he is one limited individual within a whole but rather because he is betrayed by his very ability to survey the whole to imagine himself the whole.

The fact that human vitality inevitably expresses itself in defiance of the laws of measure can be observed without the presuppositions of the Christian faith. The analysis of this fact in Greek tragedy has already been observed. But it is impossible without the presuppositions of the Christian faith to find the source of sin within man himself. Greek tragedy regards human evil as the consequence of a conflict between vitality and form, between Dionysian and Olympian divinities. Only in a religion of revelation, whose God reveals Himself to man from beyond himself and from beyond the contrast of vitality and form, can man discover the root of sin to be within himself. The essence of man is his freedom. Sin is committed in that freedom. Sin can therefore not be attributed to a defect in his essence. It can only be understood as a self-contradiction, made possible by the fact of his freedom but not following necessarily from it.

Christianity, therefore, issues inevitably in the religious expression of an uneasy conscience. Only within terms of the Christian faith can man not only understand the reality of the evil in himself but escape the error of attributing that evil to any one but himself. It is possible of course to point out that man is tempted by the situation in which he stands. He stands at the juncture of nature and spirit. The freedom of his spirit causes him to break the harmonies of nature and the pride of his spirit prevents him from establishing a new harmony. The freedom of his spirit enables him to use the forces and processes of nature creatively; but his failure to observe the limits of his finite existence causes him to defy the forms and restraints of both nature and reason. Human self-consciousness is a high tower looking upon a large and inclusive world. It vainly imagines that it is the large world which it beholds and not a narrow tower insecurely erected amidst the shifting sands of the world.

It is one of the purposes of this volume to analyse the meaning of the Christian idea of sin more fully and to explain the uneasy conscience expressed in the Christian religion. It must suffice at this point to record the fact that the Christian view of human nature is involved in the paradox of claiming a higher stature for man and of taking a more serious view of his evil than other anthropology.

IV

THE MODERN VIEW OF MAN

The modern view of man is informed partly by classical, partly by Christian and partly by distinctively modern motifs. The classical element tends to slip from the typical classical, Platonic and Aristotelian rationalism to a more naturalistic rationalism. That is, the Epicurean and Democritan naturalism, which remained subordinate in the classical period of Greek thought, becomes dominant in the modern period. This modern naturalism is in accord with the Christian concept of man as "creature" but it contradicts the Christian concept of man as "image of God" which the early Renaissance emphasized in opposition to the Christian idea of man as creature and man as sinner. The curious compound of classical, Christian and distinctively modern conceptions of human nature, involved in modern anthropology, leads to various difficulties and confusions which may be briefly summarized as follows: (*a*) The inner contradictions in modern conceptions of human nature between idealistic and naturalistic rationalists; and between rationalists, whether idealistic or naturalistic, and vitalists and romanticists. (*b*) The certainties about human nature in modern culture which modern history dissipates, particularly the certainty about individuality. (*c*) The certainties about human nature, particularly the certainty about the goodness of man, which stands in contradiction to the known facts of history.

(*a*) One of the unresolved antinomies in modern culture is the contradictory emphasis of the idealists and the naturalists. The former are inclined to protest against Christian humility and to disavow both the doctrine of man's creatureliness and the doctrine of his sinfulness. This was the mood of the Renaissance, the thought of which upon this issue was determined by Platonic, neo-Platonic and Stoic conceptions. Bruno is concerned to establish the infinity of human self-consciousness; and the infinity of space is merely an interesting analogue of this infinity of spirit in his pantheistic system. He prizes the achievements of Copernican astronomy because Copernicus "emancipated our knowledge from the prison house in which, as it were, it saw stars only through small windows." In the same manner Leonardo da Vinci is more concerned·to prove that the mathematical method which unlocks nature's mysteries and discloses her regularities and dependable recurrences is a fruit and symbol of the greatness of the human mind, than that it is a tool of nature's mastery. Petrarch sees nature as a mirror in which man beholds his true greatness.

Yet there was a minor note in the Renaissance which finally led to the naturalistic rationalism of the eighteenth century. It expresses itself in Francis Bacon's primary interest in nature, and in Montaigne's effort to understand man in the variety of his natural differentiations. Bacon is afraid lest the "unquietness of the human spirit," that is the very hankering after infinity which Bruno praises as the true mark of humanity, will "interfere most mischievously in the discovery of causes," that is, with the sober inductive processes of science. Thus modern culture slips from the essential Platonism of the early Renaissance to the Stoicism of Descartes and Spinoza and the seventeenth century generally and then to the more radical, materialistic and Democritan naturalism of the eighteenth century. Modern man ends by seeking to understand himself in terms of his relation to nature, but he remains even more confused about the relation of reason in nature and reason in man than the Stoics were. The thought of the French enlightenment is a perfect exposition of this confusion. The idealistic reaction to this naturalism is to be found in German idealism, where, with the exception of Kant, reason and being are more unqualifiedly equated than in Platonism. Descartes, the fountain source of modern culture, manages to conceive of man purely in terms of thought, nature in terms of mechanics and to find no organic unity between the two, thus bearing within himself both the contradictions and the extravagances of modernity.

In terms of social history, this course of modern thought from an idealistic protest against the Christian conception of man as creature and as sinner to the naturalistic protest against man as the "image of God" may be interpreted as the anti-climactic history of bourgeois man. The middle-class world begins with a tremendous sense of the power of the human mind over nature. But having destroyed the ultimate reference by which medieval man transcended nature spiritually, even while acknowledging his dependence practically, the bourgeois and technical world ends by seeking asylum in nature's dependabilities and serenities. Modern capitalism really expresses both attitudes at the same time. The spirit of capitalism is the spirit of an irreverent exploitation of nature, conceived as a treasure-house of riches which will guarantee everything which might be regarded as the good life. Man masters nature. But the social organization of capitalism at least theoretically rests upon the naive faith that nature masters man and that her pre-established harmonies will prevent the human enterprise from involving itself in any serious catastrophes (physiocratic theory).

The conflict between idealistic and naturalistic rationalists is complicated by a further factor: the protest of the romantic naturalists who interpret man as primarily vitality and who find neither a pale reason nor a mechanical nature an adequate key to man's true essence. This romantic interpretation of man is in some respects the newest element in modern anthropological doctrines, for it is only partially foreshadowed in either classical or Christian thought. Its bitterest fruit is modern fascism. Marxist thought complicates the pattern further; for it interprets man, as he is, primarily in vitalistic terms and rightly discounts the pretenses of rational man who does not know his own finiteness; but the man who is to be will build a society which will be governed by the most remarkable rational coherence of life with life and interest with interest. The conflict between rationalists and romanticists has become one of the most fateful issues of our day, with every possible religious and political implication. Modern man, in short, cannot determine whether he shall understand himself primarily from the standpoint of the uniqueness of his reason or from the standpoint of his affinity with nature; and if the latter whether it is the harmless order and peace of nature or her vitality which is the real clue to his essence. Thus some of the certainties of modern man are in contradiction with one another; and it may be questioned whether the conflict can be resolved within terms of the presuppositions with which modern culture approaches the issues.

(*b*) The concept of individuality in modern culture belongs to that class of certainties of modern man about himself which his own history has gradually dissipated. The tremendous emphasis upon individuality in the Renaissance is clearly a flower which could have grown only on Christian soil, since the classical culture, to which the Renaissance is an ostensible return, lacked this emphasis completely. The Italian Renaissance avails itself primarily of neo-Platonic conceptions to establish its idea of the dignity and the liberty of man. But these conceptions would not yield the idea of individuality if Christian ideas were not presupposed. The Renaissance is particularly intent upon establishing the freedom of the human spirit in opposition to Christian doctrines of divine predestination.[1]

Pico della Mirandola extols the freedom of the human spirit in concepts drawn from Platonism. God said to man, according to Pico: "You alone are not bound by any restraint, unless you will adopt it by the will which we have given you. I have placed you in the centre

---

[1]Some of the important documents in this cause were: Manetti's *De dignitate, ex excellentia hominis;* Valla's *De libero arbitrio;* Pompanazzi's *De fato, libero arbitrio et predestinatione;* and Pico della Mirandola's *Oratio de hominis dignitate.*

of the world that you may the easier look about and behold all that is in it. I created you a creature, neither earthly nor heavenly, neither mortal nor immortal, so that you could be your own creator and choose whatever form you may assume for yourself."

While classical thought was used by the Renaissance to challenge the Christian idea of man's dependence and weakness, by emphasis upon his uniqueness and the freedom of his spirit, classicism was obviously not able to suggest the concept of individuality which the Renaissance held so dear. This idea must be regarded as partly a Christian inheritance and partly a consequence of the emergence of the bourgeois individual from the historical and traditional cohesions, patterns and restraints of the medieval world. This bourgeois individual felt himself the master of his own destiny and was impatient with both the religious and the political solidarities which characterized both classical and medieval life. Speaking in social terms one may say that he lost this individuality immediately after establishing it by his destruction of the medieval solidarities. He found himself the artificer of a technical civilization which creates more enslaving mechanical interdependencies and collectivities than anything known in an agrarian world. Furthermore no one can be as completely and discreetly an individual as bourgeois individualism supposes, whether in the organic forms of an agrarian or the more mechanical forms of a technical society.

Considered in terms of philosophical issues bourgeois individualism had an insecure foundation, not only in the Platonism and neo-Platonism in which it first expressed itself but also in the later naturalism of the eighteenth and nineteenth centuries. Idealism begins by emphasizing man's freedom and transcendence over nature but ends by losing the individual in the universalities of rational concepts and ultimately in the undifferentiated totality of the divine. Naturalism begins by emphasizing natural variety and particularity. Thus it was Montaigne's interest to picture the multifarious forms of social and moral custom under the influence of the diversities of geography. But variety in nature comes short of individuality. There is no place for individuality in either pure mind or pure nature. As the idealists lose individuality in the absolute mind, so the naturalists lose it in "streams of consciousness" when dealing with the matter psychologically, and in "laws of motion" when thinking sociologically. Thus the individualism of the Renaissance and of the eighteenth century is dissipated culturally, just as bourgeois libertarian idealism disintegrates politically and succumbs to fascist and Marxist collectivism. A genuine individuality can be maintained only in terms of religious presuppositions which can do justice to the immediate involvement of human individuality in all the organic forms and social tensions of history, while yet appreciating its ultimate transcendence over every social and historical situation in the highest reaches of its self-transcendence. The paradox of man as creature and man as child of God is a necessary presupposition of a concept of individuality, strong enough to maintain itself against the pressures of history, and realistic enough to do justice to the organic cohesions of social life.

(c) The final certainty of modern anthropology is its optimistic treatment of the problem of evil. Modern man has an essentially easy conscience; and nothing gives the diverse and discordant notes of modern culture so much harmony as the unanimous opposition of modern man to Christian conceptions of the sinfulness of man. The idea that man is sinful at the very centre of his personality, that is in his will, is universally rejected. It is this rejection which has seemed to make the Christian gospel simply irrelevant to modern man, a fact which is of much more importance than any conviction about its incredibility. If modern culture conceives man primarily in terms of the uniqueness of his rational faculties, it finds the root of his evil in his involvement in natural impulses and natural necessities from which it hopes to free him by the increase of his rational faculties. This essentially Platonic idea manages to creep into many social and educational theories, even when they are ostensibly naturalistic and not Platonic. On the other hand, if it conceives of man primarily in terms of his relation to nature, it hopes to rescue man from the dæmonic chaos in which his spiritual life is involved by beguiling him back to the harmony, serenity and harmless unity of nature. In this the mechanistic rationalist and the Rousseauistic romantic of the French enlightenment seem to stand on common ground. Either the rational man or the natural man is conceived as essentially good, and it is only necessary for man either to rise from the chaos of nature to the harmony of mind or to descend from the chaos of spirit to the harmony of nature in order to be saved. The very fact that the strategies of redemption are in such complete contradiction to each other proves how far modern man is from solving the problem of evil in his life.

A further consequence of modern optimism is a philosophy of history expressed in the idea of progress. Either by a force immanent in nature itself, or by the gradual extension of rationality, or by the elimination of specific sources of evil, such as priesthoods, tyrannical government and class divisions in society, modern man expects to move toward some kind of perfect society. The idea of progress is compounded of many elements. It is particularly important to consider one element of which modern culture is itself completely oblivious. The idea of progress is possible only upon the ground of a Christian culture. It is a secularized version of Biblical apocalypse and of the Hebraic sense of a meaningful history, in contrast to the meaningless history of the Greeks. But since the Christian doctrine of the sinfulness of man is eliminated, a complicating factor in the Christian philosophy is removed and the way is open for simple interpretations of history, which relate historical process as closely as possible to biological process and which fail to do justice either to the unique freedom of man or to the dæmonic misuse which he may make of that freedom.

There are of course pessimistic reactions to this optimism about both the individual and the total human enterprise. In the mechanistic naturalism of Hobbes and the romantic naturalism of Nietzsche a thoroughgoing pessimism is elaborated. One of the modern fruits of Nietzschean thought is Freudian pessimism. Here we have no good opinion about human nature; yet there is no uneasy conscience in this pessimism. The egotism and the will-to-power which Christian thought regards as the quintessence of sin and which, in the view of bourgeois liberalism, is a defect to be sloughed off by a new education or a new social organization, is regarded as normal and normative. Hobbes accepts and Nietzsche glorifies the will-to-power. In Hobbes a political vantage point against individual egotism is gained but none against the collective egotism, embodied in the state. In Nietzsche's transvaluation of values, the characteristics of human life which make for conflict between life and life are raised to the eminence of the ideal. The fateful consequences in contemporary political life of Hobbes's cynicism and Nietzsche's nihilism are everywhere apparent.

By way of validating the relevance of the Christian conception of man as a possible source of light for the confusion of modernity, we must consider the problems of modern culture, briefly sketched here, more fully in the three following chapters.

CHAPTER II

THE PROBLEM OF VITALITY AND FORM
IN HUMAN NATURE

ALL creatures express an exuberant vitality within the limits of certain unities, orders and forms. Animal existence exhibits a uniform and resolute will to survive; but the strategy of that will, whether for the individual or the species, expresses itself variously according to the particular form of existence within the species and genus. Vitality and form are thus the two aspects of crea-tion. Human existence is obviously distinguished from animal life by its qualified participation in creation. Within limits it breaks the forms of nature and creates new configurations of vitality. Its tran-scendence over natural process offers it the opportunity of interfer-ing with the established forms and unities of vitality as nature knows them. This is the basis of human history, with its progressive alter-ation of forms, in distinction from nature which knows no history but only endless repetition within the limits of each given form.

Since man is deeply involved in the forms of nature on the one hand and is free of them on the other; since he must regard deter-minations of sex, race and (to a lesser degree) geography as forces of ineluctable fate, but can nevertheless arrange and rearrange the vitalities and unities of nature within certain limits, the problem of human creativity is obviously filled with complexities. Four terms.

must be considered in his situation: (1) The vitality of nature (its impulses and drives); (2) the forms and unities of nature, that is, the determinations of instinct, and the forms of natural cohesion and natural differentiation; (3) the freedom of spirit to transcend natural forms within limits and to direct and redirect the vitalities; (4) and finally the forming capacity of spirit, its ability to create a new realm of coherence and order. All these four factors are involved in human creativity and by implication in human destructiveness. Creativity always involves both vitality and form (in the phrase of Schiller, the *Formtrieb* and the *Stofftrieb*, though the identification of vitality with purely natural dynamic, *Stofftrieb*, betrays Schiller's romantic bias). Nature and spirit both possess resources of vitality and form. The resources of nature may be more negative. The vitalities of nature and its forms may be the indispensable presuppositions of human creativity rather than its active agents; but they cannot be disregarded. In the same manner all the four elements are involved in human destructiveness, though again the vitalities and the unities of nature may play a more negative part in human destructiveness than those of spirit. The natural impulse of sex is, for instance, an indispensable condition of all higher forms of family organization as it is the negative force of destructive sex aberrations. In the same way the natural cohesion of tribe and race is the foundation of higher political creations as also the negative determinant of interracial and international anarchy.

Modern culture, particularly in its controversies between rationalists and romanticists, has illumined various aspects of the problem of vitality and form and of the relative contributions of nature and spirit to both form and vitality. But it has not been able to arrive at any satisfactory solution of the problem because its interpretations of man were derived from metaphysical theories, idealistic and naturalistic, in which one aspect of reality was made the principle of interpretation of the whole. Its theories of man conformed to these metaphysical theories. The idealists identified spirit too simply with reason and reason too simply with God. In idealism the essential man is therefore the rational man and his reason is either the source of both vitality and form or it is the source of the order and form which transmutes the anarchic vitality of nature into genuine creativity. The possibility of spiritual destructiveness cannot be envisaged because spirit as reason is regarded as the very principle of order.

In opposition to idealistic rationalism romanticism emphasizes either the primary importance of natural vitality as a source of human creativity or the significance of the natural unities and forms as sources of order and virtue. But romanticism does not recognize to what degree the freedom of the spirit has entered into the natural vitalities which it extols and to what degree nature's unities and cohesions are subject to necessary revision by human freedom. The problem of vitality and form is thus a cause of never-ceasing debate in which half-truths are set against half-truths. Modern culture is unable to escape the confusion arising from these misconceptions. This confusion must be regarded as part of the decadence of a Christian civilization which, in its uncorrupted form, had a principle of interpretation which transcended both form and vitality. The God of the Christian faith is the creator of the world. His wisdom is the principle of form, the *logos*. But creation is not merely the subjection of a primitive chaos to the order of *logos*. God is the source of vitality as well as of order. Order and vitality are a unity in Him. Even the *logos,* identified with the second person of the Trinity in Christian faith, is more than *logos*. The Christ is the redeemer who reveals God in His redemptive vitality, above and beyond the revelation of the created order. "The world was made by Him" indeed. He is the pattern, the logos of creation. But He is also the revelation of the redemptive will which restores a fallen world to the pattern of its creation.

Concomitant with this faith in the unity of God's will and wisdom, man is interpreted as a unity of will in which human vitality, natural and spiritual, is set under the ordering will of God. No pattern of human reason but only the will of God can be the principle of the form and order to which human life must be conformed. In that sense the Christian faith is set against all idealism and participates in the romantic and materialistic protest against it. The forms, unities and patterns of human reason are themselves involved in historical relativity according to Christianity. The pretension that they are not, is, in the view of Christian faith, one of the primary proofs of the sinfulness of the human spirit which, in its pride, claims unconditioned validity for its systems of logical coherence and rational unities.

On the other hand, natural vitality is not evil of itself; and redemption does not therefore consist in a rational enervation of or transcendence over natural impulse. This emphasis of Christianity is largely responsible for the superior vigour of historical action revealed by western civilization in contrast to the Orient. Romantic vitalism must be regarded as a decadent form of this vitality or as a primitivistic emphasis upon natural forms and unities, once the Christian unity of vitality and form had been destroyed. It must also be regarded as partially a justified protest against the classical view of human nature, a view which insinuated itself into Christian culture. This rationalized Christianity failed to do justice to the natural vitalities in man and tended to attribute all creativity too simply to the capacities of human reason. The romantic protest against classicism pretends to be primarily a protest against Christianity. This was inevitable because idealistic versions of Christianity had become the vehicles of the classical tradition in the Christian era. Nevertheless there are elements in Biblical Christianity which embody what is true in romanticism and refute what is false in idealism and rationalism.

When these elements are separated from the Christian tradition the romantic protest tends to become nihilistic and primitivistic. It degenerates into a nihilistic defiance of all form and order and makes vitality self-justifying. Or it seeks to make primitive and natural forms of order and cohesion the only possible principles of harmony. This ambiguous character of romanticism and vitalism adds to the tragedy of our era; for it aggravates social anarchy in the effort to arrest it. The gradual transmutation of Nazi racialism and primitivism into an imperialism which consciously and unconsciously disavows its earlier theories of racial cohesion, proves how impossible it is for man, in his freedom, to return to the harmless unities of nature or early society.

II

THE RATIONALISTIC VIEW OF HUMAN NATURE

We have previously noted the abiding influence of Platonism upon the classical view of man, and traced the tendency of the classical view to insinuate itself into both the Christian and the naturalistic view of man. In a sense Platonism draws the most obvious and immediately plausible conclusion about the character of human creativity. Since man is creative because he has the capacity to form and reform the impulses of nature into new and more inclusive patterns, the most obvious conclusion is to identify his creative capacity with reason and to define creativity as the capacity to give form and order to a previously given and assumed vitality of nature. Ideally the soul is the natural principle of order in the body. But in the *Phædo* Plato admits that the soul "is almost always opposing and coercing the elements of which she is believed to be composed, in all sorts of ways throughout life, sometimes more violently with the pains of medicine and gymnastics; sometimes more gently; now threatening, now admonishing the desires, passions, fears as if talking to a thing which is not herself." This inner conflict is an obvious fact which proves that man alone, among all animals, stands in contradiction to himself. The possibility for this contradiction is given by the self-transcendence of the human spirit, the fact that man is not only soul, as unity of the body, but spirit, as capacity to transcend both the body and soul. But Plato does not recognize that the anarchic impulses which the "soul" brings into subjection are more than mere bodily impulses. They are impulses which have been given their freedom by the fact that man is spirit as well as nature. Plato thus falsely identifies anarchy with bodily impulse. Answering the question "Whence come wars and fightings and factions?" he answers erroneously, "Whence but from the body and the lusts of the body."

This theory of human nature is of course in harmony with the Platonic metaphysics, according to which creation consists of the activity of divine reason which coerces the formless stuff, previously given, into the order of its ideas and forms. In this aspect of his thought Plato lays the foundation for all those forms of western rationalism in which spirit is identified with reason; and creativity is equated with the capacity to discipline a previously given vitality into order. The relation of reason to impulse is negative. Plato speaks of the "ten thousand cases of opposition of the soul to the things of the body." It is this side of classical thought which prompts the romantic charge that reason enervates and destroys the instincts.

In the Platonic doctrine of ἔρως, we have, however, a different emphasis. *Eros* represents the natural vitalities sublimated rather than repressed by reason. Plato's "intellectual love" is a sublimation and not a repression of natural vitality and desire. In his famous figure of the charioteer and the two horses, representing the three aspects of the soul, reason as the charioteer drives the steeds toward divine beauty "not clogged with the pollutions of mortality." This represents a positive rather than negative relation between reason and nature, though it must be admitted that one of the steeds in Plato's simile is a "crooked lumbering animal, put together anyhow" and so recalcitrant that the charioteer is forced "with a still more violent wrench to drag the bit out of the teeth of the wild steed, cover his abusive tongue and jaws with blood and force his legs and haunches to the ground."[1] In the *Symposium* the relation of intellectual love to natural desire is explained in the following terms: "Those who are pregnant in the body only betake themselves to women and beget children—this is the character of their love; their offsprings will, as they hope, pre-

[1] This simile is recorded in the *Phædrus.*

serve their memory and give them the blessedness and immortality
which they desire in the future. But souls which are pregnant—for
there certainly are men who are more creative in their souls than
in their bodies—conceive that which is proper for the soul to conceive
or contain. And what are these conceptions? wisdom and virtue in
general." The error in the Platonic analysis is nicely betrayed in the
observation that men, who are supposedly pregnant in body only,
nevertheless beget children "to preserve their memory and give them
the blessedness of immortality," an ambition which hardly belongs
to the realm of pure physical impulse.

The Platonic *eros* doctrine has the virtue, however, of qualifying
the purely negative definitions of the relation of reason to nature in
Platonism and of recognizing nature as a source of vitality subject
to rational sublimation. The basic forms of idealism in modern
culture, derived from Kant and from Hegel, are either more dualistic
or more monistic than Platonism, as qualified by its doctrine of *eros*.
In Kantian thought reason furnishes both the forms and the vitality
of human creativity; and the vitality of the sensible world is not
admitted into the realm of human creativity. The intelligible world
furnishes the forms in terms of those universally applicable canons
of reason to which the will of man must submit. It furnishes the
vitality also; for the vital force of moral action is a reverence for
law which borrows nothing from natural vitality but is generated out
of the resources of the intelligible world. Kantian idealism throws
the impulses of nature more completely into an outer darkness than
any form of Greek classicism.

Hegelian idealism on the other hand derives the total dynamic of
life, spiritual and natural, from the operations of reason. In Hegelian
panlogism, *logos* is, as it were, both *logos* and *eros*. Reason transmutes and tames all the vitalities of human existence. Hegelianism
is thus a rationalized version and corruption of the Christian view
of the unity of human life and of the dynamic quality of historic
existence. In it the Christian idea of divine creation and providence
is reduced to categories of rationality; and the Christian concept of

the unity of body and soul is interpreted in terms which make all natural impulses derivatives of rational processes.

It is significant that Hegelian idealism arouses the protest of Marxism rather than romanticism. For Marxism is not concerned, as is romanticism, to emphasize the vitality of natural impulses against the peril of their enervation by mind. Its interest is rather to assert the creative power of subrational dynamics, as expressed particularly in collective economic activity, against the imperial pretensions of reason to be the sole source of creativity, pretensions which achieve their most typical expression in Hegelianism.

III

THE ROMANTIC PROTEST AGAINST RATIONALISM

The history of modern culture is, as we have noted, the story of a running debate between those who interpret man as reason and those who seek to explain him in terms of his relation to nature. But the latter history of this culture is not so much a debate between these two schools of thought as a rebellion of romanticism, materialism and psychoanalytic psychology against the errors of rationalism, whether idealistic or naturalistic, in its interpretation of human nature. In this revolt the older naturalism of bourgeois liberalism is more frequently on the side of classicism than on the side of the more robustious modern naturalists of romantic, materialistic and psychoanalytic persuasion. At best it stands between the battle lines. It had never suspected the depth and complexity of vital impulse below the level of reason with which romantic naturalism is concerned.

(*a*) The romantic protest takes various forms. In one of its aspects it is an assertion of the vitalities of nature against the peril of enervation through rational discipline. In this aspect romanticism is concerned to prove, in the words of Schiller, that *Fleiss in den Formen kann zuweilen die massive Wahrheit des Stoffes vergessen lassen.*[1]

[1] In *Letters on the Æsthetic Education of Mankind.*

The final form of this protest is achieved in the thought of Nietzsche, who asserts the "wisdom of the body," the will-to-power (the vitality of what he assumes to be physical impulse), against the discipline of reason. In Nietzsche the romantic protest achieves nihilistic proportions because he regards vitality as self-justifying and sets the robust expression of instincts against all possible forms and disciplines. Originally he was primarily concerned with the protagonism of the "Dionysian" urge against the rational disciplines of a "Socratic" culture.[2] His protests were subsequently directed more and more against Christian discipline, which he probably understood primarily as Schopenhauer interpreted it, and against every type of form and discipline.[3] No complete moral nihilism is of course possible. Some recognition of the principle of form and order is inevitable even in the most consistent vitalism. In Nietzsche this is done in minimal terms by his insistence that the will-to-power of his superman will create aristocratic societies of higher worth than the rationalized societies in which the morality of "herd animals" has gained ascendancy.

(*b*) Another aspect of the romantic-materialistic revolt, and one in which Marxism takes a more primary role than romanticism, is the discovery of the dishonesty of reason in its pretension of mastery over, or creation of, the vital impulses of physical life. This note is somewhat in conflict with the romantic fear of the enervation of impulsive spontaneity and vitality through rational discipline. The gravamen of its charge is that the conscious life of man is the instrument and prostitute of profound unconscious urges for which it provides rationalizations rather than disciplines.

In Freud these impulses are interpreted in individualistic and

[2]In his *Birth of Tragedy*.

[3]To choose but one among many similar reiterations, Nietzsche wrote: "Consciousness of values as norms of conduct is a sickliness and evidence that real morality, that is instinctive certainty of action, has gone to the devil. Strong nations and periods do not reflect about their rights, about principles or actions or about instinct and reason." *Works XV*, p. 166.

sexual terms; in Marx the impulses which the mind rationalizes and for which it provides "ideologies" are regarded as basically collective and economic. They are expressed in the productive relations of society which, according to Marxist doctrine, are the basis upon which the superstructure of culture and philosophy, of religion and morals, is reared. Every cultural achievement is thus but a rationalization of a given equilibrium of power in society in which the dominant class, which controls the equilibrium, fashions philosophical, moral and legal systems to justify its rule and maintain its privileges.

Marx has nothing in common with the simple hedonism of Freudianism. He does not believe that the basic impulses of man's subrational nature are primarily determined by a pleasure-pain strategy. He contends rather that men do seek the good but that they define the good in terms of their own interest. He thus recognizes, as no hedonist can, the profound paradox of human spirituality and morality: that the interests of the self cannot be followed if the self cannot obscure these interests behind a façade of general interest and universal values. This fact, which in Christian theology is regarded as the element of inevitable dishonesty in original sin, becomes in Marxism a tool of class conflict. It is used to transvalue the values of the dominant class and destroy their prestige. Marxism thus tentatively discovers and finally dissipates a valuable insight into human nature. It dissipates the insight because it fails to recognize that there is an ideological element in all human rational processes which reveals itself not only in the spirituality of the dominant bourgeois class, and not only in the rationalization of economic interest; but which expresses itself in all classes and uses every circumstance, geographic, economic and political, as an occasion for man's assertion of universal significance for his particular values. This defect in human life is too constitutional to be eliminated by a reorganization of society; a fact which constitutes the basic refutation of the utopian dreams of Marxism.

The errors in the Marxist analysis must not, however, obscure its genuine and necessary contribution to the understanding of man.

Marxist materialism is a necessary reaction to Hegelian rationalism and to every form of human pretension which glorifies rational man as essential man.

While romanticism is primarily concerned to assert the vitality of nature and to preserve it against the peril of enervation, there are also elements in romanticism which relate it to the Marxist and the Freudian criticisms of reason's pretended mastery over vital impulse. Nietzsche understands the dishonest pretensions of rational consciousness very well. He writes: "Do not deceive yourself: what constitutes the chief characteristic of modern souls and modern books is not the lying, but the innocence which is part and parcel of their intellectual dishonesty. . . . Our cultured men of today, our 'good men do not lie, that is true; but it does not redound to their honour. The real lie, the genuine, determined honest lie (on whose value you can listen to Plato) would prove too tough and strong an article for them by a long way; it would be asking them to do what people have been forbidden to ask them to do, to open their eyes to their own selves, and to learn to distinguish between 'true' and 'false' in their own selves."[4]

Nietzsche's understanding of the hidden lie, of man's capacity for self-deception, relates him not only to Marx and Freud but to the Christian conception of original sin. But a tentative affinity of thought at this point is quickly transmuted into conflict when Nietzsche seeks to overcome the hidden lie by the robust and "honest" lie. This element in Nietzsche's thought is partly responsible for the brazen dishonesty of contemporary fascist politics. It is needless to point out that the "honest" lie represents no real gain. The dishonest pretensions of human nature are not cured by disavowing the value of truth. We solve no problem by disavowing values to which we are only partially loyal and for which we pretend a greater loyalty than we actually give. We must return to this problem when we consider the problem of sin and truth in terms of the Christian faith (Vol. II, Ch. 7).

[4]*Genealogy of Morals, Third Essay*, Par. 19.

(*c*) Another aspect of the romantic protest against rationalism and idealism, chronologically prior to those previously considered, disputes the claim of reason to be the organizing and forming principle of human life. In this school of romantic thought the unities and forms of nature are emphasized against the disintegrating and divisive tendencies of conscious reason. Bergson, as a modern representative of this school of romanticism, calls attention to the perfect unity of the primitive tribe and of the ant-hill, in which natural impulse guarantees social cohesion. He regards primitive religion as "a precaution against the danger man runs as soon as he thinks at all of thinking of himself alone," as a "defensive reaction against the dissolvent power of intelligence."[5]

Bergson sees that the unities of natural impulse in primitive life are too narrow. He therefore seeks a way of escape in mystical religion from the closed morality and "static religion" of primitive life. Significantly "static religion" is, for Bergson, a substitute for purely natural organic cohesion, after heightened individual self-consciousness has intervened to destroy this cohesion. His absolute distinction between "closed" religion and "open," that is mystical, religion, the one serving the purpose of preserving the narrow unities and forms of nature, and the other breaking these forms and creating universal forms and values, advances his thought beyond usual romantic primitivism but betrays the inability of romanticism to understand the paradox of the form-creating and form-destroying capacity of human spirituality.[6] The static, that is, tribal, religion of Bergson's conception develops imperial tendencies and pretensions of universality which point to the anarchic and dæmonic capacities of even primitive man. On the other hand Bergson's mystical religion must either forswear all historical interest, as classical mysticism does, or run the danger of insinuating partial and relative historical values into its devotion to the universal. Man is, in other words, never pure nature or pure

[5] *Two Sources of Religion and Morality,* pp. 112, 113.
[6] *Cf.* for profound analysis of this paradox, Paul Tillich, *The Interpretation of History,* Part II, Ch. 1.

spirit. All his activities in history are involved in the paradox of creativity and destructiveness, arising from his ability: (*a*) to affirm and to break the unities and forms of natural cohesion; (*b*) to affirm them excessively so that they become forces of anarchy; (*c*) to create higher rational unities and realms of coherence but to corrupt these in turn by insinuating partial and narrow loyalties into them.

In the romanticism of Schopenhauer the protest against the divisiveness of self-conscious reason results in an ascetic rather than primitivistic morality. The unity of vitality (the world as will), which Schopenhauer sets against the diversification and disunity of conscious and rational existence, is not the narrow unity of life with life in primitive social forms but the absolute unity of vitality in the noumenal world, before reason has objectified it into separate entities of will. For Schopenhauer the dæmonic fury of human egotism, its tendency to destroy all forms and unities, is created by the effort of the whole vitality of life, the primal and undifferentiated will, to pour itself through the too narrow vehicle of a single individuality. He writes: "Therefore the will everywhere manifests itself in the multiplicity of individuals. But this multiplicity does not concern the will itself but only its phenomena. The will itself is present whole and undivided in every one of these, and beholds around it the innumerable repeated images of its own nature; but this nature itself, the actual real, it finds only in its inner self. Therefore every one desires everything for himself, desires to possess or at least to control everything." Thus "every individual, though vanishing altogether and diminished to nothing in a boundless world, yet makes itself the centre of the world, has regard for its existence and well-being before anything else in the world—is ready to annihilate the world to maintain its own self, this drop in the ocean, a little longer."[7] For this disease Schopenhauer has no other cure but the denial of the will-to-live, its turning upon itself. He does not however explain from what vantage point the will can gain a fulcrum upon its in-

[7]*The World as Will and Idea* (*English and Foreign Philosophical Library*), p. 428.

dividual expression and press individuality back into its primal and undivided unity. His system of thought leads to essentially Buddhist conclusions; but the Occidental-Christian emphasis upon vitality is too strong to allow these conclusions to emerge in unqualified terms. His redeemed world is undifferentiated will and not, as in Oriental thought, a world in which all vitality has been destroyed.

Obviously the romanticism of Schopenhauer and that of Nietzsche have nothing in common except their common definition of life as being primarily will. In the one case individual vitality is expressed in defiance of all forms and in the other individual vitality is destroyed because its expression in human life is believed to lead inevitably to just such dæmonic fury as Nietzsche glorifies. The negativism which Nietzsche falsely regards as the genius of Christianity is therefore really the Schopenhauerian Buddhistic variant of Christianity.

The contrast between Nietzsche and Schopenhauer sharply focuses the two contrasting strategies of the romantic attack upon rationalism. In Nietzsche the unities and forms which reason creates are regarded either as spurious masters or as perils of the original vitality in man. In Schopenhauer reason is seen as the divisive and disintegrating force of a noumenal unity and form. In other types of romanticism this original unity is conceived as a characteristic of primitive life. The fact that romanticism, in various schools of thought, charges rational self-consciousness with completely contradictory tendencies: with the enervation on the one hand and the accentuation of the natural vitalities on the other; with the creation of too broad and too narrow forms for the expression of the will-to-live or the will-to-power, proves the impossibility of penetrating to the paradox of human spirituality from the perspective of romanticism.

IV

THE ERRORS OF ROMANTICISM

But romanticism errs not only in the contradictory criticisms which it levels at rationalism in general and idealism in particular. It also errs in interpreting the vitality of man, of which it constitutes itself the champion. Its error consists not so much in reducing that vitality to bio-mechanical proportions as bourgeois naturalism tends to do. Its basic error lies in its effort to ascribe to the realm of the biological and the organic what is clearly a compound of nature and spirit, of biological impulse and rational and spiritual freedom. Man is never a simple two-layer affair who can be understood from the standpoint of the bottom layer, should efforts to understand him from the standpoint of the top layer fail. If rationalism tends to depreciate the significance, power, inherent order and unity of biological impulse, romanticism tends to appreciate these without recognizing that human nature knows no animal impulse in its pure form.

Every biological fact and every animal impulse, however obvious its relation to the world below man, is altered because of its incorporation into the human psyche. The freedom of man consists not only, as it were, of the windows of mind which look out from his second story; but also of vents on every level which allow every natural impulse a freedom which animals do not know. Romanticism is therefore wrong in ascribing either the unity or the vitality of animal impulse in man to pure nature. The unity of social cohesion even in the primitive tribe is differentiated from the unity of the wolf pack. Pride of self and contempt of the other is required to maintain it; and social convention enters into the mechanics of its social solidarity. Man has difficulty in controlling the vital force of the sex impulse not because nature has endowed it with an impetus beyond the requirements of human life; on the contrary the sex impulse is controlled with difficulty because it is not imbedded in a total order of natural process in man as in animal life. Each physical impulse, freed of the restraints which hedge it about in nature, can therefore develop imperial tendencies of its own. The difficulty which man experiences in bringing his various impulses into some kind of harmony is therefore not caused by the recalcitrance of nature but occasioned by the freedom of spirit. Even the so-called inertia of nature has spiritual qualities. The anarchy of narrow loyalties in the field of inclusive unities, created by rational freedom, is always partly the consequence, not of the inertia of nature but of the freedom which enables man to accentuate and emphasize natural unities of family and tribe and use them as vehicles of his pride.

The vitality of the total, organized personality is as filled with spiritual factors as the force of specific and particular impulses. Nietzsche seeks to equate his basic concept of vitality, the will-to-power, with purely natural impulse by interpreting the whole of nature as an area of conflict between competing wills.[1] Nietzsche's Zarathustra says; "I am body through and through and nothing else besides. Soul is only a word for something in the body. . . . There is more intelligence in your body than in the highest wisdom. . . . The creating body created the spirit as a tool of its will." Yet pure nature knows no will-to-power. It is informed by the will-to-live, that is by each organism's impulse to survive. The romantic definition of basic natural vitality as "will" is obviously an error prompted by interpreting nature through categories of uniquely human vitality, in which spirit has given natural impulse a conscious organization and direction unknown in animal existence.

Nietzsche's insistence that wisdom, courage and strength are to be found in the purely biological impulses may be a consciously perverse symbolism, prompted by his hatred of rationalism. For in his first great work, *The Birth of Tragedy,* he deliberately relates his interpretation of life to the Dionysian, the form-defying ambitions and lusts of the spirit, which Greek tragedy seeks to interpret. Dionysus is a god. He is spirit and not flesh. The pride and ambition which defy the rule of Zeus in Greek drama are obviously "fruits of the spirit" and Nietzsche makes no effort to interpret them otherwise.

[1]He writes: "Physiologists' must beware of regarding the impulse of survival as the basic drive of organic life. All life desires above all to express its power. Life is itself will-to-power. The impulse of survival is only an indirect and frequent consequence of this will." *Kritik und Zukunft der Kultur,* Ch. IV, Par. 13.

One must suspect that, unlike other romantics, Nietzsche sees the distinction between pure physical impulse and lusts of the spirit clearly enough, but obscures it for polemic purposes.

Rousseau, in contrast to later romantics, also knows this distinction. He recognizes pride and the will-to-power as the spiritual corruption of a simpler animal egoism which he defines with a strikingly unbiological term as "self-respect." He would separate this simple animal impulse of survival "which leads every animal to look to its own preservation" from "the purely relative and factitious feeling which arises in the state of society and leads each individual to make more of himself than any other," in other words, from the very will-to-power which later romantics interpret in purely biological terms. But he imagines that reason "can modify by compassion" the natural impulse of survival and thus "create humanity and virtue" and fails to see that the same capacities of spirit would transmute the will-to-live into a will-to-power.[2]

In this interpretation of human vitalities in purely biological terms, Freudian psychology is in perfect accord with romanticism. The basic biological impulses, according to Freudian psychology, are sexual. But the *id* which is their abode is described as "a chaos, a cauldron of seething excitement." It has "no organization and no unified will, only an impulsion to obtain satisfaction for the instinctual needs according to the pleasure principle."[3] The instinctual drives of the *id* may not be highly organized but they have remarkably subtle strategies for escaping the censor of the conscious ego. They are in other words armed with the guile of spirit. The "little we know about it (the *id*) we have learned from the study of dreamwork," Freud declares (p. 103). This is a significant admission which reveals the basic error in Freudian psychology. How remarkable that the world of dreams, that curious twilight zone between consciousness and unconsciousness should be the portal of entry into the meaning of purely biological impulses. Here Freud might have learned

[2] *Social Contract* (*Everyman's Edition*), p. 197.
[3] Freud, *New Introductory Lectures on Psychoanalysis*, p. 104.

something from Job, who seeks to flee into the simplicity of simple biological existence from the strains of self-consciousness. He seeks this asylum in sleep: "But when I said my bed will comfort me, my couch will ease my complaint, then thou scarest me with visions and terrifiest me with dreams." Dreams reveal something quite different from purely biological impulses. Or can it be supposed that animals are troubled by the Œdipus complex and suffer from a guilty conscience because incestuous impulses struggle for expression in the depths of their unconscious?

The whole of Freudian psychology, not in what it declares but in what it implies, is really a striking proof of how remarkably spirit and nature, animal impulse and spiritual freedom, are compounded in human existence. The *id* reveals subtleties and strategies which do not belong to nature; and on the other hand Freud warns that we must remember that "parts of the ego and the super-ego are unconscious" (p. 105). Freudianism pretends to explain all the complexities of man's spirit in biological terms but fails to explain how biological impulses should have become transmuted into such highly complex spiritual phenomena.[4]

v

ROMANTIC ELEMENTS IN MARXISM

The Marxist interpretation of man's subrational life is of course sharply distinguished from the romantic one. Since the emphasis lies not so much upon the impulses of individuals but upon the common

[4] An interesting admission by Freud of an error he had made in his calculations points much further than Freud realizes. In reporting on his analysis of the Œdipus complex he declares: "Let it suffice to say that, to our astonishment, the result was the reverse of what we had expected. It is not repression that creates anxiety; it is there first and creates repression" (*Ibid.*, p. 120). If Freud could have realized how basic a concomitant of human freedom anxiety is, and how little it has to do with "external danger" it would have become apparent that all the aberrations with which he deals are not the consequence of the repressions of his "super-ego" but arise out of the very character of human freedom. A

drives of social classes, and since these drives are interpreted primarily in economic terms, the interpretation of man's infrarational life avails itself of materialistic rather than biological concepts. It is never pure nature which furnishes the vitality of historical action, according to Marxist theory. "In nature," declares Engels, "insofar as we disregard the reaction of man upon it, there exist only unconscious blind agents which influence one another and through whose reciprocal interplay general laws assert themselves. . . . On the other hand in social history the active agents are always endowed with consciousness, are always men working toward definite ends, with thought and passion. . . . But this difference does not alter the fact that the course of history obeys general laws. . . . Out of the conflicts of innumerable individual wills and acts there arises in the social world a situation which is quite analogous to that in the unconscious and natural one. The ends of actions are willed; but the results, which really flow from these actions, are not willed, or, insofar as the results seem to agree with the willed ends, ultimately they turn out to be quite contrary to the desired consequences."[1]

This description of historical process, the accuracy of which can

---

modern and very intelligent Freudian, Karen Horney, seeks to prove that both the "will-to-power" which Alfred Adler regards as the basic impulse and the libidinal impulse in Freud must be regarded as derivatives from a more basic anxiety. "Neither Freud nor Adler has recognized the rôle which anxiety plays in bringing about such drives" (*The Neurotic Personality of Our Time,*" p. 187). Miss Horney regards Freud's theory as too narrowly biological: "He tends to attribute sociological phenomena to psychic factors and these primarily to biological factors" (p. 28). But Miss Horney in turn has a purely sociological explanation for anxiety: "Modern culture is economically based upon the principle of competition. . . . The potential hostile tension between individuals results in constant generation of fears" (p. 284). In substituting this socio-economic interpretation of the root of anxiety for a purely biological one, Miss Horney comes only slightly nearer to the truth. Modern psychoanalysts might learn much about the basic character of anxiety and its relation to human freedom from the greatest of Christian psychologists, Soren Kierkegaard, who devoted a profound study to this problem: *Der Begriff der Angst.*

[1] F. Engels, *Ludwig Feuerbach* (Duncker ed.), p. 56.

hardly be denied, assigns the vital propulsion of historical creativity to conscious human will and associates the principle of form and direction with a higher suprahuman logic which overrules the wills of men. This logic, the dialectic of history, which must be regarded as a rationalized and mechanized version of the Christian concept of providence, brings Marxism into terms of analogy with Stoic rationalism; but with the difference that its rationalized providence is a law of history and not of nature. It therefore does not make the harmony and unity of nature a premature goal of human activity. Or, stated in other words, Marxism remains within terms of Hegelian rationalism up to this point. It does not deny a rational principle of form. It objects, however, to the Hegelian derivation of the propulsive power of history from pure reason. The propulsive power lies in the dynamics of historical economic relations. Reduced to biological proportions, that would mean in the impulse of hunger. But significantly Marxism does not reduce the vitality of human history to such proportions. It is never simply the hunger impulse, but some organization of society, designed to satisfy it, which determines human thought. "It is precisely the changes in nature brought about through men and not nature as such alone which is the most essential and primary foundation of human thought," declares Engels.[2]

Beginning with this assumption that the vital force of history is an impulse of nature, previously organized and formed by human consciousness in history, Marxism seeks to do justice to both natural vitality and rational freedom in its interpretation of human action and history. It finally fails in this effort only because its metaphysical presuppositions do not allow it to interpret human nature in terms which are consistent with its conception of the relation of natural necessity and spiritual freedom in its social philosophy.

In its social philosophy Marxism is obviously far from interpreting materialism in terms of mechanism. It does not fail to do justice to the element of freedom in human consciousness. "According to the

---

[2] In *Dialectik und Natur*, quoted by Sidney Hook in *Toward an Understanding of Karl Marx*, p. 165.

materialistic conception of history," Engels writes, "the production and reproduction of life constitutes in the last instance the determining factor of history. Neither Marx nor I ever maintained more. Now when some one comes along and distorts this to mean that the economic factor is the *sole* determining factor, he is converting the former proposition into a meaningless, abstract and absurd phrase."[3] Though increasing misery is, on the one hand, the source of the proletariat's rising revolutionary will, Lenin protests against "subservience to the spontaneity of the labor movement," against "belittling the role of the conscious element" and insists that revolutionists must be judged by the quality of their revolutionary will rather than by their economic circumstance.[4] In the same spirit, Engels recognizes that historical factors, into which conscious human decisions have entered, become in turn determining factors in history, together with purely economic causes. He writes: "An historical factor, once it has been brought into the world by another, ultimately economic fact, is able to react upon its surroundings and even affect its own causes."[5]

According to such interpretations Marxism knows nothing of a simple vitality of nature but only vitalities which are formed partly by a superhuman historical logic and partly by human consciousness itself.

But this position is not consistently maintained. Rational consciousness which plays such a role in historical decisions is nevertheless debased into the role of a mere tool of unconscious forces. Marx declares: "The phantasmagorias in the brains of men are necessary supplements . . . of their material life-processes as empirically establishable and bound up with material premises. Morals, religion, metaphysics and other ideologies and the forms of consciousness corresponding to them here no longer retain a look of independence. They have no history, they have no development; but men in developing

---

[3]From letter to J. Bloch, quoted by Hook, *ibid.,* p. 179.
[4]Lenin, *Works,* Vol. IV (Engl. trans.), p. 122.
[5]In letter to F. Mehring, quoted by Hook, *ibid.,* p. 342.

their material production and their material intercourse, alter along with this reality of theirs, their thought and the product of their thought. It is not consciousness which determines life but life which determines consciousness."[6]

If the role of consciousness is inconsistently emphasized and depreciated in Marxist social theory, Marxist psychology and epistemology have the virtue of complete consistency, in the interest of materialistic determinism. Its epistemology is crudely sensationalistic and the psychology reduces rational processes to biological dimensions. Engels declares: "Our consciousness and thought, however supernatural they may seem, are only evidences of a material bodily organ, the brain. Matter is not a product of mind but mind is itself the highest product of matter."[7]

Marxism consequently has at least one characteristic in common with the older liberalism. It reveals a voluntarism, however qualified, in its social theory which its psychology does not support. Within the limits of its philosophy it cannot conceive of the real freedom and transcendence of the human spirit. It introduces sufficient inconsistency into its social theory to give a fairly true picture of historical events, falsified only to the degree in which it uses mechanical concepts to comprehend the paradox of historical freedom and historical destiny. But in its view of man's stature, it is forced to deny the depth of spirit in the structure of human personality. It is consequently unable to understand the real character of human evil. The greed of the dominant bourgeoisie, which symbolizes the principle of evil in Marxist theory, is obviously something more than organized hunger. The possessive impulse is itself more spiritual than physical; and it is obviously only the tool for the lust of power in many instances. But Marxism has no understanding of the will-to-power. That is why it can hope for a complete social harmony as soon as the physical needs of all men are equally satisfied—and can construct a new society in Russia in which the will-to-power of a

[6]*Capital (Modern Library)*, p. 8.
[7]*Ludwig Feuerbach*, p. 64.

new oligarchy expresses itself without social restraint and with tragic fury.

Marxism understands the spiritual character of dishonesty as little as the spiritual character of the possessive and the power impulse. Its great insights into the ideological character of all cultural enterprises are vitiated by its interpretation of consciousness as merely the reflection and the product of material conditions. Marxism, in other words, attributes the human tendency to hide egoistic interests behind ideals of supposedly general validity, to the mere finiteness of the human mind, its dependence upon its environment. But it fails thereby to explain why the human spirit should feel under the necessity of making such pretensions. Why does not man merely seek his own interest as animals do? Precisely because his spirit transcends his impulses of survival sufficiently to envisage a more general realm of value than his own life, he must seem to be loyal to this more inclusive realm even when he is not. The same spiritual capacity which necessitates dishonesty also adds an element of conscious deception to the errors of unconscious dishonesty. Engels recognizes a part of this truth, but only a part, in the words: "Ideology is a process which of course is carried on with the consciousness of the so-called thinkers, but with a false consciousness. The real driving force which moves it remains unconscious; otherwise there would be no ideology."[8] Engels is right in seeing that there is a true consciousness beyond the false consciousness, though that insight does not agree with the general Marxist position that all consciousness is merely the reflection of the balance of interest in which a man stands. But he is wrong in assuming that the rationalization of interest is possible only if it remains unconscious. It is both conscious and unconscious. Marxist political polemic, incidentally, constantly implies a denial of this definition of completely unconscious rationalization, by treating the ideologies of the foe with a moral scorn which only conscious wrongdoing deserves.

[8]In letter to F. Mehring, quoted by Hook, *op. cit.*, p. 341.

THE SOCIAL BASIS OF CONFLICTING THEORIES

The ambiguous and equivocal position of the older rationalistic naturalism in the conflict between idealism and romanticism, psychoanalysis and materialism, has been previously mentioned, and attributed to the covert rationalism in this naturalism. But neither the neutrality of the older naturalism nor the fury of the attack from the more recent romantic and materialistic type of naturalism can be understood in purely cultural terms. The real dynamic of the struggle must be explained in socio-economic terms. The naturalism which dominated eighteenth-century thought was the philosophical expression of rising middle-class life. This class, in the period of its revolt against feudalism, made naturalistic philosophy a vehicle of its appreciation of the vitalities of nature and the relativities of history against the conservatism of a Christian-classical rationalism. This feudal conservatism used the idea of immutable and perennially valid rational-social forms as a support for the society which it had established and the reconstruction of which it resisted. But these same middle classes have now become the dominant forces in modern society, at least in what is still left of bourgeois civilization. They have therefore allowed their sense of vitality and relativity, their understanding of man in his relation to the processes of nature and history, to be subordinated to the rationalistic sense of established form. Since this bourgeois rationalism was indebted to Stoic and Epicurean, rather than Platonic, rationalism from the very beginning, it had never had a strong sense of tension between natural vitality and rational discipline. The real tensions of life were obscured in its thought. It lacked all sense of the tragic while it was rising to power; and it could not consequently be expected to appreciate the tragic conflicts of life, particularly the paradox of creativity and destruction, in the period of its triumph. For this reason the Nietzschean and Marxist protest against both Christianity and rationalism has more affinities with the essential insights of Christianity than the less obviously anti-Christian thought of the bourgeois world.

The romantic and materialistic protest against the pretensions of rational man as essential man and against the perils of the enervation of vitality by reason is borne by the two classes in modern society: the lower middle classes and the industrial workers, who are forced by historical necessity to challenge the economic and political supremacy of the higher middle classes. The lower middle classes express themselves in various forms of romanticism culminating in fascist politics; while the industrial workers gravitate naturally toward the philosophy of materialism and communist politics. These protests gain in plausibility as the power and the prestige of the bourgeois civilization decays; for the truth embodied in a culture maintains itself, and hides the error in which all historical truth is involved, more by the prestige and stability of the civilization in which it is incarnated than by the inherent plausibility of its ideas.

Unfortunately, in spite of the important truths about human nature and history which romanticism and materialism have discovered, these philosophies are becoming instruments of a deepening decadence on the one hand and of abortive regeneration on the other. They do not see the problem of human nature in sufficient depth and therefore remain in the confusion, and sometimes accentuate the errors, in which modern culture has been involved from the beginning. Romanticism asserts both the vitality of nature and its primitive and organic unities against the universalities of rationalism. It therefore either defies every principle of form and order (as in Nietzscheanism) or it emphasizes primitive and inadequate natural forms of unity (*Blut und Boden*). It thus becomes an instrument of decadence, hastening the destruction of bourgeois civilization without offering a way to a new order. Significantly the lower middle classes (individualists who desperately flee from their isolation into unities of race and nation, and persons without a sense of history who rediscover history in terms of primitive tribalism) are the instruments of this decadence.

Marxist materialism on the other hand contains a genuine principle of construction. It is itself a type of rationalism; for it believes in the forming and creative capacity of reason, though not of human reason. The creative human force in history lies below the level of reason in the vital impulses which are expressed in the dynamic of class relations. But it believes that these vital impulses are under the simple control of a higher logic, a dialectic of history. Under the illusion that it can tame the destructiveness of man by a simple change in social organization, that it can purge human creativity of its destructiveness, it prompts modern rebels against an established social and cultural order to a dæmonic fury, assuring them that their destruction will result in a new society in which the vital forces of human existence will be brought under, and remain within, the forming power of a dialectical suprahuman historical logic. If romanticism leads in politics to primitivistic tribalism and concomitant anarchy, Marxist materialism believes that the anarchy of class conflict in modern society can be guided, by those who understand its underlying logic, into a resolution of all conflict.

It is not altogether strange that Marxist politics should result in political realities in Russia, not too distinguishable from the fruits of fascism. For in both cases the paradoxical relation of the creative and the destructive forces in human life is not fully understood; nor is the relation of form to vitality in human creativity fully comprehended. The romantic fascist, conscious of the element of pretension in the culture of bourgeois rationalism, dispenses with all norms and rational principles of order, insisting upon the self-justifying character of the romantic-natural order of race and blood, if only it is expressed with sufficient vitality. The Marxist rebel, also conscious of the element of pretension in the social standards of the rationalist, but oblivious to the inevitability of a degree of pretension in all forms of human spirituality including his own, blandly hopes for a new social order in which human creativity will express itself without destructiveness; and human vitality will be captured and contained in a perfect social harmony. The provisional cynicism of the Marxist is thus given a moral sanction and facade of a too simple principle of universal form and order; just as the deeper cynicism of the romanticist, unable to exist in terms of pure nihilism, is compounded with a too primitive and narrow principle of natural cohesion and order. In both cases the moral façade allows human impulses to express themselves without sufficient discipline. Hence the similarity in the political fruits of these two creeds. It must be admitted, however, that the moral cynicism and nihilism of romantic fascism is more unqualifiedly destructive than the provisional cynicism and ultimate utopianism of communism.

It might be added that the insights of Freudian psychology, considered in terms of social history, may be regarded as elaborations of the basic romantic-materialistic protest against rationalistic interpretations of human nature and history. In the Freudian protest those aspects of a common rebellion are emphasized which are available to the members of the dominant social classes rather than to the lower middle class and proletarian rebels. In Freudianism the dark labyrinths of man's unconscious impulses are illumined in such a way that he loses confidence in the pretensions of rational man and the disciplines of culture and civilization. Since these insights are expressed within the terms of the given social order and do not envisage moral or political alternatives, they lead to a deeper pessimism which despairs not of a particular civilization or culture but of civilization itself. This may be the consequence of the sense of impotence of individuals who are socially too bound to their culture and civilization to allow themselves to envisage alternatives. It may also be a way of deflecting insights into the pretensions of a particular historical form and discipline so that the individual who is still attached to it socially and benefits from its privileges, need not undergo the pain of seeking socio-moral alternatives. In *Civilization and Its Discontents* Freud arrives at conclusions almost as nihilistic in their implications as Nietzsche's. He believes that the discipline of the super-ego (significantly regarded not as transcendent spirit but as a social construct) leads inevitably to complexes and aberrations. Provisionally inclined to draw anarchistic conclusions from these premises, Freud is ultimately unable either to deny the necessity of social discipline or to find a real cure for the psychopathic aberrations which are, in his opinion, inevitable concomitants of such discipline. This insoluble problem leads him into the cul-de-sac of pessimism.

In a sense his pessimistic conclusions reveal the basic spiritual problem of the upper middle classes as clearly as Marxism reveals that of the proletarian classes and fascism that of the lower middle classes. Freudianism is a typical product of the uneasy conscience of that portion of the upper middle class which has discovered the realm of chaos under the pretenses and partial achievements of rational order and discipline, but is unable or unwilling to find a basic solution for the problem which it has discovered.

The fact is, that it is not possible to solve the problem of vitality and form, or fully to understand the paradox of human creativity and destructiveness within the limits of the dimension in which modern culture, whether rationalistic or romantic, views this problem. Within those limits modern culture is forced to choose between four equally untenable viewpoints: (*a*) It exalts destructive fury because it is vital, as in fascism; or (*b*) it imagines a harmony of vital forces in history which the facts belie, as in liberalism; or (*c*) it admits the dishonest pretensions of rational discipline and the reality of human destructiveness provisionally but hopes for a complete change in the human situation through a revolutionary reorganization of society, as in Marxism; or (*d*) it despairs of any basic solution for the problem of vitality and discipline and contents itself with palliatives, as in Freudianism.

CHAPTER III

INDIVIDUALITY IN MODERN CULTURE

INDIVIDUALITY is a fruit of both nature and spirit. It is the product of nature because the basis of selfhood lies in the particularity of the body. The self is most obviously separated from other selves by the simple fact that it is grounded in a physical organism which maintains its discrete existence and has its particular and dated history. Yet nature rises only gradually to the reality of individuality. In the inorganic world substances or forces are integrated and disintegrated so as to produce capriciously "unique" events (the upheaval of a particular mountain, for instance, and its gradual corrosion) but no unique or irreproducible unities. The inorganic world is thus subject to recurrences which can be charted with mathematical exactitude; hence the intimate relation between physics and mathematics.

In the organic world nature rises to the particularity of organisms, characterized by an interdependent and indestructible unity. The plant lives as a unity and its death means the destruction of that particular unity, its component elements sinking back into the inorganic world. On a still higher level animal life achieves a higher measure of discrete particularity, through an organism with a specific centre of unified interdependence, a central nervous system. Through this nervous system the animal achieves a higher degree of separation from its environment; yet its actions are governed by instincts which bind the individual animal to the general characteristics of the species. Variations in colour, size and, possibly, temper are capricious rather than significant and are subject to predictable recurrences. In animal life it is the species rather than the individual which is really unique. The particular animal merely expresses through endless repetition the special life-strategy of the species.

Genuine individuality, embodying both discreteness and uniqueness, is a characteristic of human life. It must consequently be regarded as the product of spirit as well as of nature. Nature supplies particularity but the freedom of the spirit is the cause of real individuality. Man, unlike animal existence, not only has a centre but he has a centre beyond himself. Man is the only animal which can make itself its own object. This capacity for self-transcendence which distinguishes spirit in man from soul (which he shares with animal existence), is the basis of discrete individuality, for this self-consciousness involves consciousness of the world as "the other." The animal knows its particular needs and the particular objects in its environment which satisfy those needs. Its consciousness therefore does not transcend the natural process in which it is involved. Animal consciousness is merely the expression of a central organic unity of an organism in relation to its immediate environment. Human consciousness involves the sharp distinction between the self and the totality of the world. Self-knowledge is thus the basis of discrete individuality.

Human capacity for self-transcendence is also the basis of human freedom and thereby of the uniqueness of the individual. Human consciousness not only transcends natural process but it transcends itself. It thereby gains the possibility for those endless variations and elaborations of human capacities which characterize human existence. Every impulse of nature in man can be modified, extended, repressed and combined with other impulses in countless variations. In consequence no human individual is like another, no matter how similar their heredity and environment. To a certain degree man is free to reject one environment for another. If he dislikes the spiritual environment of the twentieth century he may consciously choose to live by the patterns of the thirteenth century. If he finds his physical environment uncongenial he has the capacity to modify it. The pride of modern man has sometimes tempted him to forget that there are limits of creatureliness which he cannot transcend and that there are inexorable forces of nature which he cannot defy. It is nevertheless important to remember that human spirituality is sharply distinguished from animal existence by the measure of human freedom and the consequent degree of discrete and unique individuality in man.

Human individuality, being a product of spirit as well as of nature, is subject to development. Primitive man is inserted with comparative frictionless harmony into the "primeval we" of group life.[1] He emerges from this group consciousness only gradually as an individual. But what emerges is an original endowment, present from the beginning. The uniqueness of this special endowment is proved not only by the fact that it develops in human life only but by the character of primitive existence. The primitive community is forced to establish certain common usages and methods of restraining natural impulse whereas animal existence, having no freedom, faces no problem of achieving unity. The lack of social freedom in a primitive community is a testimony of the inchoate freedom of primitive man. This freedom makes for a wide variety of the expression of impulses. Since the primitive community lacks the intelligence to achieve unity within variety it must insist upon uniformity, enforcing standards which may have emerged at first by pure historical caprice but which are gradually submitted to crude pragmatic tests of usefulness.[2]

[1] Cf. *inter alia,* Fritz Kunkel, *Charakter, Einzelmensch und Gruppe.*
[2] Efforts to explain the emergence of "mind," that is of human freedom, in purely sociological terms are self-contradictory, sometimes to an amusing degree. Thus Professor George H. Mead, who elaborates a social behaviourist viewpoint, widely held in America, reasons in his *Mind, Self and Society:* "[Our view] must be clearly distinguished from

ii

THE CHRISTIAN SENSE OF INDIVIDUALITY

It would be impossible at this point to trace the development of individuality through the centuries of early civilization. What is important for us is that both the idea and the fact of individuality achieve their highest development in the Christian religion and that modern culture, beginning with the Renaissance, seeks to raise the idea of individuality beyond the limits set for it in the Christian faith by the law of love on the one hand and by the idea of the creatureliness of man on the other; and ends by losing the idea and the fact altogether.

Before tracing this remarkable self-destruction of individuality in modern culture it is necessary to anticipate later chapters by a brief exposition of the Christian view of the individual. Christianity is responsible for a heightened sense of individuality because, according to the Christian faith, the human spirit in its freedom is finally bound only by the will of God, and the secret of its heart is only fully known and judged by the divine wisdom. This means that human life has an ultimate religious warrant for transcending the

---

the partially social view of mind. According to this view, mind can get expression only within or in terms of an organized social group, yet it is nevertheless in some sense a native endowment, a congenital or hereditary biological attribute of the individual organism. . . . According to this latter view the social process presupposes and in a sense is the product of mind; in direct contrast is our opposite view that mind presupposes and is the product of the social process. The advantage of our view is that it enables us to give a detailed account of, and actually to explain the genesis and development of mind" (p. 224). This viewpoint, which has nothing to commend it but rigorous consistency, sacrifices its consistency when Professor Mead explains in a footnote: "Hence it is only in human society, only within the peculiarly complex context of social relations and interactions which the human central nervous system makes physiologically possible, that minds arise or can arise; and thus also human beings are evidently the only biological organisms which are or can be self-conscious or possessed of selves." P. 235.

custom of tribes, rational rules of conduct, and all general and abstract norms of behaviour. Yet Christian morality at its best is not antinomian because it is bound to the will of God as revealed in Christ: "All things are yours but ye are Christ's," said St. Paul. In the mysticism of Plotinus we find something of the same sense of the transcendence of the human spirit. But mysticism results only in an immediate heightening of the sense of man's spiritual unique-ness and in an ultimate loss of the uniqueness of the individual. Unique individuality is identified with natural creatureliness in mysticism and is therefore regarded as the very root of evil which must be overcome. In the words of Meister Eckhardt: "Thou must be pure in heart; and only that heart is pure which has exterminated creaturehood."[1] According to the Christian faith each individual life is subjected to the will of God. It is this obedience to the divine will which establishes the right relation between the human will in its finiteness and the whole world order as ruled by God. According to mysticism, even when interpreted in Meister Eckhardt's semi-Christian sense, virtue can be achieved only by the annihilation of the individual's will: "The poor man is not he who wants to do the will of God but he who lives in such a way as to be free of his own will and from the will of God, even *as he was when he was not.*"[2] Mysticism in other words insists on the full dimension of height in the human spirit but identifies unique individuality with a creature-liness which must be overcome. Ultimately the individual is absorbed into the divine. In various nature religions the human spirit may transcend a given circumstance but it is bound to the spirit of its tribe, nation, culture or era. Thus only Christianity (and Judaism inasfar as it participates in the prophetic-Biblical tradition and does not allow itself to be bound to a law of a nation) sees and establishes the human spirit in its total depth and uniqueness.

Naturally this heightened sense of individuality is not without its

[1]*Meister Eckhardt*, comp. by Franz Pfeiffer, trans. by C. deB. Evans, Vol. I. p. 48.
[2]*Ibid.*, p. 220.

perils. If the religious sense of responsibility to God and contrite humility before God is weakened, Christian individuality may become the source of anarchy. This may explain some of the cruel and dæmonic aspects of the history of western Christendom.

During the whole period of medieval Catholicism Christian individuality never came to a consistent expression. This was partly due to socio-economic causes. The agrarian-feudal economy of medievalism was in still intimate relation to the previous tribal unity of the Teutonic tribes; and social complexity had not yet forced the full emergence of individual consciousness. On the other hand the Catholic religion prevented the emergence of a high sense of individuality, partly by the amalgam of Greek rationalism in its theology which subjected the individual to the universal rules of the natural law; and partly by its religious authoritarianism which interposed the religious institution between the soul and God. Since the will of God which transcended all rational abstractions was nevertheless completely interpreted by an historic institution, involving casuistic applications of general norms to specific situations, the individual always remained conscious of the general categories, social, moral and political of which he was an exemplar. He never expressed himself fully as an individual.

The modern sense of individuality therefore begins on the one hand in Protestantism and on the other hand in the Renaissance. From the standpoint of the typical modern, Protestantism and Renaissance are merely two different movements in the direction of individual freedom, the only difference between them being that the latter is a little more congenial to the modern spirit than the former. The real significance of the two movements lies in the fact that one represents the final development of individuality within terms of the Christian religion and the other an even further development of individuality beyond the limits set in the Christian religion, that is, the development of the "autonomous" individual. It is this autonomous individual who really ushers in modern civilization and who is completely annihilated in the final stages of that civilization.

The heightened sense of individuality in Protestantism is expressed theologically in the Reformation principle of the "priesthood of all believers." The emphasis lies not so much upon the individual's capacity to know the truth as upon his indivisible responsibility to God, and upon an assurance of mercy for his sins which no institution can mediate, if individual faith is wanting. Involved in this conception is a strong sense of the peril of meaninglessness in the freedom of human spirituality which only the individual's direct relation to God can overcome. Luther puts the matter in a typically robust illustration: "When you lie upon your deathbed you cannot console yourself by saying 'The pope said thus and so.' The devil can drill a hole through that assurance. Suppose the pope were wrong? Then you will be defeated. Therefore you must be able to say at all times: 'This is the word of God.'"

The Protestant Christian sense of the individual's immediate responsibility to God implies and develops a strong anti-legalism; not only because it is felt that no particular external norm can guarantee the quality of motives which prompt the conforming deed, but also because legal and rational moral norms are regarded as inadequate guides of virtue amidst the infinite possibilities of good and evil which every action presents in both its internal and external facets. Protestantism significantly places the rational concept of the "natural law" in a more insignificant position than in Catholic thought. It has too strong a sense of the individual occasion, and the uniqueness of the individual who faces the occasion, to trust in general rules. The will of God is the norm, the life of Christ is the revelation of that will, and the individual faces the awful responsibility of seeking to do God's will amidst all the complexities of human existence with no other authoritative norm but that ultimate one.

Despite the religious profundity of this conception of a human spirit, which transcends all circumstances and norms so much as to be responsible to no one but God, Protestantism has frequently contributed to the anarchy of modern life by its inability to suggest and to support relative standards and structures of social virtue and political justice. It has thus indirectly contributed to the romantic defiance of all rational and traditional norms in the sphere of politics and morals. In that sense the profoundest expression of Christian individuality is itself partly responsible for the anarchy of modern life. The individual who is admonished, "All things are yours but ye are Christ's," may, in a period of religious decay, easily lose the sense of ultimate religious responsibility expressed in the words, "But ye are Christ's," and remember only the law-defying implications of the first part of the dictum: "All things are yours."

III

THE IDEA OF INDIVIDUALITY IN THE RENAISSANCE

If Protestantism represents the final heightening of the idea of individuality within terms of the Christian religion, the Renaissance is the real cradle of that very unchristian concept and reality: the autonomous individual. The Renaissance emphasis upon individual autonomy is partly a reaction to Catholic authoritarianism. Its part in the emancipation of learning from the tyranny of religious dogmatism is so great that most of the uncritical devotees of the "scientific spirit" of modernity have not discerned the peril in this idea of autonomy. Ostensibly Renaissance thought is a revival of classicism, the authority of which is either set against the authority of Christianity or used to modify the latter. Yet classic thought has no such passion for the individual as the Renaissance betrays. The fact is that the Renaissance uses an idea which could have grown only upon the soil of Christianity. It transplants this idea to the soil of classic rationalism to produce a new concept of individual autonomy, which is known in neither classicism nor Christianity.

The nexus between the Christian and the Renaissance individual is not the Protestant idea of the individual's sole responsibility to God but the medieval mystical idea of the infinite potentialities of the human spirit. A straight line leads from Meister Eckhardt to Nicholas of Cusa, one of the great creative spirits of the Renaissance, via the "Brothers of the Common Life" and John Ruysbroek.[1] To the mystics who followed Eckhardt, Christ was the symbol of the divine potentialities of man. "The Father," wrote Eckhardt, "is begetting his Son unceasingly and furthermore I say he begets me his Son, his very own Son." There is no upper limit for the potentiality of the human spirit: "The just soul is like to God, by the side of God, on a level with God, not under nor yet over."[2]

In the thought of Eckhardt this divine potentiality does not make for individuality but ultimately destroys it. How the Renaissance transmutes the idea of man's divine potentiality into the concept of individuality and uniqueness is beautifully illustrated in the prayer of Nicholas of Cusa: "Thy true countenance is without any limitations and has neither quantitative nor qualitative, neither temporal nor spacial qualities; for it is the absolute form, the countenance of countenances. . . . Every countenance which gazes into Thine own therefore beholds something not different from its own because it beholds its own truth. . . . O Lord, how wonderful is Thy countenance which must be conceived as youthful by the youth, as mature by the man and as old by the old. In every countenance the countenance of countenances is veiled as in a mystery. Unveiled it cannot be seen until man enters that secret and dark stillness which is beyond all countenances and in which nothing is left of the knowledge and concept of countenances."[3] This is a remarkable sentiment of a Christian mystic standing at the threshold of the Renaissance. He feels and expresses no opposition to Christian thought; yet the Renaissance emphasis upon unique individuality breaks the bounds of both Christian and mystic thought. The prophetic-Biblical note of God as the judge of men "whose thoughts are not our thoughts" is wholly lost in the contemplation of God who is the fulfillment of each unique human individuality but not the judge of its sin. The

---

[1]*Cf.* Ernst Cassierer, *Individuum und Kosmos in der Philosophie der Renaissance,* p. 35.
[2]*Op. cit.,* Vol I, p. 162.
[3]From *De visione Dei,* Ch. 6. Quoted from Cassierer, *op. cit.,* p. 34.

mystic concept of an eternity which finally swallows up all individuality is significantly retained as an afterthought.

Giordano Bruno is less Christian and more neo-Platonic than Cusa and his primary interest is in the divine potentiality of the human spirit rather than its uniqueness. His concern is to assert that man "becomes a god through intellectual contact with that transcendent object and has no thought but of divine things and shows himself insensible by that which ordinary men feel most of all."[4] But in him also the mystical doctrine of the divine potentiality of the human spirit is subtly made the bearer of the new doctrine of the uniqueness of human individuality: "Poetry is not born in rules; rules are derived from poetry. But how are true poets to be recognized? By their song."[5] Bruno arrives at the idea of a completely autonomous individual; and this idea inspires his resistance to authoritarianism. The source of the soul's duty lies in the soul's own nature. And this nature is not some general law of rationality as in Stoic or Kantian thought. An inner light guides every man. Since for Bruno infinity of space is a symbol of the infinite potentialities of the soul, it might be supposed that the doctrine of immortality would be important for his thought. His attitude toward the hope of immortality is, however, ambiguous. Here his pantheism overcomes his strong sense of individuality, just as Nicholas of Cusa crowns his view of the fulfillment of each individuality in the divine with a mystic vision of "dark stillness" which swallows up all individuality.

On this point the Renaissance anticipates the tendency of later rationalism to destroy the concept of individuality; and proves that it has a less tenable ground for this concept than the Biblical religion. In Biblical religion the idea of individuality is preserved in the hope of the resurrection. The thoroughly unrational idea of the "resurrection of the body" has the virtue of expressing a dark and unconscious recognition of the sources of individuality in nature as well as in spirit. Without the particularity of the body the spirit of man is easily lost in the universality of divine spirit, in the undifferentiated being

[4]William Boulting, *Giordano Bruno*, p. 178.   [5]*Ibid.*, p. 180.

of eternity. Naturally a consistent rationalism finds it impossible to affirm eternal significance for the particularities which have emerged in temporal existence.

The Renaissance concept of individuality, rooted in the idea of the greatness and the uniqueness of man, naturally implies his liberty. It was therefore one of the primary interests of Renaissance thinkers to prove that divine foreknowledge does not circumscribe human liberty of action or invalidate man's creative role in history. The freedom of the will was a problem of primary interest to the thinkers of the Italian Renaissance.[6]

The Renaissance emphasis upon individuality is obviously not prompted by any simple set of ideas, for it presses various philosophies into its service. The sober, sceptical and earth-bound Montaigne expresses the idea as fully as the God-intoxicated Bruno. Montaigne's primary interest is in the endless variety and relativity of forms in which human life expresses itself. He is scornful of every effort to bring these multifarious forms under general categories, whether moral, legal or rational. Montaigne's sense of individuality is partly an extension of this interest in variety. Human beings exhibit an endless diversity: "Plutarke saith in some place that he findes no such great difference between beast and beast, as he findeth diversitie between man and man. . . . I could finde in my heart to endeare upon Plutarke; and say there is more difference between such and such a man than there is diversitie between such a man and such a beast."[7] In a sense Montaigne pays tribute to individualization inasfar as it is the fruit of natural history, of the diversity of geographic and historical circumstances; while the leaders of the Italian Renaissance are primarily interested in the individualization of spirit, in the mystery of introspection and the art of self-portraiture. Yet Montaigne is equally interested with Petrarch and the Italian Renaissance in the art of autobiography, boasts that, "I present myself standing

[6]Two treatises of Italian thinkers are particularly devoted to this theme: Pompanazzi's *De fato, libero arbitrio et praedestinatione* (1436) and Valla's *De libero arbitrio* (1520).

[7]*The Essays of Montaigne,* trans. by John Florio, Book I, Ch. XLII.

up and lying down, front and back, right and left and in all my natural attitudes,"[8] and justifies the importance of such a study by the conviction that "every man has in himself the whole form of human nature."[9] The idea, despite Montaigne's naturalism, is really derived from a combination of nominalistic and mystic thought and we find it more fully elaborated in the romanticism of a later period, in Goethe's and Schleiermacher's view of the individual as a revelation of the universal.

IV

BOURGEOIS CIVILIZATION AND INDIVIDUALITY

Since the Renaissance doctrine of individuality avails itself of various philosophical and theological ideas, Christian and classic, pantheistic and naturalistic, mystic and nominalistic, we cannot attribute the emergence of the doctrine to the potency of any of these ideas. Its cultural roots lie, paradoxically, to a larger degree in the Christian religion itself than in the classical influences which corroded the medieval form of the Christian religion. But this does not answer the question why this particular emphasis should have come to expression at just this time and should have dominated the culture of modernity until a recent date. The answer must be found in the social rather than in the purely cultural history of the era. The rise of the sense of individuality corresponds with the emergence of the commercial, the bourgeois classes. The Italian city states were the seed-plot of bourgeois culture. While the rest of Europe was still under the dominance of the landed aristocrat, the Italian cities provided the rising business man with the opportunity of forming his own culture; and it is significant that the forms of this culture anticipated in many particulars the culture of the Enlightenment which signalized the triumph of the business man in the rest of Europe.

The business man developed a form of economic power which

[8]*Ibid.*, Book III, Ch. 8.　　　[9]*Ibid.*, Book III, Ch. 2.

depends upon individual initiative and resourcefulness rather than upon hereditary advantages; and which creates dynamic rather than static social relationships. It naturally sees human history as a realm of human decisions rather than of inexorable destiny. In the same way it regards nature as an instrument rather than the master of the human will. The rise of the natural sciences was at first merely a by-product of this sense of human self-reliance, for nature was regarded merely as the mirror of the greatness of man. But as science gradually contributed to man's actual mastery of natural forces it gave a new impetus of its own to the idea of human self-sufficiency.

This pride and power of man, who surprises himself by the influence of his decisions upon history and the power of his actions upon nature, who discovers himself as a creator, is subtly merged with the Christian idea of the significance of each man in the sight of God. It is indeed a this-worldly version of the latter. That is proved by the fact that neither the non-Christian nations nor the Catholic nations, in the culture of which Christianity was modified by classical influences, participated in any large degree in the dynamics of modern commercial-industrial civilization. It is proved also by the bewildering complexity of interactions between Protestant religious individualism and the secular individualism of bourgeois culture. The modern individual could not have arisen in any but a Christian culture; yet the progress of his thought destroys the Christian basis of individuality; and the development of his civilization destroys the social and economic basis for the effectiveness of individual initiative, resourcefulness and decisive action.

The social and economic destruction of individuality is a consequence of the mechanical and impersonal elaborations of a commercial culture which reach their culmination in the development of an industrial civilization. Modern industrialism pushes the logic of impersonal money and credit relationships to its final conclusion. The processes of production and exchange, which remain imbedded in the texture of personal relationships in a simpler economy, are gradually emancipated and established as a realm of automatic and rationalized relations in which the individual is subordinated to the process. The same historical dynamic, which corrodes the traditional social unities, loyalties and inertias of medieval agrarianism and thus allows the business man to emerge and assume a creative role in history, continues the process of corrosion until communities and nations are bound together primarily by ties of mechanical interdependence and tempted to conflict by the frictions which this interdependence entails.

Inevitably the early vision of capitalistic philosophers (Adam Smith) of a process of production and exchange which would make for automatic harmony of interests is not realized. Man controls this process just enough to disturb its harmony. The men who control and own the machines become the wielders of social power on a vaster scale and of more dynamic quality than previous history has known. They cannot resist the temptations of power any more than the older oligarchies of history. But they differ from previous oligarchies in that their injustices are more immediately destructive of the very basis of their society than the injustices of a less dynamic age. Modern society is consequently involved in processes of friction and decay which threaten the whole world with disaster and which seem to develop by a kind of inexorable logic of their own, defying all human efforts to arrest the decay.

The bourgeois individuals who initiated the age with such blithe confidence in the power of human decisions over historical fate see an historical process unfold in which individuals appear as hapless and impotent victims of an ineluctable destiny. Most of their decisions tend, in fact, to aggravate the difficulties of modern society; for those who hold significant economic and social power make decisions in the interest of maintaining their power so that the decisions fall into a general pattern of social anarchy. Thus the bourgeois individual who emerges from the social cohesions, restraints and inertias of medievalism and imagines himself master of nature and history, perishes ingloriously in the fateful historical necessities and the frantically constructed tribal solidarities of the age of decay.

The lower middle classes fashion this solidarity out of corrupted forms of romanticism; and the proletarian class conceives a philosophy of history which supplants the bourgeois sense of historical mastery with a sense of submission to historical destiny. Unfortunately this class is sufficiently corrupted by the mechanism of the age to deny what is true as well as what is false in bourgeois individualism. Therefore it conceives of historical destiny in mechanical terms and tries to comprehend history in terms of "laws of motion."

v

THE DESTRUCTION OF INDIVIDUALITY IN NATURALISM

The mistake of the Renaissance was to overestimate the freedom and the power of man in history. This power and freedom in history is ambiguous. His actions and decisions are less unique than he imagines them to be. That is proved by the fact that the character of his decisions can be averaged statistically and predicted with fair exactitude according to the circumstances in which they are made. His privileges and securities, or lack of them, his mode of work, whether rural or urban, are fairly determinative in prompting his decisions. They are, moreover, less potent in determining historical direction than the Renaissance had assumed. They are in each instant compounded with, modified, and frequently overruled by partly conscious and partly unconscious hopes, fears and strivings of his fellow creatures. Frequently his own conscious decisions are overruled by his own unconscious fears. In such a moment the individual remains individual only in the highest reaches of transcendent spirit, where he is able to defy historical fate and appeal to a realm of meaning in which his life has a significance which history denies. Yet his ability to make decisions in history depends upon this same sphere of transcendence. Any individual who is completely immersed in historical process is naturally forced to accept the moral, political and religious norms which the caprices of that process make definitive at a given moment. His ability to challenge the victory of a culture or civilization depends upon a measure of freedom over its presuppositions and credos. Frequently, and possibly usually, this means complete dependence upon some competing philosophy of life and history. This dependence may sustain him as long as his own cause still promises a measure of success. An irrevocable defeat of a socio-historical cause which gives meaning to the life of the individual must create a complete sense of meaninglessness unless the individual is sustained by a religion which interprets such defeats from the aspect of the eternal.

If, however, the eternity to which the individual flees is an undifferentiated realm of being, which negates all history and denies its significance, the individual is himself swallowed up in that negation, as the logic of mysticism abundantly proves. Consequently it is only in a prophetic religion, as in Christianity, that individuality can be maintained. This faith alone does justice to both the natural and the spiritual bases of individuality. Since it takes history seriously, it affirms the significance of the distinctive character achieved by each individual within the tensions of historical existence, tensions which have their root in natural, geographic, economic, racial, national and sexual conditions. But since it interprets history from the standpoint of the eternal (*i.e.* since it sees the source and end of history beyond history) it gives the individual a place to stand within a world of meaning, even when and if the particular historical movement into which he is integrated should fail completely.

No philosophy or religion can change the structure of human existence. That structure involves individuality in terms of both the natural fact of a particular body and the spiritual fact of self-transcendence. But religions and philosophies have an important bearing upon the possibility of the ego, maintaining itself in such a position of transcendence. Naturalistic philosophies may (and in modern nationalism do) destroy individuality by emphasizing consanguinity and other natural forces of social uniformity as the only basis of meaning; spiritualistic philosophies may on the other hand prompt the transcendent ego (spirit) to flee from history with all its perils of particularity and its uncertain vicissitudes into a realm of meaning which negates history and individuality. Both the concept and reality of individuality are a characteristic product of the Christian faith because it is only within terms of that faith that an individual may stand both inside and outside of history. He stands inside because his faith affirms the meaningfulness of history and he stands outside because his faith asserts that history is borne by an eternal will.

The history of modern culture has a peculiar pathos because the same Renaissance tendencies which had asserted and modified the Christian idea of individuality in such a way as to accentuate the individual's historic power and freedom unduly finally led to the destruction of any genuine concept of individuality. Since this cultural destruction of individuality was both antecedent to and synchronous with the development of a mechanical civilization, it may have contributed to, and in turn been influenced by, the latter's practical annihilation of individual freedom and uniqueness.

The logic of this annihilation can be simply stated. The naturalistic portion of modern culture seeks to reduce the whole dimension of spirit in man to an undifferentiated "stream of consciousness" if indeed it does not seek to reduce consciousness itself to purely mechanical proportions. Idealism on the other hand is interested in spirit as mind; but it generally dissipates the distinctive qualities of human selfhood in the abstract universalities of mind. Between them the reality of selfhood remains in constant peril.

Beginning with Thomas Hobbes a fairly consistent denial of the significance of selfhood, certainly of transcendent individuality, runs through the empirical and naturalistic tradition. In Hobbes's sensationalistic psychology and materialistic metaphysics there is no place for human individuality. His individuals are animal natures whose egohood consists in the impulse of survival. Human reason serves the purpose of extending this impulse beyond the limits known in nature, thus creating conflict between equally valid claims of various individuals; but there is no rational transcendence over impulse where these claims might be arbitrated. They must therefore be suppressed and arbitrated by a political power, which is the sole source of all morality. Fear of mutual destruction prompts the historical decision, the social contract, by which government comes into being. But this decision lies significantly in a mythical past. This philosophy may be regarded as symbolic of the curious vagary of naturalistic thought which, throughout subsequent ages, interprets human history as the consequence of pure human decisions without having an individual with sufficient transcendence over the social process to make significant decisions.

John Locke is sufficiently influenced by Cartesian thought to define the self as a "thinking thing" and to insist on personal identity as a reality: "The self is that conscious thinking thing whatever substance made of (whether spiritual or material, simple or compounded, it matters not) which is sensible or conscious of pleasure or pain, capable of happiness or misery and so is concerned for itself so far as that consciousness extends. . . . This consciousness is annexed to and the affection of one individual immaterial substance."[1] His concern is to prove that it is consciousness and "not numerical substance" which accounts for identity. This description of consciousness would apply with equal validity to animal consciousness, *i.e.*, to any organism with a central nervous system. But Locke's theory of self-consciousness follows Descartes, in insisting upon self's intuitive awareness of itself: "If I doubt all other things that very doubt makes me perceive my own existence and will not suffer me to doubt that."[2] This awareness of the existence of the self is hardly an adequate description of the whole dimension and uniqueness of human self-consciousness. It is nevertheless a recognition of human uniqueness found in neither Hobbes nor Hume, particularly when Locke's argument for the existence of God as related to his idea of the thinking self is taken into consideration. The idea of self-awareness does not, however, enter into Locke's conception of personal identity from which he explicitly subtracts the element of self-tran-

[1] *An Essay Concerning Human Understanding,* Book II, Ch. 25.
[2] John Locke, *ibid.,* Book IV, Ch. 9.

scendence involved in memory: "Could we suppose any spirit stripped wholly of all its memory or consciousness of past actions" this "would make no variation in personal identity."[3] It is perfectly true that this would make no difference in the identity of what may be called the "empirical ego," the self as involved in the unity of the body. But it is precisely the pure or transcendent ego, which stands above consciousness as the consciousness of consciousness and which expresses itself in terms of memory and foresight, which is the real centre of human personality.

David Hume, in this as in other respects, purges Locke's thought of Cartesian elements in the interest of a purer empiricism and denies the possibility of any awareness of the ego: "When I enter most intimately into what I call myself I always stumble on some particular perception or other, of heat or cold, light or shade, pain or pleasure. I can never catch myself at any time without a perception and can never observe anything but the perception."[4] This observation may be regarded as a valid criticism of Descartes' conception of a pure ego which subsists within itself without relations. The ego is always the centre of relations so that it is perfectly correct to observe, "I do not catch myself without a perception"; but Hume's final conclusion, "and can never observe anything but a perception," is obviously not a logical deduction from the former observation; nor is it in accord with the facts. Yet even if Hume were correct in his interpretation of the empirical ego as a stream of impressions it would still be pertinent to inquire into the nature of the "I" which he implies when he says: "When I enter most intimately into what I call myself." It is reality of that "I" as subject which challenges the validity of all purely empirical interpretations of the ego.[5]

However great may be the achievements of modern psychology, it is not unfair to say that the psychological systems which remain within the confines of the naturalistic tradition never get beyond

[3]*Ibid.,* Book II, Ch. 25.
[4]David Hume, *A Treatise of Human Nature,* Vol. I, Part IV, Sec. 6.
[5]*Cf.* C. D. Broad, *The Mind and Its Place in Nature,* Ch. 6.

the varying interpretations of Hobbes, Locke and Hume. Behaviour-istic psychology is an elaboration of Hobbes's position. The position of Locke is taken by all "dynamic" psychologists who emphasize the initiative of the ego and the unity of its processes. Of those who fol-low Hume it may suffice to present one particularly illustrious exam-ple: William James. James denies both the unity of consciousness and the transcendent ego: "If there were no passing states of con-sciousness, then indeed we might suppose an abiding principle, abso-lutely one with itself, to be the ceaseless thinker in each of us. But if the states of consciousness be accorded as realities no such 'sub-stantial' identity in the thinker need be supposed. Yesterday's and today's states of consciousness have no substantial identity, for when one is here the other is irrevocably gone. . . . The logical conclusion seems to be that the states of consciousness are all that psychology needs to do her work with. Metaphysics or theology may prove the soul to exist; but for psychology the hypothesis of such a substan-tial principle of unity is superfluous."[6]

James's assurance, that the hypothesis of a substantial principle of unity is superfluous, is an interesting example of an ever recurring effort of psychology as a natural science (and of all natural science for that matter) to affirm its character as a pure science by its metaphysical scepticism. But, unfortunately, this scepticism leads to implied metaphysical credos. An object which has both surface and depth cannot be correctly interpreted in terms of one dimension when it has in fact two. That is why science which is only science cannot be scientifically accurate. This is particularly true of *Geistes-wissenschaft* in contrast to physical science. It is more particularly true of psychology which deals with a dimension of depth in the human spirit, transcending the scientific method. Every rigorous effort to remain within the confines of pure science reduces psychol-ogy to physiology, and physiology to bio-mechanics. The ultimate unity and transcendence of the human ego are indeed beyond pure

<hr/>

[6]*Psychology, Briefer Course*, p. 203. James sums up his position in the succinct phrase "The thoughts themselves are the thinkers." P. 216.

science. Yet it is a necessary undertaking to inquire into the realities of that region "beyond."[7]

Psychological theory of the past decades exhibits, of course, a wide variety of schools which range from mechanistic to organismic interpretations, and from atomistic and behaviouristic interpretations of consciousness to interpretations which emphasize configurative wholeness (*Gestalt* psychology). It is interesting, however, that naturalistic psychology rises with difficulty to the concept of organic unity in consciousness and only occasionally makes the self and self-consciousness an object of particular study.[8] The real profundities of self-consciousness, the complex problems of personality, in the breadth of its relations to the world of nature and history on the one hand and in the depth of its dimension as self-conscious ego on the other, are the concern of only those schools of psychology which frankly leave the confines of natural science and regard psychology as a cultural science, which means that their psychological investigations are guided and prompted by philosophical and therefore semi-religious presuppositions.

VI

THE LOSS OF THE SELF IN IDEALISM

Long before the emergence of a particular "cultural science" emphasis in psychology, philosophy had of course dealt with the problems

---

[7]This is a fact more generously recognized in European than in American psychological schools. *Cf.* G. E. Stout, *Manual of Psychology:* "The last word about freedom lies with neither psychology nor ethics. Its full discussion involves an examination of the relation of thought and will of the individual mind and the reality of the universe. This relation is utterly inexplicable from the point of view of any finite science. The more closely and conscientiously we seek to explain it by the ordinary categories of any special science the more plain it becomes that so regarded it is a miracle, indeed the miracle of miracles. Psychology cannot explain how it is possible that an individual can consciously mean or intend something." P. 735.

[8]One of the few studies of self-consciousness is by M. W. Calkins, *A First Book in Psychology*.

of human consciousness and sought to interpret the nature of the human spirit and its relation to nature, history and the universe. The significant fact from the standpoint of our study is that, while naturalistic philosophies tend to reduce the human ego to a stream of consciousness in which personal identity is minimal, idealistic philosophies tend in varying degrees to identify consciousness with mind and to equate the highest reaches of conscious mind with a divine or absolute mind, or at least with some socially or politically conceived universal mind.

The self is primarily an active rather than contemplative organic unity. But it is more than an organic unity. It has the spiritual capacity of transcending both the natural process in which it is immersed and its own consciousness. As consciousness is the principle of transcendence over process, so self-consciousness is the principle of transcending consciousness. Idealistic philosophy always has the advantage over naturalism in that it appreciates this depth of human spirit. But it usually sacrifices this advantage by identifying the universal perspective of the self-transcendent ego with universal spirit. Its true self therefore ceases to be a self in a true sense and becomes merely an aspect of universal mind. This self of idealistic rationalism is both less and more than the real self. It is less in the sense explained by Kierkegaard: "The paradox of faith is this that the individual is higher than the universal, that the individual determines his relation to the universal by his relation to the absolute, not his relation to the absolute by his relation to the universal."[1] In idealism the true self is that reason which relates the self to the universal. But since the true self in idealistic thought is neither more nor less than this universal reason, the actual self is really absorbed in the universal. The actual self is, however, less, as well as more, than reason; because every self is a unity of thought and life in which thought remains in organic unity with all the organic processes of finite existence. Failure to recognize this latter fact falsifies the prob-

[1]From *Fear and Trembling,* quoted by W. Lowrie, *Kierkegaard,* p. 264.

lem of sin in all idealistic philosophy. Sin becomes the inertia of man's "animal nature" in contrast to the universalities of mind.[2] Idealism fails to recognize to what degree finiteness remains a basic characteristic of human spirituality. The self has in other words a narrower natural base and a higher and narrower pinnacle of spirit than the breadth of perspective of its rational processes. The self is a narrow tower with a wide view. In idealism the self is lost in the breadth of its view; and the breadth of its view is identified with ultimate reality. Idealism conceives the self primarily as reason and reason primarily as God.[3]

It could not be maintained that all forms of idealism lose the individual in universal mind. There are pluralistic forms of idealism with a strong sense of individuality as for instance those of Leibnitz and Herbart. There are furthermore forms of idealism strongly under the influence of Christian theism in which the pantheistic tendencies of idealism are challenged.[4] Yet the indictment is true with reference to all forms of absolute idealism. In Kant's critical idealism the self is not lost in universality but maintains a shadowy existence between the universality of the intelligible self and the particu-

[2]Bosanquet uses the betraying phrase "animal nature" consistently. See, inter alia, *Philosophical Theory of the State*, p. 143.

[3]James Ward defines reason as follows: "Reason is concerned with the world in its totality either as being a system or as having a meaning." *The Realm of Ends*, p. 418. The error of all rationalism is to identify "totality as being a system" with "totality as having a meaning." The system in totality, its "logos," is the structure and coherence as analysed by reason. The Christian faith asserts that totality cannot be comprehended or exhausted in this structure and that therefore meaning cannot be identified with rational coherence. The validity of this distinction is attested by the fact that the self stands outside its own rational processes sufficiently to ask whether its reason can comprehend the structure of reality and whether that structure includes the totality of reality. In terms of our simile the self is a high tower which not only looks at the world to understand its "what" but beyond the world to inquire into its "why." The former may give clues to the latter but can give no final answer in regard to the "why."

[4]As for instance in James Ward's profound theistic pluralism expounded in *The Realm of Ends*.

larity of the empirical (*i.e.,* the sensible) self. It exists by virtue of its acceptance of the moral law of the intelligible self.[5] It is the unvarying tendency of idealistic thought thus to translate the Christian moral paradox "who loseth his life will find it" into an ontological one and to claim that true selfhood and true individuality are something quite other than actual selfhood and individuality. Bosanquet states the logic of absolute idealism perfectly in the words: "God, it has been said, could only impart Himself by imparting a self; and we may urge the complementary truth that the self can only be a self by being THE self."[6] This conclusion is arrived at in steps which may be most succinctly stated in a series of brief quotations: (1) "We want to think of the individual primarily as mind."[7] (2) "The best general description of mind is to call it a world; and a world which constitutes a mind is not limited according to hard and fast rules—there are many conditions under which a single mind is constituted by and controls more bodies than one."[8] (3) The individual is therefore "a world that realizes, in a limited matter, the logic and the spirit of the whole, and in principle there is no increase of comprehension and no transformation of the self, that is inconceivable as happening to him."[9] (4) "Individuality is positive and constructive; and if self-consciousness is negative against the idea of the self, individuality must not be construed in analogy with it. . . . Its exclusiveness judged by the principle of its self-identity is a defect."[10]

It is instructive to observe how near Bosanquet's rationalism is to the classical mystical belief that selfhood as such is evil. Mysticism hopes that the self will be swallowed up into an undifferentiated divine unity and Bosanquet hopes it will be lost in the attainment of a rationality "beyond the reflective consciousness of self

[5]Hegel's theory of the transmutation of the individual of "unhappy consciousness" to the "changeless consciousness" which is its "true self" is analysed more fully in Ch. IV.

[6]Bernard Bosanquet, *The Principle of Individuality and Value,* p. 342.

[7]*Ibid.,* p. 282.   [9]*Ibid.,* p. 288.

[8]*Ibid.,* p. 287.   [10]*Ibid.,* pp. 285–6.

and not-self." In terms of the Christian faith man always remains a creature and there is, therefore, no possibility of achieving a position "beyond the reflective consciousness of self and not self." The ideal possibility is a loving relationship between the self and the other self in which alienation but not discrete identity is transcended.

The impossibility of doing justice to the Christian idea of self-hood within terms of absolute idealism is perfectly illustrated in Josiah Royce's heroic efforts to do so in his *The World and the Individual,* particularly because he tries so desperately to preserve an adequate concept of individuality. Royce rightly insists that he does not lose the self as mysticism does; and most of his polemic is directed against the mystic doctrine of an ultimate undifferentiated reality in which all individuality is lost. His Absolute is a mosaic which requires the variety of individuality for its richness. But by individuality Royce means merely particularity and not the distinctive depth of spirit which distinguishes human individuality from the particularity of nature: "Any finite idea is so far a self; and I can, if you please, contrast my present self with my past or my future self, with yesterday's hopes or with tomorrow's deeds, quite as genuinely as with your inner life or with the whole society of which I am a member, or with the whole of life of which our experience of nature is a hint, or, finally with the life of God in its entirety."[11] Finite self-hood is thus in the same category as any finite reality while ultimate selfhood is nothing short of the Absolute. For the Absolute is defined as "our very own selfhood in fulfillment."[12] Royce is less concerned about the exclusive aspect of self-consciousness, as a root of evil, than is Bosanquet. He writes: "But if one persists in asking, 'What has sundered us from the Absolute and narrowed our consciousness as it is narrowed?' my only general answer is, Such narrowness must find its place within the Absolute life in order that the Absolute may be complete. One needs then no new principle to explain why, as Plotinus asked, the souls fell away from God. From the point of view of the Absolute the finite beings never fall away. They are

[11]*The World and the Individual,* Book II, p. 273.   [12]*Ibid.,* p. 302.

where they are, namely in and of the Absolute Unity."[13] Put in terms of Christian doctrine, Royce's view is that each man is Christ from the perspective of God while he is both creature and sinner only from his own perspective. Or it might be fairer to say that in his view man's finiteness is sinful only as its exclusiveness and discreteness have not yet been transcended in a rational perspective which logically culminates in God's perspective.[14] Thus universal mind is the "Christ" of redemption.

The logic of idealism in annihilating individuality probably achieves its most consistent (and absurd) expression in the thought of the Italian idealist, Gentile—who "denies reality to the thinking personality."[15] Thus the circle is completed and the idealist agrees with the radical empiricist that "the thoughts themselves are the thinkers."

That the idealistic denial of individuality has immediate socio-political as well as ultimate cultural significance in the history of western civilization is proved by the fact that it has made a tremendous contribution of dubious worth to the modern deification of the state. Whenever idealism seeks to escape the undifferentiated Absolute of mysticism and desires to prove that it is a counsel of historical action rather than pure contemplation, its rational universal becomes embodied in that very dubious god, the modern state. In the words of Bosanquet: "The idea is that in it [the state] or by its help, we find at once discipline and expansion, the transfiguration

[13]*Ibid.*, p. 303.

[14]How little, despite his fervent Christian piety, Royce understands the basic presuppositions of the Christian view of man is revealed in his equating of the Biblical and the Platonic view of man: "The two doctrines which, in European history, have most insisted upon the duality of our higher and our lower selfhood, *viz.* the ethical teachings of Plato and the Gospel of the Christian church, have agreed in insisting that the higher self is a resultant of influences which belong to the eternal world and which the individual man is powerless to initiate. In Plato's account of the process of the soul's release from its own lower nature, the eternal Ideas appear as the supernatural source of truth and goodness. . . . Christianity has emphasized, in all its essential teachings, a similar source and meaning in speaking of the higher self." *Ibid.*, p. 251.

[15]Roger Holmes, *The Idealism of Giovanni Gentile*, p. 175.

of partial impulses and something to do and care for such as the nature of the human self demands. If, that is to say, you start with a human being as he is in fact and try to devise what will furnish him with an outlet and a stable purpose capable of doing justice to his capacities, a satisfying object of life, you will be driven by the necessity of the facts as far as the state and perhaps further."[16] The state in its inclusiveness and stability represents the "real will" of man against his momentary and fragmentary will. The irony of this deification of the state by Hegel and his followers is that the whole dæmonic fury of the state, as a partial historical force, more universal than the individual but less universal in either value or extent than it claims to be, is not recognized by the same idealists who are so very sensitive to the fragmentary and finite aspects of individual existence. In Bosanquet's thought this tremendous problem of the sinfulness of the state as a partial reality which claims absolute value is both expressed and veiled in the innocent qualification, "you will be driven by the necessity of the facts as far as the state, AND PERHAPS FURTHER." A great deal further, one is bound to say, and not probably but certainly.[17]

From the Christian point of view the whole pathos of original sin expresses itself in the pretensions of idealistic thought. The individual is sacrificed to the rational universal conceived in either political or trans-historical terms, for fear that anything less than this total immolation will result in the chaos of particularity and the sin of "exclusive consciousness." But human pride manages to reclaim the supposedly divine and universal reason as not only some universal humanity but as a very particular type of universality conforming to the prejudices and perspectives of the philosopher who conceives

[16]*The Philosophical Theory of the State*, p. 140.
[17]E. F. Carritt calls attention to the frequency of similar qualifying clauses in Bosanquet's thought upon the state, declaring that his thought differs from Hegel's primarily "by the insertion of these rather puzzling qualifications." They are puzzling, for if taken seriously they invalidate the whole thesis on the state held by this school of idealism. *Morals and Politics*, p. 160.

it. James Ward describes this anti-climactic note in Hegel's thought with nice irony: "The earth, he says, is the truth of the solar system —the sun, the moon and the stars are only conditions for the earth which they serve. Among the continents of the earth Europe, by virtue of its physical characteristics, forms its consciousness, its rational part, and the centre of Europe is Germany. With his own philosophy he has the sublime assurance to think that philosophy closes; and in the restoration of Prussia under Stein he thought the culmination of the world's history was attained."[18]

VII

THE LOSS OF THE SELF IN ROMANTICISM

Naturalism loses the individual because it does not view life in sufficient depth to comprehend the self-transcendent human spirit. This spirit is a reality which does not fit into the category of natural causality which is naturalism's sole principle of comprehending the universe. Idealism on the other hand discovers the human spirit in its height of transcendence over natural process, but loses it again because the uniqueness and arbitrariness of individuality do not conform to its pattern of rationality, which is its sole principle of interpreting reality. It is instructive in this connection that even a pluralistic philosophy such as Leibnitz's, with its emphasis upon individuality, can find a place for the individual only by seeing it as a microcosmic type of the macrocosm. This interpretation allows a monist such as Christian Wolff, with a slight shift of emphasis, to reabsorb the individual into, and identify him with the universal. In the words of Kierkegaard's criticism of the idealistic passion for a universal system: "Before the system completes itself, every scrap of existence must have been swallowed up in the eternal; there must not be the slightest remainder; not even so much as a bit of dingle-dangle represented by the Herr Professor who writes the system."[1]

[18]*The Realm of Ends*, p. 180.
[1]From "Unscientific Postscript" as trans. by David E. Swenson in *Anthology of Modern Philosophy*, edited by D. S. Robinson, p. 649.

Within the alternatives of naturalism and idealism the modern man therefore faces either the submergence of both his individuality and his spirit in natural causality or the submergence of his individuality and the deification of his spirit in the universality of reason. Confronted with annihilation through either abasement or deification it is natural that modern culture should have sought for another way out. It found this way in romanticism.

Beginning with Paracelsus in the period of the Renaissance, romanticism has played a subordinate role in the history of modern culture only to emerge in these latter days as the conqueror over rationalism. (The political form and tool of romanticism is fascism.) Romanticism was originally par excellence the champion of the individual. It seemed to understand him in terms of both the particularity of his physical existence and the unique self-knowledge of his spiritual life, because the romantic tradition is curiously compounded of Rousseauistic primitivism and Christian pietism. It seeks, speaking symbolically, wisdom in the body rather than the mind (Nietzsche). But it does not reduce man's physical existence to bio-mechanical proportions. On the contrary it means by body: feeling, imagination and will; which it prefers to spirit, particularly to spirit conceived as mind. The romantic quarrel with rationalism is really a quarrel of the soul (psyche) in its intimate union with the body, against spirit conceived as ratio. But through its union with Christian pietism romanticism emphasizes the self-transcendence of this soul to such a degree that its body-soul is really spirit in its particularity and individuality in contrast to spirit as rational and universal. This "spiritual" emphasis is frequently more implicit than explicit. Nietzsche, for instance, extols animal cruelty; but the cruelty he values is not known among animals but only among men with their spiritual endowments. Furthermore he explicitly rejects the animal's impulse of self-preservation and substitutes the spiritual "will-to-power"[2] as the basic vitality of existence.

From the standpoint of the vicissitudes of the idea of individuality

[2]*Beyond Good and Evil*, p. 20.

in modern culture the significance of romanticism is that it exalts the individual more unqualifiedly, but also loses him more quickly and completely than any form of rationalism. The process of this romantic destruction of individuality can be briefly summarized as follows: Individuality is directly related to the eternal source of meaning and given unqualified significance, while idealism ascribes significance to the individual only as he is related to a rational universal value of history. Sooner or later the romantic thinker must, however, recoil from the pretension of this purely individual self-deification; and all but Nietzsche do recoil. They seek to increase the plausibility and reduce the pretension of this self-glorification by looking for the "larger individual"; which they find in the unique nation. This collective individual then supplants the single individual as the centre of existence and the source of meaning. In the pursuit of seeking something larger than a person as his centre, the romanticist meets the absolute idealist who is intent upon finding something a little more domestic and manageable than the Absolute as the source of value. Thus they both discover the nation, approaching it from different sides but agreeing in its deification. The fact that race or nation is a form of universality which seems small enough to be regarded by the romantic as a fruit of natural cohesion (consanguinity) and large enough to seem to the idealist a characteristic product of reason, unites these two forces, romanticism and idealism, behind the single historical reality of the nation. This is the cultural, though not the socio-political, history of modern nationalism in a nutshell. The compound of Nietzschean and Hegelian philosophy in modern nationalistic hysterias is an expression of this strange unity. In the earlier history of romanticism the two elements were combined in the thought of Fichte.

This brief summary requires further explication. The romantic tradition, we have said, is compounded of Rousseauistic primitivism on the one hand and Christian pietism on the other. From Rousseau it derives its emphasis on the non-rational forces in human personality, upon emotion, imagination and will. From pietism it takes the sense of the individual's unmediated relation to God; which it secularizes so that the individual is not only directly related to God, as the source and centre of meaning, but becomes himself self-justifying and autonomous.

The romantic sense of individuality is primarily derived from what the pietist, Spener, termed the "spiritual priesthood." This pietist version of the Protestant principle of the priesthood of all believers differs slightly but significantly from the original. Luther's religious individualism emphasized the person's unique relation of faith and responsibility to God.[3] The pietists emphasized, rather, the possibility of a direct and unmediated experience of unity between the believer and God. "Every individual," said Zinzendorf, "experiences the Saviour himself and does not merely repeat what he has heard from his neighbor."[4] This sense of individuality in pietism represents a compound of Protestant and mystic doctrines. But it is more Protestant than mystic because the union of the individual with God is achieved through the grace of God rather than man's own mystic discipline. It is through "the overwhelming greatness and power of the Lord" that the individual rises "from the natural state to the state of grace" (Francke). Pietistic individualism is therefore not subject to the peril of mystic dissipation of individuality. On the other hand it easily transgresses the bounds which orthodox Protestantism sets between creature and Creator. Zinzendorf's assurance, "I am a part of the body of Christ," analogous to Meister Eckhardt's "Christ is born in me" becomes the basis of the romantic doctrine of individuality. Schleiermacher, who represents the historical nexus between pietism and romanticism, states this doctrine in the words: "Thus there dawned upon me what is now my highest intuition. I saw clearly that each man is meant to represent humanity in his own way, combining its elements uniquely so that it may reveal itself in every mode, and all that can issue from its womb be made actual in the

[3]Luther said: "Just as no one can go to Hell or Heaven for me, so no one can believe for me and so no one can open or close Heaven or Hell for me and no one can drive me either to believe or disbelieve."

[4]Otto Uttendoerfer, *Zinzendorf's Weltbetrachtung*, p. 305.

fullness of unending space and time. . . . But tardily and only with great difficulty does man reach the full knowledge of his individuality. He does not always dare to look toward it as his ideal but prefers to turn his eyes upon the good which he possesses in common with humanity. Clinging to this common element with love and gratitude he often doubts whether he should separate his individual self from it."[5]

One might imagine that romanticism thus possessed an ideal understanding of the natural and the spiritual sources of individuality, the particularity of the body and the ultimate self-transcendence of the human spirit. But individuality has an even shorter life in romanticism than in rationalism. In rationalism the whole history of an era is required to dissipate the Renaissance emphasis upon individuality. In romanticism individuality is emphasized and lost in the life of practically each romantic thinker. Rousseau quickly subordinates the will of the individual to the mystically conceived general will, regarded as the real will of the individual. The German romantics are interested in originality and uniqueness rather than in individuality, despite their protestations. Schleiermacher explains that by "individuals" he means not solely persons but also collective individuals, such as races, nations and families. "It is precisely individuality," wrote Schlegel, "which is the eternal and original thing in men. . . . The cultivation and development of this individuality, as one's highest vocation, would be a divine egoism."[6] But Schlegel finds in the uniqueness of the landscape of his homeland as significant an expression of individuality as in individual personality. Herder, Lavater, Haman and Novalis were interested in the æsthetic implications of this doctrine of the significance of variety. "The more personal, local, peculiar (*eigentuemlich*) of its own time a poem is," said Novalis, "the nearer it stands to the centre of poetry."[7]

The romantic doctrine led to complete relativism in morals, religion and politics. "Why," said Schleiermacher, "in the province of

[5]*Monologen*, II. Trans. by Horace L. Friess (Open Court Publ. Co.).
[6]*Athaneum*, III, 15.
[7]Quoted by Arthur O. Lovejoy, *The Great Chain of Being*, p. 307.

morals does this pitiable uniformity prevail which seeks to bring the highest human life within the compass of a single lifeless formula?"[8] a sentiment which betrays the affinity between Schleiermacher and Nietzsche and foreshadows the latter's doctrine of the autonomous and self-justifying superman with his contempt for the morality of the herd.

The romantic relativism in religion and politics is particularly instructive because it clearly reveals the romantic logic, leading to the self-destruction of the concept of individuality. The religious relativism of the romantics reveals how far they have departed from the Christian faith. In Christianity the unique individual finds the contingent and arbitrary aspect of his existence tolerable because it is related to, judged and redeemed by the eternal God, who transcends both the rational structure and the arbitrary facts of existence in the universe. In romantic religion the unique and arbitrary character of existence does not find its limit and fulfillment in an eternal world of meaning but expresses itself in terms of limitless pretension. "Every man," said Lavater, "has his own religion just as he has his own face and every one has his own God just as he has his own individuality."[9] While Schleiermacher does not follow this position through to such an explicit polytheism, he thinks in the same terms. "If you want to grasp the idea of religion as a factor in the infinite and progressive development of the World Spirit then you must give up the vain and empty desire for one religion," he declares.[10] This means that the only meaning of life is that there should be a variety of meaning. This untenable position, beginning in relativism, ends in nihilism. Here again Nietzsche follows the logic, suggested by Schleiermacher, to its consistent conclusion: "The world seen from within, the world defined and designated according to its 'intelligible character,' would simply be the 'Will to Power' and nothing else. What? Does this not mean in popular language:

[8]*Reden ueber die Religion*, II.
[9]*Antworten auf wichtige und wuerdige Fragen und Briefe weiser und guter Menschen*, Vol. I, p. 66.
[10]*Reden ueber die Religion*, p. 36.

God is disproved but not the devil? On the contrary, my friends! On the contrary! And who the devil also compels you to speak popularly?"[11]

If religious relativism is the natural and logical expression of the romantic doctrine of individuality with its premium upon uniqueness and variety as such, its worship of the unique race and nation is an inevitable effort to reduce the pretension and absurdity of this polytheism, an effort which leads tragically to the complete annihilation of the idea of individuality in personal terms. An individual cannot bear to make himself the centre of meaning without qualification. Inevitably he must seek support from something greater and more inclusive than himself. Schleiermacher follows this idea perfectly in supplementing his conception of individuality. A few months after the battle of Jena he wrote to a friend: "Remember that the individual cannot stand alone, cannot save himself, if that in which each and all of us are rooted—German freedom and German feeling—be lost; and it is these that are threatened."[12]

The whole pathos of the unique individual projecting himself into eternity in one moment and in the next seeking for a simple historical companionship which will give his life meaning, is expressed in Schleiermacher's confession: "Here alone [in nationality] can you make yourself completely understood; here you can turn to a common feeling and to common ideas; for your ideas are welcomed by your brothers because they are the same as yours."[13] In other words national self-worship is a more plausible form of self-glorification than mere emphasis upon individual uniqueness. The nation, said Schleiermacher, is the largest form of individuality as the person is the smallest. Yet in this largest form one finds oneself writ large, for the ideas of "your brothers are the same as yours." Following the same thought Herder rather regretted that Christianity had supplanted the more primitive polytheistic religions of the nations fearing that

[11]*Beyond Good and Evil*, p. 52.
[12]Fredericka Rowan, *Life of Schleiermacher as Unfolded in His Autobiography and Letters*, Vol. II, p. 55.
[13]*Predigten*, Vol. I, p. 230.

with them "they lost their spirit and character, yes, I might say, their language, their heart, their country and their history."[14]

While Nietzsche maintains a more resolute individualism and bravely asserts the autonomous individual against every type of universality, including the relative universality of the nation, it is significant that in these latter days even his version of romanticism has been subtly compounded with nationalistic furies. There is a peculiar irony in the fact that his doctrine, which was meant as an exposure of the vindictive transvaluation of values engaged in by the inferior classes, should have itself become a vehicle of the pitiful resentments of the lower middle classes of Europe in their fury against more powerful aristocratic and proletarian classes.

In the heyday of romanticism when the individuality of the nation begins to devour the individuality of the person, an effort is still made to remain within terms of a nationalistic polytheism and not to claim ultimate value for the national uniqueness which the individual appreciates simply because it is his own. Herder states this doctrine held by all the classical romanticists: "Ministers might deceive each other, political machines might be set against each other until one destroys the other. Not so with fatherlands. They lie peacefully side by side and aid each other as families. It is the grossest barbarity of human speech to speak of fatherlands in bloody battle with each other."[15] Unfortunately the barbarity which Herder deplores belongs inevitably to human history and not merely to human speech, and precisely because it is not possible to appreciate and preserve particularity and uniqueness, whether individual or national, without either bringing it into relation with, and subordination to, an ultimate centre and source of meaning or allowing the particular and the unique value to become itself an imperialistic centre of ultimate meaning.[16]

The full force of this development has become apparent only in

[14]K. Pinson, *Pietism as a Factor in the Rise of German Nationalism*, p. 92.
[15]Pinson, *op. cit.*, p. 101.
[16]Professor Lovejoy describes this development accurately: "A type of national culture valued at first because it was one's own, and because the

our own day. But it betrayed itself even in the heyday of classical romanticism. Thus Schleiermacher neatly anticipates the anti-Semitism of modern German fascism with the idea that, once a people has arrived at a high stage of development, "it is disgraceful for it to embrace within it anything alien to it, no matter how excellent that may be in itself, for its particular character it has received from God Himself."[17] This domestic imperialism is in strange contradiction with Schleiermacher's boast: "This *is* the very thing of which I chiefly boast, that my love and friendship always have so high a source that they have never been blended with any vulgar sentiment, have never been the offspring of habit or tender feeling but ever an act of purest freedom oriented toward the individuality of other human beings. . . . Wherever I notice an aptitude for individuality, inasmuch as love and sensitiveness its highest guarantees are present, there also I find an object of my love."[18]

In the thought of Fichte, who represents a watershed between rationalism and romanticism, the universalism of rationalism becomes compounded with the nationalistic particularism of romanticism and issues in a dubious spiritual national imperialism. For Fichte conscience is the voice of the universal and the eternal in man: "Thus do I approach that Infinite Will; and the voice of conscience in my soul, which teaches me in every situation of life what I have here to do, is the channel through which again His influence descends upon me. That voice made audible by my environment and translated into my language is the oracle of the Eternal world which announces to me how I am to perform my part in the order of the spiritual universe, or in the Infinite Will who is

---

conservation of differences was recognized as good for humanity as a whole, came in time to be conceived of as a thing which one had the mission to impose upon others, or to diffuse over as large a part of the world as possible. Thus the wheel ran full circle; what may be called a particularistic uniformitarianism, a tendency to seek to universalize things originally valued because they were not universal, found expression in poetry, in a sort of philosophy in the policies of great states and the enthusiasm of their populations." *The Great Chain of Being*, p. 313.

[17]*Predigten*, Vol. IV, p. 75.   [18]*Monologen*, p. 46.

Himself that order."[19] On one side of his thought the demands of
the Eternal drive Fichte into otherworldliness: "My sensuous existence may, in the future, assume other forms but they are just as
little true to life as its present forms. By that resolution I lay hold
on eternity and cast off this earthly life and all other forms of
sensuous life which may yet lie before me in futurity, and place
myself far above them. I become the sole source of my own being
and its phenomena, and henceforth, unconditioned by anything
about me, I have a life in myself."[20]

On this side of Fichte's thought he belongs in the category of
the idealists, previously discussed, who transmute the human ego
into virtual divinity, to unconditioned reality. But the vicissitudes
of his contemporary Germany prompt Fichte to follow the romantics
in their emphasis upon the nation as the largest individuality of history. Conscious of the very relative character of national existence in
comparison with the infinite will which is, for him, the true source
of value, Fichte conveniently discovers that only Germans can love
their nation especially, without treason to the heavenly vision of the
universal, because Germany as the birthplace of philosophy is a true
instrument of universal values.[21]

[19]Fichte, *The Vocation of Man,* trans. by William Smith (Open Court
Publ. Co.), p. 152.
[20]*Ibid.,* p. 142.
[21]*Cf.* "The German patriot wishes that this purpose be attained first of
all among the Germans and that from them it spread to the rest of mankind. The German can desire this, for in his midst philosophy has had
its origin and it is developed in his language. It may be assumed that in
that nation which has had the wisdom to conceive philosophy there
should also rest the ability to understand it. Only the German can desire this, for only he, through the possession of philosophy and the possibility given thereby to understand it, can comprehend that this is the
immediate purpose of mankind. This purpose is the only possible pa-
triotic goal. Only the German can therefore be a patriot. Only he can,
in the interest of his nation, include all mankind. Since the instinct of
Reason has become extinct and the era of Egotism has begun, every other
nation's patriotism is selfish, narrow, hostile to the rest of mankind."
Quoted by H. C. Engelbrecht in *Johann Gottlieb Fichte,* p. 98 (Columbia
University Press).

Romanticism is, in short, nearer to the Christian faith and a more perverse corruption of it than idealistic philosophies. It understands, with Christianity, the unique and arbitrary character of historical existence and knows that the rational universalities of philosophical systems can neither fully contain nor comprehend the unique quality of the givenness of things nor yet themselves fully transcend the contingency and irrationality of existence. With Christianity, it consequently discovers the subtle self-deception and hypocrisy of rationalistic cultures, which manage to insinuate their own particular values into the supposed impartial and objective universal values of their philosophy. (The relation of democracy to bourgeois culture for instance.) It is this penetration into the dishonesty of rational idealists which establishes affinities between Nietzsche and classical Christianity, despite his strictures against the "bad conscience" which Christianity prompts. On the other hand romanticism, at least in its fully developed Nietzschean form, substitutes brutality for hypocrisy and asserts the particular and unique, whether individual or collective, in nihilistic disregard of any general system of value.

The simple fact is that both the obviously partial and unique and the supposedly universal values of history can be both appreciated and judged only in terms of a religious faith which has discovered the centre and source of life to be beyond and yet within historical existence. This is the God who is both Creator and Judge revealed in Biblical faith. Romanticism understands the fact of the goodness of creation in all of its particularity and individuality; but it has no perspective beyond creation. Idealism seeks a rational point of vantage beyond the created forms and thus has an inchoate conception of God as judge. But the judge turns out to be man's own reason. The individuality of man is tenable only in a dimension of reality in which the highest achievements of his self-knowledge and self-consciousness are both known and judged from a source of life and truth beyond him.

The idea of individuality which is the most unique emphasis of modern culture, is thus a tragically abortive concept, which cannot be maintained as either fact or as idea within the limits of the cultural presuppositions of modernity. The social history of modern life moves from the individualism of the early commercial period to the collectivism of industrialism. The individual who emancipates himself from the social solidarities of agrarian feudalism and the religious authoritarianism of medievalism is, within a brief span of history, subjected to the mechanical solidarities of industrial collectivism. His revolt against this collectivism betrays him into the even more grievous tyranny of primitive racialism and imperial nationalism.

The cultural history of modern man gives him no resource to modify or to defy this tendency. In idealism the individual is able to transcend the tyrannical necessities of nature only to be absorbed in the universalities of impersonal mind. In the older naturalism, the individual is able for a moment to appreciate that aspect of individuality which the variety of natural circumstances creates; but true individuality is quickly lost because nature knows nothing of the self-transcendence, self-identity and freedom which are the real marks of individuality. In romantic naturalism the individuality of the person is quickly subordinated to the unique and self-justifying individuality of the social collective. Only in Nietzschean romanticism is the individual preserved; but there he becomes the vehicle of dæmonic religion because he knows no law but his own will-to-power and has no God but his own unlimited ambition.

Without the presuppositions of the Christian faith the individual is either nothing or becomes everything. In the Christian faith man's insignificance as a creature, involved in the process of nature and time, is lifted into significance by the mercy and power of God in which his life is sustained. But his significance as a free spirit is understood as subordinate to the freedom of God. His inclination to abuse his freedom, to overestimate his power and significance and to become everything is understood as the primal sin. It is because man is inevitably involved in this primal sin that he is bound to meet God first of all as a judge, who humbles his pride and brings his vain imagination to naught.

CHAPTER IV

THE EASY CONSCIENCE OF MODERN MAN

Our introductory analysis of modern views of human nature has established the complacent conscience of modern man as the one unifying force amidst a wide variety of anthropological conceptions. In the words of T. E. Hulme: "All thought since the Renaissance, in spite of its apparent variety, forms one coherent whole. . . . It all rests on the same conception of the nature of man and all exhibits the same inability to recognize the meaning of the dogma of original sin. In this period not only have its philosophy, its literature and its ethics been based upon this new conception of man as fundamentally good, as sufficient, as the measure of things; but a good case can be made out for regarding many of its characteristic economic features as springing entirely from this central abstract conception."[1]

The most surprising aspect of the modern man's good conscience is that he asserts and justifies it in terms of the most varied and even contradictory metaphysical theories and social philosophies. The idealist Hegel and the materialist Marx agree in their fundamental confidence in human virtue, disagreeing only in their conception of the period and the social circumstances in which and the method by which his essential goodness is, or is to be, realized. The

[1]*Speculations*, p. 52.

romantic naturalist Rousseau agrees with the rationalistic naturalists of the French enlightenment, though in the one case the seat of virtue is found in natural impulse unspoiled by rational disciplines and in the other case it is reason which guarantees virtue. Among the rationalistic naturalists again there is agreement upon this point whether they are hedonistic or Stoic in their conceptions and whether they believe that reason discovers and leads to a natural harmony of egoistic impulses or that it discovers and affirms a natural harmony of social impulses.

The whole Christian drama of salvation is rejected ostensibly because of the incredible character of the myths of Creation, Fall, Atonement, etc., in which it is expressed. But the typical modern is actually more certain of the complete irrelevance of these doctrines than of their incredibility. He is naturally not inclined to take dubious religious myths seriously, since he finds no relation between the ethos which informs them and his own sense of security and complacency. The sense of guilt expressed in them is to him a mere vestigial remnant of primitive fears of higher powers, of which he is happily emancipated. The sense of sin is, in the phrase of a particularly vapid modern social scientist, "a psychopathic aspect of adolescent mentality."

The universality of this easy conscience among moderns is the more surprising since it continues to express itself almost as unqualifiedly in a period of social decay as in the eighteenth- and nineteenth-century heyday of a bourgeois culture. The modern man is involved in social chaos and political anarchy. The Marxist escape from this chaos has developed in Russia into a political tyranny of unparalleled proportions. Contemporary history is filled with manifestations of man's hysterias and furies; with evidences of his dæmonic capacity and inclination to break the harmonies of nature and defy the prudent canons of rational restraint. Yet no cumulation of contradictory evidence seems to disturb modern man's good opinion of himself. He considers himself the victim of corrupting institutions which he is about to destroy or reconstruct, or of the confusions of ignorance which an adequate education is about to overcome. Yet he continues to regard himself as essentially harmless and virtuous. The question therefore arises how modern man arrived at, and by what means he maintains, an estimate of his virtue in such pathetic contradiction with the obvious facts of his history.

One possible and plausible answer is that the great achievement of modern culture, the understanding of nature, is also the cause of the great confusion of modern man: the misunderstanding of human nature. Nature is a one-dimensional world of seemingly necessary effects consequent upon particular causes. Though a profounder observation may reveal that no observable cause is a sufficient explanation of a subsequent effect and that each effect is but one of many possible consequences in the causal chain, this metaphysical scruple, pointing to a realm of freedom even in nature, has given but slight pause to a culture which is primarily informed by the methods and presuppositions of physical science. Whatever the ultimate problem of the relation of *nous* to *physis*, of spirit to nature, the modern man is certain that the two scientific methods of detailed empirical observation and mathematical calculation give him knowledge of the unique and particular event on the one hand and of the regularities and dependable recurrences of nature on the other.

The two methods are the sources of his two sometimes conflicting and sometimes mutually supporting assurances of security. The empirical method points to nature as a realm of order, having its own laws which cannot be fathomed by a priori deductions. Let man disavow his proud pretensions and follow the course of nature patiently! Here modern culture follows Epicurean naturalism. The mathematical method, on the other hand, impresses man with his own powers of reason and with the marvellous coincidence of rational calculation and natural process, prompting a new Stoic identification of reason and nature. Nature and reason are thus the two gods of modern man, and sometimes the two are one. In either case man is essentially secure because he is not seriously estranged from the realm of harmony and order. Either it is nature which is itself that harmony; in which case mere ignorance has tempted man to stray from her innocency and the return to it is easy. Or if, on the other hand, nature is regarded as a realm of chaos, the realm of reason is an easily accessible asylum from, and force of conquest over, the conflicts and disharmonies of nature. A culture which underestimates the problem of freedom and necessity in nature is bound to depreciate the reality of freedom in man. The modern man is, in short, so certain about his essential virtue because he is so mistaken about his stature. He tries to interpret himself in terms of natural causality or in terms of his unique rationality; but he does not see that he has a freedom of spirit which transcends both nature and reason. He is consequently unable to understand the real pathos of his defiance of nature's and reason's laws. He always imagines himself betrayed into this defiance either by some accidental corruption in his past history or by some sloth of reason. Hence he hopes for redemption, either through a program of social reorganiza-tion or by some scheme of education.

II

THE EFFORT TO DERIVE EVIL FROM SPECIFIC
HISTORICAL SOURCES

The inclination of modern man to find the source of evil in his life in some particular event in history or some specific historical corruption is a natural consequence of his view of himself in a simple one-dimensional history. But this modern error merely accentuates a perennial tendency of the human heart to attribute wrong-doing to temptation and thus to escape responsibility for it. Every man has at some time or other repeated the excuse of the first man: "The woman whom thou gavest to be with me, she gave me of the tree and I did eat." The important point in all these explanations is that they fail to explain why the particular sources of evil in history, bad priests, evil rulers, and ruling classes, should have had the power and the inclination to introduce evil into history. In the eighteenth century human evil was variously attributed to the corrupting influence of religion or to tyrannical governments and ignorant legislators who had disturbed the harmony of nature. In the nineteenth century Marx traced the self-alienation of man from his true essence to the rise of the class organization in society. Each of these explanations has the virtue of throwing light upon the character of particular social evils and may point the way to their mitigation or elimination. But none of them explain how an evil which does not exist in nature could have arisen in human history.

The belief that priests and their religion were the source of social evil was a natural conviction of a generation which was forced to contend against the religious sanction of established social injustice. The eighteenth century regarded religion as the source of both political tyranny and social conflict. Holbach wrote: "History points out some of these vice-regents of deity who in the exacerbations of their delirious rage have insisted upon displacing him by exalting themselves into gods, exacting the most obsequious worship, who have inflicted the most cruel torment upon those who have opposed themselves to their madness." This self-deification of the religious leader is also the source of political tyranny, according to Holbach: "Theology—far from being useful to the human species, is the true source of all those sorrows which afflict the earth—of those governments which oppress him."[1] In the same spirit Helvetius protests against the fanaticism of religion and the social conflict which results from it: "What does the history of religions teach us? That religions have kindled the torch of intolerance everywhere. They have filled the plains with corpses, bathed the countryside in blood, destroyed cities, devastated empires. Religions have never improved men. Their improvement is the work of law. Religions determine our beliefs but laws determine our habits and customs."[2] The eighteenth century saw quite truly that there is a religious element in all tyranny and fanaticism. But it attributed this fact to the corruptions of par-

[1] *System of Nature*, Vol. III, pp. 60, 152.
[2] *De l'Homme*, Section VII, Cd. I.

ticular historical religions. It ought to have asked why it is that man is prompted and tempted to claim a dignity and eminence which no man ought to possess; and to affirm a finality for his convictions which no relative human judgment deserves. The world of pure nature knows nothing of priest-kings or fanatic prophets. "Nature interrogated by princes," declares Holbach, "would teach them that they are men and not gods";[3] but it does not seem to occur to him to inquire why men should have both the capacity and the inclination to claim divinity for themselves and infallibility for their opinions, the very inclination which Christianity defines as original sin. One of the instructive and pathetic aspects of contemporary history is that the same modern man who hoped for emancipation from tyranny and fanaticism by the destruction of historic religion, should in this latter day of modernity be drawn to the worship of Hitlers and Stalins and a whole variety of new priest-kings who manage to assert their ridiculous pretensions without the benefit of clergy. A particular manifestation of evil in human history cannot be regarded as the source of a general evil inclination. It is, on the contrary, but the fruit and consequence of a profounder root of evil.

The naturalists of the eighteenth century, following Epicurus, thought they could beguile man from his fears, hatreds, ambitions and fanatic furies by dwelling on the serenity and harmony of nature and upon its freedom from those ultimate perils which men fear most. They thought it possible to destroy the depth of human spirituality by proving that there is no depth in nature. They did not realize that, even if the spirits with which the human imagination peoples the world of nature were purely figments of the imagination, it would still be important to know why the imagination of man runs riot in this way and why it is impossible for men to enjoy the bovine serenity of the animal world. Epicurus thought he could exorcize the fear of death by proving that there is no peril on the other side of the grave, since death for man is merely the dissolution which all nature knows. But Epicurus overlooked the significance

[3] *Op. cit.*, p. 109.

of the fact that man should inevitably fear death while animals do not.

These eighteenth-century savants did not realize that man cannot, by taking thought, reduce himself to the proportions of nature and that he does not have the freedom to destroy his freedom over natural process, any more than he has the freedom to overcome his precarious dependence upon nature. Human fears arise precisely in this situation of strength and weakness; and the boundless character of human ambitions is the consequence of man's effort to hide his weakness, deny his dependence and insignificance and thus to quiet his fears.

Modern culture makes exactly the same mistake in dealing with the problems of government as in dealing with the fanaticism and fury of historic religions. It attributes evils to specific historical causes without inquiring how such particular causes could have arisen. The eighteenth century attributed tyranny and injustice to governments as well as to historic religions; and it was never very clear about the relation between the political and the religious sources of injustice. Furthermore in attributing social evil to the machinations of "bad governors" and "evil legislators," it assumes a voluntarism in its social theory which its deterministic psychology denies. While it reduces human freedom to such minimal proportions as will conform to its naturalism, its social theory assumes man's mastery over his social destiny. It fails to understand how every social decision is modified and circumscribed by natural circumstances and historical tendencies, beyond the control of human decision. There is a peculiar pathos in the social contract theories of government, which dominate the thought of the seventeenth and eighteenth centuries. They all attribute a more absolute freedom to man in history than the obvious facts of history justify; and certainly more freedom than is justified by their own philosophy.

This paradox is most striking in the thought of the father of modern empirical naturalism, Thomas Hobbes. When analysing human nature Hobbes is intent upon reducing man's uniqueness to a minimum. Reason merely extends the natural will to live: "Reason is no less of the nature of man than passion, and it is the same in all men, because all men agree in the will to be directed and governed in the way to that which they desire to attain, namely their own good which is the work of reason."[4] The freedom of man is not distinguished in essence from that of animal life: "Neither is the freedom of willing and not willing greater in man than in other living creatures. . . . Such a liberty as is found free of necessity is found in neither men nor in beasts. But if by liberty we mean the faculty or power of doing what they will, then certainly that liberty is to be allowed to both and both may equally have it."[5]

Human history begins nevertheless with an act of decision. For Hobbes this decision, the social contract, is intended to avoid anarchy by the creation of an absolute government, to the authority of which all social decisions are submitted. The primary purpose of government, created by the social contract, is to establish precisely the kind of sovereignty which the French naturalists regard as the "Fall" in history, the error from which man must retrace his way back to nature.

Hobbes ostensibly regards the peril of anarchy as a peril of nature. He meets this peril by a free decision of human history, which involves him in the contradiction of assuming a distinction between historical man and natural man in his social philosophy which he denies in his psychology. Furthermore the peril of anarchy is really in human history rather than in nature. Hobbes is forced to admit this in spite of his psychological denial of human freedom. He writes: "It is true that certain living creatures as bees and ants live sociably with one another . . . and therefore some may perhaps desire to know why mankind cannot do the same." He answers this question by admitting that "men are continually in competition for honour and dignity and consequently . . . there ariseth envy and hatred and finally war" and that "these creatures having not as man the use

[4] *Elements of Law*, IV.
[5] *Elements of Philosophy*, Part IV, Ch. 25, Part 12.

of reason, do not see, or think they see, any fault in the administration of their common business."[6] This difficulty in the thought of Hobbes perfectly illustrates the conflict between the voluntarism of modern social theory and the determinism of its psychology, a contradiction which becomes a permanent source of confusion in modern thought. Man actually has a greater degree of freedom in his essential structure and less freedom in history than modern culture realizes.

Beginning with John Locke the idea of the social contract is appropriated for democratic rather than absolutistic theories of civil government. In the opinion of Locke the autocratic government defined by Hobbes is still in the realm of nature, and he requires a different social contract in order to establish democratic government, in which the power of the ruler is brought under social control. Locke finds the condition of nature "inconvenient" rather than anarchic and his natural law is not abrogated by civil law. Rather civil law must be regarded as a "proper remedy for the inconvenience of the state of nature which must certainly be great where men may be judges in their own cases." Whatever the explicit presuppositions of this democratic theory, Locke's real concern is for what Christian theology would call the peril of sin in human society but which Locke defines as the "inconvenience" of a state of nature. Since the peril arises from the fact that men "are judges in their own cases" it is not a peril of nature but of human freedom. In democratic theory, government is thus, as in Christian thought, a dyke against sin; the only difference being that Locke wrongly attributes sin to nature rather than to freedom. Unlike either Hobbes or most Christian theologians, Locke rightly fears the perils of tyranny more than the perils of anarchy. But with Hobbes, and unlike Christianity, he falsely ascribes the perils of social life to "nature." He seeks to overcome these perils, whether of tyranny or anarchy, by decisions in history. These decisions have a freedom ascribed to them which neither naturalism's own psychology nor the facts of history validate,

[6]*Leviathan*, Part II, Ch. 17.

and they have a degree of virtue attributed to them which history belies. In spite of himself the democratic naturalist thus trusts reason rather than nature in his effort to overcome human evil by new political institutions.

The French enlightenment partially follows the democratic doctrines of Locke's empiricism; but on the whole it is informed by a simpler naturalism. It ascribes political injustice to some error in history by which tyrannical governments have been established; and it hopes to return to justice by a return from history to nature. The nature to which it wishes to return is usually conceived more in Epicurean and Democritan than Stoic terms; which is to say that it regards nature as a realm of necessity in which the will-to-live of competing organisms is held in a simple harmony. This harmony can be restored, once the interference of governments is eliminated. "Moralists continually declaim against the badness of men," declares Helvetius, "but this shows how little they understand the matter. . . . The thing to complain of is not the badness of men but the ignorance of legislators who have always put the interests of individuals in opposition with general interest." In this theory the natural egoism of man is regarded as harmless so long as bad rulers and legislators do not interfere with the balance of competing egotistic impulses as it exists in nature. It is, of course, not explained how man happens to have the freedom to interfere with nature's laws. He is told that he must not and cannot interfere with nature; but none of these guides to a new morality seems to understand that if man cannot interfere it is superfluous to advise him that he must not. The contradiction is vividly revealed in the words of Diderot: "It would be very singular that all planets, all nature, should obey eternal laws and that there should be a little animal five feet high, who in contempt of these laws could act as he pleased, solely according to his caprice."

The logic of this position finally leads to a fully developed "physiocratic" theory; and it is this theory which Adam Smith ultimately elaborated into the philosophy of modern capitalism. The theory moves in the general direction of anarchism, as is evident in the thought of W. Godwin and others. The idea is that if only government will not interfere with the operation of natural laws in the economic sphere justice will be established through a harmony pre-established in nature. It is instructive that while modern political life can boast of genuine advances in justice, through the equaliza-tion of political power advocated by the democrats, modern economic life was allowed to develop cruel and iniquitous disproportions of power through the *laissez-faire* theories advocated by the physio-crats. Whatever their errors, the democrats started with more realistic assumptions than the physiocrats. Both were equally wrong how-ever in attributing social sin merely to social institutions and in hoping for a sinless man in a just society. W. Godwin, who, like Condorcet, mixed democratic and physiocratic theories in his thought, expressed this hope in the words: "All men would be fearless [in the new society] because they would know that there would be no legal snares lying in wait for their lives. They would be courageous because no man would be pressed to earth that another might enjoy immoderate luxury—jealousy and hatred would cease, because they are the offsprings of injustice."[7]

Profoundly as Marxism is distinguished from eighteenth-century liberalism in its social philosophy, its view of human nature is strik-ingly similar. It merely derives human evil, not from faulty political organization but from a prior fault in economic organization. Tyrannical governments are the consequence and the instruments of class domination. Man was alienated from his natural goodness at that period in history when the equalitarian and communistic or-ganization of the primitive tribe grew into the class organizations of the more advanced societies. The final elimination of classes will restore the natural goodness of man and thus obviate the necessity of coercion and, therefore, the need of the state. The Marxist theory of human consciousness, its virtual reduction of conscious behaviour to the "laws of motion" of the physical world, makes it difficult to

[7]*Enquiry Concerning Political Justice,* Vol. II, p. 29.

understand by what capacity man escaped from the restrictions of the primitive "we-consciousness" of the early tribe and how he achieved the ability and inclination to lord it over his fellow man. In the Marxist theory of man's alienation from his true communal essence there is an implicit, though not explicit, affinity with the doctrines of Rousseau. Social evil is attributed not so much to a specific evil in the history of man as to the elaborations of civiliza-tion itself. But the Marxist, unlike the romanticist, seeks to go for-ward rather than backward to a new innocency, a distinction which probably establishes the primary difference between communist and fascist social theories.

III

NATURE AS A SOURCE OF VIRTUE

The hope of modern culture of eliminating human wrong-doing through the political and economic reorganization stands in more or less confused relation with its other hope of eliminating social evil by more individual methods of return to the simple harmony of nature. The modern naturalist, whether romantic or rationalistic, has an easy conscience because he believes that he has not strayed very far from, and can easily return to, the innocency of nature. The most consistent naturalism from the ethical point of view is the naturalism of romanticism. For Rousseau and his followers the way back to nature was the method of throttling and destroying the uniquely human elaborations of nature in the freedom of man. "Retire to the woods," he declared, "there to lose sight and remembrance of the crimes of your contemporaries and be not apprehensive of degrading your species by renouncing its advances in order to renounce its vices." This romantic primitivism has the one advantage over ration-alism of recognizing that the freedom of the so-called rational man is not harmless and that it is not easily conformed to the order of either nature or reason. But it fails to recognize that the freedom of man is the source of all his creativity as well as of his vices. It there-

fore seeks abortively to turn human history back upon itself by
"renouncing its advances in order to renounce its vices." It is both
more profound and more perverse than the more rationalistic-
mechanistic forms of naturalism. It is profound because it understands, as the other naturalists do not, that there is a wide gulf between the purely natural impulse of survival and the distinctively
human and spiritual impulse of pride and power, or, in the language
of Rousseau, between "the natural feeling which leads every animal
to look to its own preservation" and the "factitious feeling which
arises in the state of society which leads every individual to make
more of himself than any other." This difference between the natural
will-to-live and the spiritual will-to-power remains an unexplored
mystery to non-romantic forms of naturalism.

The perversity of romantic naturalism consists in its primitivistic
effort to regain the innocency of nature. Rousseau does not, of course,
remain true to a consistent primitivism. His theory of social contract
does not conform to his injunction, "retire to the woods." It is,
rather, an effort to reconstitute the harmony of nature on a new
level of historical decision. He thinks it possible to compound all
individual wills into a frictionless harmony of a "general will" upon
this new level. There is significantly no clarity in his thought about
the character of this general will. Is it the will of the majority? Or
does it merely represent some ideal possibility of perfect harmony
between life and life? This lack of clarity reveals the inability of
romanticism to understand the nature of human freedom. It does
not realize that there is no definition of a general and unifying purpose at which any society may arrive, which the individual does
not transcend sufficiently to be able to criticize. He is not only able to
criticize it and to seek to amend it; but he may feel under a high
sense of obligation to do so.

Practically Rousseau's "general will" becomes merely the will of
the majority. Since there is no principle of criticism in his philosophy
for this general will, his conception of the general will becomes an
instrument of tyranny in the hands of a given and momentary ma-

jority. This tyranny of the majority is easily transmuted into the tyranny of a minority, which uses the instruments of modern democracy to give its purposes the semblance of majority consent. Thus Rousseau's too simple solution of a perplexing problem contributes to the emergence of modern political dæmonries. The relation between the primitive and the demonic in the history of modern culture is a significant revelation of the danger which arises when human freedom is not understood. Every effort to return by a too simple route to the harmony and harmlessness of nature inevitably results in dæmonic politics in which human ambitions and lusts defy the restraints of both nature and reason.

The naturalism of Rousseau's rationalistic contemporaries offers the individual an even simpler way back to the harmlessness of nature. Nature is governed by the impulse of survival and no distinction is made in this rationalism between this impulse and human ambitions. "It is the essence of man to love himself," writes Holbach, "to tend to his own conservation, to seek to render his own existence happy; thus interest and desire is the only motive of all actions."[1] It is the business of reason to discover or to rediscover the "necessary" harmonious relations which exist in nature by virtue of this egoism, to "teach that everything is necessary" to "take for the basis of morality the necessity of things."[2] The only prerequisite for achieving this harmlessness of nature is the elimination of precisely the government which Hobbes institutes in order to overcome the chaos of conflicting egoistic desires. With naive inconsistency Holbach implies the reality of human freedom while he ostensibly denies it. The same man who is asked to base his morality on the "necessity of things" is scolded: "Thou wicked unfortunate who art everywhere in continual contradiction with thyself."[3]

In the simple hedonistic naturalism of Holbach and Helvetius reason simply leads man back to the laws of nature and its harmony but it is not explained how he could ever have departed from them.

[1] *System of Nature,* Vol. II, p. 8.
[2] *Ibid.,* Vol. III, p. 91.   [3] *Ibid.,* Vol. III, p. 91.

In the more sophisticated hedonism of the nineteenth century reason so directs the desire for happiness that it includes the general welfare in the interest of the agent. The hedonism of nineteenth-century utilitarianism assumes the harmlessness not of the egoist as such but of the prudent egoist. This utilitarianism really transcends both hedonism and naturalism. The reason of which James Mill speaks completely transcends the self-interest of individuals. He is convinced that "every man possessed of reason is accustomed to weigh evidence and to be guided and determined by its preponderance" and that "the greater number will judge right and that the greatest force of evidence wherever it is, will produce the greatest impression."[4] In John Stuart Mill the obligation toward the general welfare is held within a hedonistic scheme only with the greatest difficulty. This naturalism is Stoic rather than Epicurean, despite its protestations. It is still the philosophy of an easy conscience but it regards reason rather than nature as the seat of virtue. That this virtue is not as perfect as had been assumed dawns upon the last of the great utilitarians, Jeremy Bentham, who discovers the "principle of self-preference," that is, the principle that "man prefers his own happiness to that of all sentient beings put together."[5] Against this egoistic tendency Bentham is forced to set political rather than purely rational restraint. He does this by inventing the "principle of the artificial identification of interest," which means that he will use government to distribute rewards and punishments in such a way as to counteract the tendency of the individual to seek his own advantage at the expense of the general welfare.

The other possibility of reason improving upon nature and thus achieving the virtue of man is that it will favour the social as against the egoistic impulses. There seems to be in reason a principle of selection which enables it to choose between various forces of nature. Thus David Hume declares: "that a man had but bad grace who delivers a theory however true, which, he must confess, leads to practice dangerous and pernicious. Why rake into those corners

[4]*Liberty of the Press*, p. 22.   [5]*Works*, Vol. X, p. 80.

of nature which spread a nuisance all around? Why dig up the pestilence from the pit in which it is buried?"[6]

The function of reason is to select and affirm the social and generous impulses as against the more egoistic ones. Hume writes: "It is sufficient for our present purposes if it be allowed, what surely without the greatest absurdity cannot be disputed, that there is some benevolence, however small, infused into our bosom, some spark of friendship for humankind, some particle of the dove kneaded into our frame along with elements of the wolf and the serpent. Let these generous sentiments be supposed ever so weak . . . they must still direct the determinations of *our mind* and, where everything else is equal, produce a cool preference of what is useful and serviceable to mankind above what is pernicious. . . . Avarice, ambition, vanity and all passions vulgarly though improperly comprised under the denomination of self-love are here excluded from our theory concerning the origin of morals, not because they are too weak but because they have not a proper direction for that purpose."[7] It must be noted that, in conformity with the classical tradition, the antisocial impulses in man are attributed to nature (wolf and serpent) and not to the unique freedom of the human spirit. Furthermore Hume is quite complacent about the possibility of checking egotism by education. He thinks that though "we are naturally partial to ourselves and to our friends we are capable of learning the advantages of a more equitable conduct."[8]

The belief that human virtue is guaranteed by the rational preference for the benevolent as against the egoistic impulses becomes a definite strand in modern thought. Saint Simon erected his structure of a "New Christianity" upon it and Auguste Comte made it the cornerstone of his positivist sociology. Comte imagined he had found a new path to virtue by exploiting and extending parental affection: "The love of his family leads Man out of the original state of self-love and enables him to attain finally a sufficient measure of social

[6]*General Principles of Morals*, Sec. VI, Part 2.
[7]*Ibid.*, Sec. IX.   [8]*Ibid.*, Sec. III, Part 1.

love." The family "completes the training by which nature prepares us for universal sympathy."[9] Comte failed to observe that his great discovery was vitiated by the fact that the family is also the source of that "alteregoism" which is a more potent source of injustice than the egotism of the individual. He realizes that rational discipline may extend social sympathy; but he does not see that human imagination may not only extend the boundaries which nature sets but may also impart such an intensity to the narrow loyalties, within the bounds of natural consanguinity, as to transmute them into forces of anarchy within the general community.

In all forms of naturalism in which reason is regarded as a secondary resource of virtue, as the eye without which natural impulse might be too blind to achieve "harmony between the parts," there is some difficulty in defining a consistent relation between reason and impulse. Sometimes it is regarded as a transcendent perspective which is able to prefer benevolence to self-love and the social to the egoistic impulses. Sometimes it holds a balance between them. In the thought of Bishop Butler it is not clear whether it is the business of reason to maintain such a balance or to find the identity between self-love and social harmony. Sometimes it is the business of reason to extend the impulse of self-preservation beyond itself until it includes the "general weal." All these interpretations, though usually claiming to be naturalistic, are inconsistently so because they fail to be consistently hedonistic. They introduce some criterion of reason as the norm of conduct and fail to maintain the pleasure principle consistently as either the norm or the motive of conduct.

The fact that such a great proportion of modern thought since the eighteenth century preserves man's good opinion of himself in terms of a dubious naturalism which is not certain whether virtue is to be found in reason or in nature nor how the two are related to each other, is indicative of the degree to which modern man's easy conscience is derived from a false estimate of his transcendence over nature.

[9] *A General View of Positivism*, pp. 100, 102.

The thought of a typical naturalistic philosopher of the twentieth century, John Dewey, advances remarkably little beyond the perplexities and confusions of the previous centuries. He has the same difficulty in finding a vantage point for reason from which it may operate against the perils of nature and the same blindness toward the new perils of spirit which arise in the "rational" life of man. Dewey is in fact less conscious of the social perils of self-love than either Locke or Hume. In his thought the hope of achieving a vantage point which transcends the corruptions of self-interest takes the form of trusting the "scientific method" and attributing anti-social conduct to the "cultural lag," that is, to the failure of social science to keep abreast with technology. "That coercion and oppression on a large scale exist no honest person can deny," he declares. "But these things are not the product of science and technology but of the perpetuation of old institutions and patterns untouched by the scientific method. The inference to be drawn is clear."[10] The failures of the past and present are due to the fact that the scientific method "has not been tried at any time with use of all the resources which scientific material and the experimental method now put at our disposal."[11] The subordination of intelligence to party passion is attributed to faulty social theories which represent "a kind of political watered-down version of the Hegelian dialectic" and the true liberal must make it clear that this "method has nothing in common with the procedure of organized co-operative inquiry which has won the triumphs of science in the field of physical nature."[12]

Professor Dewey has a touching faith in the possibility of achieving the same results in the field of social relations which intelligence achieved in the mastery of nature. The fact that man constitutionally corrupts his purest visions of disinterested justice in his actual actions seems never to occur to him. Consequently he never wearies in looking for specific causes of interested rather than disinterested action. As an educator, one of his favourite theories is that man's

[10]*Liberalism and Social Action*, p. 82.
[11]*Ibid.*, p. 51.   [12]*Ibid.*, p. 71.

betrayal of his own ideals in action is due to faulty educational techniques which separate "theory and practice, thought and action." He thinks this faulty pedagogy is derived from the "traditional separation of mind and body" in idealistic philosophy.[13] In common with his eighteenth-century precursors, he would use the disinterested force of his "freed intelligence" to attack institutional injustices and thus further free intelligence. Despotic institutions represent "relationships fixed in a pre-scientific age" and are the bulwark of anachronistic social attitudes. On the other hand "lag in mental and moral patterns provide the bulwark of the older institutions."[14]

No one expresses modern man's uneasiness about his society and complacency about himself more perfectly than John Dewey. One half of his philosophy is devoted to an emphasis upon what, in Christian theology, is called the creatureliness of man, his involvement in biological and social process. The other half seeks a secure place for disinterested intelligence above the flux of process; and finds it in "organized co-operative inquiry." Not a suspicion dawns upon Professor Dewey that no possible "organized inquiry" can be as transcendent over the historical conflicts of interest as it ought to be to achieve the disinterested intelligence which he attributes to it. Every such "organized inquiry" must have its own particular social locus. No court of law, though supported by age-old traditions of freedom from party conflict, is free of party bias whenever it deals with issues profound enough to touch the very foundation of the society upon which the court is reared. Moreover, there can be no "free co-operative inquiry" which will not pretend to have achieved a more complete impartiality than is possible for human instruments of justice. The worst injustices and conflicts of history arise from these very claims of impartiality for biased and partial historical instruments. The solution at which Professor Dewey arrives is therefore an incredibly naive answer to a much more ultimate and perplexing problem than he realizes. It could only have arisen in a

---

[13]Joseph Ratner, *Philosophy of John Dewey*, p. 381.
[14]John Dewey, *Liberalism and Social Action*, p. 76.

period of comparative social stability and security and in a nation in which geographic isolation obscured the conflict of nations, and great wealth mitigated the social conflict within a nation.

IV

THE OPTIMISM OF IDEALISM

Modern naturalism expresses its confidence in the goodness of man either by finding a harmony of nature, conceived in mechanistic or vitalistic terms, to which he can flee from the tensions and conflicts of freedom; or by placing its trust in some principle of order and harmony in reason in which it really has no right to believe within the limits of its naturalistic presupposition. Idealistic rationalism, on the other hand, has a much more simple approach to its moral optimism. Its confidence in the goodness of man rests upon a sharp distinction between nature and reason, between *nous* and *physis*. The order and inner coherence of reason is regarded as a safe retreat from the chaos of natural impulse; and the power of reason is considered sufficient to master and coerce natural vitality and transmute it into a higher realm of coherence. Such an interpretation of human nature has the advantage of recognizing the total dimension of the human spirit; but it makes the mistake of dividing the human *psyche* too absolutely and of identifying spirit and reason too completely. Its dualism prevents it from understanding the organic relation between nature and reason and the dependence of reason upon nature. Its identification of reason and spirit obscures the fact that human freedom actually transcends the capacities which are usually known as "rational." In other words it repeats the errors of Greek classicism. Consequently it finds a premature security for the freedom of man in the inner coherence of reason and does not see to what degree man may, in his freedom, violate, corrupt and prostitute the canons of reason in his own interest. Its rejection of Christian pessimism rests upon its belief that the rational man is also the good man.

Professor Alfred N. Whitehead, despite the qualified character of his idealism, offers a striking example of this idealistic optimism. He distinguishes between "speculative reason" and "pragmatic reason" and regards the former as the source of virtue and the latter as the root of evil. This distinction is reminiscent of Aristotle's distinction between the active and the passive *nous*. According to Whitehead, the former is the reason "which Plato shares with God," while the latter is the reason which "Ulysses shares with the foxes": "The short-range function of reason characteristic of Ulysses is reason criticizing and emphasizing subordinate purposes of nature which are agents of final causation. This is reason as a pragmatic agent. . . . The other function of reason was connected with the life work of Plato. In this function reason is enthroned above the practical tasks of the world. . . . It seeks with disinterested curiosity an understanding of the world. . . . In this function reason serves only itself. This is speculative reason." Evil arises from the "massive obscurantism of human nature" and this obscurantism in turn is defined as "the inertial resistance of practical reason with its millions of years behind it, to interference with its fixed methods arising from recent habits of speculation."[1]

Thus Whitehead, from the standpoint of a quasi-idealistic theory, believes the root of evil to lie in the inertia of that very intelligence, that pragmatic and short-range rational relation to natural impulses which, in the opinion of Professor Dewey, is man's sole rational possession. Yet both arrive at a "cultural lag" theory of human evil and both hope for a society which will ultimately be governed purely by rational suasion rather than force.[2] Their arrival at this common goal by contrasting methods is indicative of the power of moral optimism in modern culture. The rationalistic naturalists are forced to construct a very shaky and inadequate point of reference from which they can operate against the confusion of natural impulse. In Professor Dewey's case this is the device of a "free cooperative

---

[1] *The Function of Reason*, pp. 23–30.
[2] *Cf.* Whitehead, *Adventures of Ideas*, Ch. 5; John Dewey, *Philosophy and Civilization*.

inquiry," which is involved in the natural-historical process and yet somehow has a vantage point of pure disinterestedness above it. The purer rationalist splits the human spirit into a speculative and a pragmatic intelligence; and he assumes that the former has a vantage point of pure disinterestedness which no type of human intelligence ever possesses.

Idealism always has the provisional advantage over naturalism that it sees the human spirit in a deeper dimension than a pure naturalism. The proof that this is an advantage is given by the fact that naturalism is always forced to contradict itself to explain the facts of human history. The human spirit obviously transcends natural process too much to be bound by the harmony of natural necessity. This is proved both by the character of human creativity and by the emergence of a distinctively historical rather than natural chaos and destruction. The rationalist realizes that the human spirit is *nous* and not *physis*. But he immediately sacrifices his provisional advantage by identifying *nous* with *logos,* spirit with rationality. He believes therefore that the human spirit has a certain protection against the perils of its freedom within its own law-giving rationality. The possible evil of human actions is recognized but it is attributed to the body or, more exactly, to the *psyche,* that is, to the vitality of a particular form of existence.

For Spinoza, for instance, the "Fall" signifies the fact that human reason is unable to control passions completely; "for if he [Adam] had the power to make right use of his reason it was not possible for him to be deceived ... accordingly we must conclude that it was not in the first man's power to make right use of his reason but that, like us, he was subject to passions."[3] Of the three great rationalists of the seventeenth century, Spinoza, Descartes, and Leibnitz, Spinoza had the least confidence in the ability of reason to control passions and he made it a point to criticize Descartes' simple faith in the completely rational man. This realism prompted in him a provisional agreement with the Christian doctrines of humility: "For inasmuch as men

[3]*A Political Treatise,* Ch. 2, Part 8.

rarely live according to the dictates of reason . . . humility and repentance . . . work more good than evil. For if men who are powerless in mind should also become equally proud they would be
shamed with nothing."[4] But this provisional uneasiness about man
is overcome in Spinoza's thought by the admixture of Epicurean or
hedonistic naturalism in his Stoic pantheism. So completely are natural necessity and rationality identified in his thought that he is
finally unable to condemn even the actions of unreason: "For man,
be he learned or ignorant, is part of nature and everything by which
man is determined to action ought to be referred to the power of
nature. . . . For man whether guided by reason or mere desire does
nothing save in accordance with the laws of nature, this is by natural right. But most people believe that the ignorant rather disturb
than follow the course of nature. . . . Experience however teaches us
but too well that it is no more in our power to have a sound mind
than a sound body. Next, inasmuch as everything, as far as in it lies,
strives to preserve its own existence, we cannot at all doubt, were it
as much in our power to live by the dictates of reason as to be led
by blind desire, all would live by reason and order their lives wisely,
which is far from being the case."[5] In these words Spinoza becomes
almost the most perfect representative of modern culture, for he
manages to express its confidence in both nature and reason and its
slight preference for the latter over the former. He fails to understand, of course, that human egotism is something more than the
natural impulse of every organism "to preserve its own existence,"
that it has a power which defies both nature and reason; and that
the possession of a sound mind and a sound body is not completely a
matter of natural necessity in the life of man, for man is free to perfect and to destroy both physical health and mental capacity.

Leibnitz's pluralistic rationalism arrives at remarkably similar
optimistic conclusions in spite of a tremendous difference in philosophical presuppositions. For him natural necessity and rational

[4]Spinoza, *Ethics,* Part IV, Prop. LIV.
[5]*A Political Treatise,* Ch. II, par. 5–6.

universality are not in conflict, because God as a divine clock-maker has ordained that the two clocks, soul and body, should achieve a perfect coincidence in each unit. Thus "souls which act according to the laws of final causes" and "bodies which act according to the laws of efficient causes" though belonging to two realms are "in harmony with each other." The harmony is not quite perfect and what is called sin is to be regarded as "the inertia of matter," the friction between the two realms. But even this is not evil. On the contrary it is a prerequisite virtue; for without it, the soul could not express its true genius as a citizen of the heavenly city.

In the thought of German idealism, Christian conceptions of the freedom of human self-consciousness are merged with classical distinctions between the rational self and the self which is involved in natural process. In Hegel there is a profound understanding of the problems of self-consciousness which must be attributed to the Christian rather than the classical background. He nevertheless arrives at the conclusion that the highest self which knows itself is identical with universal reason. "Reason," he declares, "is the highest union of consciousness with self-consciousness, of the knowing of an object and the knowing of itself. It is the certitude that its determinations are just as much objective, *i.e.,* determinations of the essence of things as they are subjective thoughts." The ultimate heights of the human spirit are thus identical with God. "The knowing reason is therefore not the mere subjective certitude, but also truth; because Truth consists in the harmony or rather unity of certitude and Being, or of certitude and objectivity." But the self which is thus on the one hand identical with divine reason is on the other hand involved in change and particularity which leads to the "unhappy consciousness" which is "explicitly aware of its own doubleness," of "its own contradiction." It regards the "changeless consciousness as the true self" and "the other the multiform and fickle as the false self."[6] The sense of sin in Hegel, expressed in his term of "contrite" or "unhappy" consciousness is thus the sense of conflict

[6]Hegel, *Phenomenology of Mind,* trans. by J. B. Baillie, Vol. I, p. 201.

between what Professor Hocking calls "the self which is in the world and the self which contemplates the world from a point not within the world."[7] Sin, for Hegel, is thus practically identical with the emergence of man from the innocency of nature and is a prelude to virtue. Sin is a necessary and inevitable assertion of individuality against universality. But since the divided self "is aware of the Changeless, *i.e.,* of the True Self its task must be one of self-deliverance," a task which is accomplished by achieving a unity of the twofold consciousness in which it discovers that "its individuality is reconciled with the Universal." In a sense, sin, for Hegel, performs an even more positive function than in the thought of Leibnitz. Without the sinful assertion of individuality man would not express the freedom which distinguishes him from nature, nor would he be able to find the ultimate synthesis of universality and individuality which is true virtue. The self-consciousness which separates the self and distinguishes it from the world is a necessary element in the logic of consciousness by which the self ultimately finds itself in unity with the world.

Whatever the uniqueness of Hegel's thought and its admitted profundity in analysing the position of the self in the realms of both nature and spirit, it exhibits the uniform tendency of all idealism to be essentially complacent about the perils of the freedom of the human spirit. It is certain that spirit and rationality are really identical and that the laws of the latter control the freedom of the former. In Hegel this idea is accentuated because in his thought rationality is not only the principle of form but also a self-moving vitality and creativity. The full peril of Hegel's complacency is revealed in his estimate of the virtue of the state. He regards the state as the true universal in which the rational self emancipates itself from its particular self: "It provides for the reasonable will—insofar as it is in the individual only implicitly the universal will—coming to a consciousness and an understanding of itself and being found."[8]

[7] W. E. Hocking, *Thoughts on Death and Life,* p. 72.
[8] Hegel, "Philosophy of Mind," from *Encyclopedia of the Phil. Sciences,* Section II, par. 539.

Thus the belief that the individual must and can come to his true self in the universal and that this must be achieved in history leads Hegel to appreciate the morality of man most highly at precisely the point at which it is most dubious, that is in his collective will. It is at that very point at which the elimination of individual particularity in the collective ego creates a false sense of universality. The fact that the collective will of the nation remains, from the ultimate perspective, a particular will, in conflict with other wills, is obscured. Hegel does not deny that "the national spirit contains nature-necessity" and "labours under contingency" but he believes that the spirit which "thinks in universal history" thereby "lays hold of its concrete universality."[9] Yet it is in precisely this relation of the nation to universal history that the sinful pretensions of the national spirit are most fully revealed. It is just at that point that imperialism is compounded, being composed of the universalism of spirit and the will-to-live of the finite organism. Hegelian state worship is a rather pathetic fruit of idealism's unjustified confidence in the universality and virtue of reason. This reason, which remains involved in the contingencies of history becomes most dæmonic at the very point at which it pretends to have transcended all natural contingency, *i.e.,* at the point of collective particularity.

In Kant's critical idealism there is no such temptation to confound the universal and particular in history because he has no scheme for rising from nature to spirit by way of the self-sublimation of the individual ego. On the contrary in Kant a great gulf is fixed between the intelligible self and the sensible self, roughly synonymous with Hegel's "changeless" and "multiform" self, or the self which is reason and the self which is in nature. The gulf is so absolute that "if the determination of the will takes place in conformity indeed with the moral law—but not for the sake of the law, then the action possesses legality but not morality."[10] In consequence all natural vital forces in the life of man are ruled out of the field of ethics. Only respect

[9]Hegel, *ibid.,* par. 552.
[10]T. K. Abbott, *Kant's Theory of Ethics,* par. 7.

for law is an adequate moral motive, a basis for moral goodwill. Thus, in general compliance with the classical tradition, it is man's involvement in the natural process which is the cause of evil in him. The sensible self is essentially evil from the perspective of the intelligible self. Kant is thus able to arrive at provisionally pessimistic conclusions about man and declares: "Man is indeed unholy enough." But the intelligible self is holy and man must therefore "regard humanity in his own person as holy." The basis of human worth "is nothing less than a power which elevates man above himself (as a part of the world of sense). . . . This power is nothing but personality, that is, freedom and independence of the mechanism of nature, yet regarded also as a faculty of a being which is subject to special laws, namely, purely practical laws given by its own reason."[11]

This reason of the intelligible self is not as unqualifiedly identified with either God or the active self as in absolute idealism. God stands beyond it as an ultimate unity of essence and existence. On the other hand the intelligible self, though defined as the reason of the self, seems to have a more transcendent position than the self which wills obedience to the law of reason. It would appear that the self which is the lawgiver is really abstract reason, not to say abstract logic, since its primary function is to prevent contradiction within the sphere of morals. The self which obeys is primarily will; but since no vital urges of the sensible self are allowed to enter that will, it is a will generated by reason. The Kantian self is thus involved in a hierarchy of existence consisting of the self in nature, the self as rational will transcending nature, the rational or intelligible self which is the lawgiver and God who is the ultimate nexus between reason and nature. But this complexity of structure does not modify the general approach of rationalism to the problem of man. Man is cut in two. The part which is immersed in natural process is essentially evil and the part which is subject to reason is essentially good. But the freedom of man is always freedom from nature and not freedom from reason. In Kant "freedom is the *ratio essendi* of the moral

[11]*Ibid.*, par. 7.

law while the moral law is the *ratio cognoscendi* of freedom." It is thus inconceivable that the human spirit in its freedom should defy reason. Non-rational actions and immoral actions are the consequence of natural inclinations and passions which defy the laws of reason.[12]

It would not be profitable for our purposes to trace the various configurations of idealistic thought in modern culture. Whatever their variations, they are derivations from either Hegel or Kant. Sometimes, as in Fichte, they achieve a greater sense of the total unity of the human psyche by an admixture of romantic motifs. But the general emphasis remains the same. They see the problem of human freedom more clearly than naturalism. They are deeply conscious of the paradox of man's involvement in nature and transcendence over natural process. But they are never able to define sin in terms of a violation of the good within freedom itself. They cannot define sin as spiritual because they regard spirit as essentially good. They fail to see the paradox of evil arising out of freedom not as an essential or necessary consequence but as an alogical fact.

The easy conscience of modern culture is practically unanimous, but not quite. It may be more correct to say that there are practically no exceptions to the easy conscience but there are exceptions to the

[12]In the basic trends of his thought Kant exhibits the moral complacency of the rational man which modern idealism shares with all forms of rationalism. It is necessary, however, to call attention to the fact that Kant had a theory of sin in his *Religion Within the Limits of Reason Alone* which stands in complete contradiction to his general system and which can only be explained as the evidence of the influence of pietistic Christian thought upon him, an influence which did not, however, change the general system of his ethics and could not have done so without completely shattering it. Kant's theory is expounded under the caption of "The Radical Evil." Radical evil, for Kant, is man's inclination to corrupt the imperatives of morality so that they become a screen for the expression of self-love. "This evil is radical," he declares, "because it corrupts the very basis of all maxims." In analysing the human capacity for self-deception and its ability to make the worse appear the better reason for the sake of providing a moral façade for selfish actions, Kant penetrates into spiritual intricacies and mysteries to which he seems to remain completely blind in his *Critique of Practical Reason*.

general moral optimism. For there are pessimists about human nature, who are nevertheless of easy conscience, because they do not hold man himself responsible for the evils in human nature. Hobbes is a pessimist in regard to the individual; but he is completely complacent about the moral qualities of the state, which he introduces to overcome the chaos of individual life. Most of the other pessimists stand in the romantic tradition. Rousseau's romanticism is provisionally pessimistic; yet it becomes the very fountain of optimism in modern educational theory. Nietzsche's pessimism is thoroughgoing but even he is able to erect an ultimate optimism upon his conception of the superman, who transmutes the will-to-power into an instrument of social creativity and order. Freud's pessimism is most thoroughgoing, but he finds no conscience to appeal to. His "super-ego" performs the functions of Hobbes's state; but it cannot be given an unconditioned function of discipline, because it is feared that discipline will lead to new disorders in the unconscious life of the individual.

The romantic pessimism which culminates in Freud may be regarded as symbolic of the despair which modern man faces when his optimistic illusions are dispelled; for under the perpetual smile of modernity there is a grimace of disillusion and cynicism.

This undercurrent of romantic pessimism and cynicism does not, however, deflect the main stream of optimism. The fact that modern man has been able to preserve such a good opinion of himself, despite all the obvious refutations of his optimism, particularly in his own history, leads to the conclusion that there is a very stubborn source of resistance in man to the acceptance of the most obvious and irrefutable evidence about his moral qualities. This source of resistance is not primarily modern but generally human. The final sin of man, said Luther truly, is his unwillingness to concede that he is a sinner. The significant contribution of modern culture to this perennial human inclination lies in the number of plausible reasons which it was able to adduce in support of man's good opinion of himself. The fact that many of these reasons stand in contradiction to each other did not shatter modern man's confidence in them; for he could always persuade himself of the truth of at least one of them and it never occurred to him that they might all be false.

Yet they were all false. Whether they found the path from chaos to order to lead from nature to reason or from reason to nature, whether they regarded the harmony of nature or the coherence of mind as the final realm of redemption, they failed to understand the human spirit in its full dimension of freedom. Both the majesty and the tragedy of human life exceed the dimension within which modern culture seeks to comprehend human existence. The human spirit cannot be held within the bounds of either natural necessity or rational prudence. In its yearning toward the infinite lies the source of both human creativity and human sin. In the words of the eminent Catholic philosopher Étienne Gilson: "Epicurus remarked, and not without reason, that with a little bread and water the wise man is the equal of Jupiter himself. . . . The fact is, perhaps, that with a little bread and water a man ought to be happy but precisely is not; and if he is not, it is not necessarily because he lacks wisdom, but simply because he is a man, and because all that is deepest in him perpetually gainsays the wisdom offered. . . . The owner of a great estate would still add field to field, the rich man would heap up more riches, the husband of a fair wife would have another still fairer, or possibly one less fair would serve, provided only she were fair in some other way. . . . This incessant pursuit of an ever fugitive satisfaction springs from troubled deeps in human nature. . . . The very insatiability of human desire has a positive significance; it means this: that we are attracted by an infinite good."[13]

The fact that man can transcend himself in infinite regression and cannot find the end of life except in God is the mark of his creativity and uniqueness; closely related to this capacity is his inclination to transmute his partial and finite self and his partial and finite values into the infinite good. Therein lies his sin.

[13]*The Spirit of Medieval Philosophy*, pp. 270–272.

CHAPTER V

THE RELEVANCE OF THE CHRISTIAN VIEW
OF MAN

Our analysis of modern interpretations of human nature has led to the conviction that the modern mind arrives at contradictory conclusions about the relation of vitality to form in human nature; that the perennial debate between rationalists and romanticists, the one depreciating and the other glorifying the power and the virtue of subrational vitalities, is the historic evidence of this contradiction; that the modern mind fails to find a secure foundation for the individuality which it ostensibly cherishes so highly; and that its estimates of human virtue are too generous and optimistic to accord with the known facts of human history.

In analysing the modern failure in each of these areas of thought we have suggested that the difficulty arises from the lack of a principle of interpretation which can do justice to both the height of human self-transcendence and the organic unity between the spirit of man and his physical life. The modern mind interprets man as either essentially reason, without being able to do justice to his non-rational vitalities, or as essentially vitality without appreciating the extent of his rational freedom. Its metaphysics fails to comprehend the unity of mind and nature, of freedom and necessity, in the actual life of man. In similar fashion it dissipates the sense of individuality, upon which it insists with so much vehemence in the early Renaissance, because it cannot find a foundation in either nature, historical social structure, or universal mind for this individuality. It lacks an anchor or norm for the free individual who transcends both the limitations of nature and the various social concretions of history. Its inability to estimate the evil in man realistically is partly due to the failure of modern culture to see man in his full stature of self-transcendence. The naturalist sees human freedom as little more than the freedom of *homo faber* and fails to appreciate to what degree the human spirit breaks and remakes the harmonics and unities of nature. The idealist, identifying freedom with reason and failing to appreciate that freedom rises above reason, imagines that the freedom of man is secure, in the mind's impetus toward coherence and synthesis. Neither naturalism nor idealism can understand that man is free enough to violate both the necessities of nature and the logical systems of reason.

All three errors of modern estimates of man, therefore, point to a single and common source of error: Man is not measured in a dimension sufficiently high or deep to do full justice to either his stature or his capacity for both good and evil or to understand the total environment in which such a stature can understand, express and find itself. One might define this total environment most succinctly as one which includes both eternity and time; but the concept of eternity without further definition may be too ambiguous to clarify the point at issue. The eternity which is part of the environment of man is neither the infinity of time nor yet a realm of undifferentiated unity of being. It is the changeless source of man's changing being. As a creature who is involved in flux but who is also conscious of the fact that he is so involved, he cannot be totally involved. A spirit who can set time, nature, the world and being *per se* into juxtaposition to himself and inquire after the meaning of these things, proves that in some sense he stands outside and beyond them.

This ability to stand outside and beyond the world, tempts man to megalomania and persuades him to regard himself as the god around and about whom the universe centres. Yet he is too obviously involved in the flux and finiteness of nature to make such pretensions plausibly. The real situation is that he has an environment of eternity which he cannot know through the mere logical ordering of his experience. The rational faculty by which he orders and interprets his experience (sometimes erroneously regarded as the very eternity in which finiteness rests) is itself a part of the finite world which man must seek to understand. The only principle for the comprehension of the whole (the whole which includes both himself and his world) is therefore inevitably beyond his comprehension. Man is thus in the position of being unable to comprehend himself in his full stature of freedom without a principle of comprehension which is beyond his comprehension.

This is the situation which gives perennial rise to mystic faiths in both east and west, though the east is more addicted to mysticism than the west. The mystic, being conscious of standing somehow beyond the flux of events in the finite world, and fearful lest his finite effort to comprehend this eternal world merely obscure the concept of the eternal with finite perspectives, restricts himself to a purely negative definition of the eternal world. It is everything the finite world is not; or rather it is not anything which the finite world is. He thus arrives at a concept of an undifferentiated eternal unity. With this as his principle of criticism for the finite world, he is forced to regard the finite world as a corruption of, or emanation from, the undifferentiated unity of eternity. Since his own particularized existence is a part of this corrupt finite world the pure mystic, who begins by lifting self-consciousness out of the flux of temporal events, must end by negating his own conscious life as part of the temporal world and by seeking absorption into eternity.

II

INDIVIDUAL AND GENERAL REVELATION

The character of Biblical religion must be understood in contrast to this tendency toward self-immolation in mysticism. It is a religion which neither reduces the stature of man to the level of nature, nor yet destroys it in an empty and undifferentiated eternity. Biblical religion is variously defined, in distinction from other religions, as a prophetic or as an apocalyptic religion, or as a religion of revelation. In a religion of revelation, the unveiling of the eternal purpose and will, underlying the flux and evanescence of the world, is expected; and the expectation is fulfilled in personal and social-historical experience.[1]

From the standpoint of an understanding of human nature, the significance of a religion of revelation lies in the fact that both the transcendence of God over, and his intimate relation to, the world are equally emphasized. He is more completely transcendent than the eternity of mystic faith. Mysticism always regards the final depth of human consciousness as in some sense identical with the eternal order, and believes that men may know God if they penetrate deeply enough into the mystery of their own being. But on the other hand the transcendent God of Biblical faith makes Himself known in the finite and historical world. The finite world is not, because of its finiteness, incapable of entertaining comprehensible revelations of the incomprehensible God. The most important characteristic of a religion of revelation is this twofold emphasis upon the transcendence of God and upon His intimate relation to the world. In this divine transcendence the spirit of man finds a home in which it can understand its stature of freedom. But there it also finds the limits of its freedom, the judgment which is spoken against it and, ultimately, the mercy which makes such a judgment sufferable.

[1] John Oman defines the difference between mystical and apocalyptic religions as follows: "In the former case the eternal is sought as the unchanging by escape from the evanescent; in the latter it is looked for in the evanescent as a revelation of the increasing purpose in its changes." . . . "A mystical religion is, as it should always be understood scientifically, one that seeks the eternal behind the illusion of the evanescent; but in using 'apocalyptic' for any religion which looks for a revealing in the evanescent the term is extended from its customary use, which is for a religion which expects this in sudden catastrophic form, to one which expects it in any form." *The Natural and the Supernatural,* pp. 403–409.

God's creation of, and relation to, the world on the other hand prove that human finiteness and involvement in flux are essentially good and not evil. A religion of revelation is thus alone able to do justice to both the freedom and the finiteness of man and to understand the character of the evil in him.

The revelation of God to man is always a twofold one, a personal-individual revelation, and a revelation in the context of social-historical experience. Without the public and historical revelation the private experience of God would remain poorly defined and subject to caprice. Without the private revelation of God, the public and historical revelation would not gain credence. Since all men have, in some fashion, the experience of a reality beyond themselves, they are able to entertain the more precise revelations of the character and purpose of God as they come to them in the most significant experiences of prophetic history. Private revelation is, in a sense, synonymous with "general" revelation, without the presuppositions of which there could be no "special" revelation. It is no less universal for being private. Private revelation is the testimony in the consciousness of every person that his life touches a reality beyond himself, a reality deeper and higher than the system of nature in which he stands.

St. Paul speaks of this experience of God when he declares that even without a further revelation men are "without excuse" if they do not glorify God as God but become vain in their imagination and make themselves God (Romans 1:20). The experience of God is not so much a separate experience, as an overtone implied in all experience.[2] The soul which reaches the outermost rims of its own consciousness, must also come in contact with God, for He impinges upon that consciousness.

[2]Professor John Baillie writes very truly: "No matter how far back I go, no matter by what effort of memory I attempt to reach the virgin soil of childish innocence, I cannot get back to an atheistic mentality. As little can I reach a day when I was conscious of myself but not of God as I can reach a day when I was conscious of myself but not of other human beings." *Our Knowledge of God*, p. 4.

Schleiermacher describes this experience of God as the experience of "unqualified dependence." This is one of its aspects but not its totality. It is one of its aspects because there is, in all human consciousness, at least a dim recognition of the insufficient and dependent character of all finite life, a recognition which implies the consciousness of the reality upon which dependent existence depends. An equally important characteristic of the experience of God is the sense of being seen, commanded, judged and known from beyond ourselves. This experience is described by the Psalmist in the words: "O Lord, thou hast searched me, and known me. Thou knowest my downsitting and mine uprising, . . . and art acquainted with all my ways" (Ps. 139). The Psalmist exults in this relation between God and man and rightly discerns that the greatness and uniqueness of man is as necessary as the greatness of God for such a relationship: "I am fearfully and wonderfully made: marvellous are thy works; and that my soul knoweth right well." If any one should maintain that this sense of the impingement of God upon human life is a delusion by which man glorifies himself, one might call attention to the fact that in the book of Job exactly the same experience is described by one who is not grateful for it but protests against it. The constant demands and judgments of God seem to him to place life under an intolerable strain: "What is man, that thou shouldest magnify him? and that thou shouldest set thine heart upon him? and that thou shouldest visit him every morning, and try him every moment?" He feels that the divine demands are too exacting for human weakness: "let me alone; for my days are vanity," and he looks forward to the day when death will make the visitations of God impossible: "for now shall I sleep in the dust; and thou shalt seek me in the morning, but I shall not be" (Job 7:16-21). This impious protest against the ever-present accusing God is perhaps a more perfect validation of the reality of the experience than any pious words of gratitude for it.

The experience so described is in some sense identical or associated with what is usually called "conscience." The actual nature of conscience is, of course, variously defined in various philosophies. It may be regarded as the social obligations and judgments which all men must face. Or it may be defined as the obligation and judgment under which the rational or intelligible self places the empirical, the sensible or the partial self. The significance of the Biblical interpretation of conscience lies precisely in this, that a universal human experience, the sense of being commanded, placed under obligation and judged is interpreted as a relation between God and man in which it is God who makes demands and judgments upon man. Such an interpretation of a common experience is not possible without the presuppositions of the Biblical faith. But once accepted the assumption proves to be the only basis of a correct analysis of all the factors involved in the experience; for it is a fact that man is judged and yet there is no vantage point in his own life, sufficiently transcendent, from which the judgment can take place. St. Paul describes the three levels of judgment under which men stand, and the relativity of all but the last level in the words: "But to me it is a very small thing that I should be judged of you, or of man's judgment: yea, I judge not mine own self. For I know nothing by myself; yet am I not hereby justified: but he that judgeth me is the Lord" (1 Cor. 4:3–4).

It might be argued that the content of a personal experience which can be defined only through the aid of a more historical revelation of the nature of the divine, which enters this experience, while this historical revelation can gain credence only if the personal experience is presupposed, is so involved in a logical circle as to become incredible. But the fact is that all human knowledge is also so involved. All common human experience requires more than the immediate experience to define the character of the object of experience. The reality of the object of experience is not in question, but the exact nature of the reality touched is not clear until it is defined by insights which transcend the immediate perception of the object. If the reality touched is something more than a mere "object" but is itself subject, that is, if its character cannot be fully revealed to us, except as it takes the initiative, the principle of interpretation must be some-

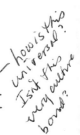

how is this universal? Isn't this very culture bound?

thing more than merely the general principles of knowledge which illumine a particular experience. The principle of interpretation must be a "revelation."

Our approach to other human personalities offers an illuminating analogy of the necessity and character of "revelation" in our relation to God. We have various evidence that, when dealing with persons, we are confronting a reality of greater depth than the mere organism of animal life. We have evidence that we are dealing with a "Thou" of such freedom and uniqueness that a mere external observation of its behaviour will not only leave the final essence of that person obscure but will actually falsify it, since such observation would debase what is really free subject into a mere object. This person, this other "Thou" cannot be understood until he speaks to us; until his behaviour is clarified by the "word" which comes out of the ultimate and transcendent unity of his spirit. Only such a word can give us the key by which we understand the complexities of his behaviour. This word spoken from beyond us and to us is both a verification of our belief that we are dealing with a different dimension than animal existence; and also a revelation of the actual and precise character of the person with whom we are dealing.

In the same way, the God whom we meet as "The Other" at the final limit of our own consciousness, is not fully known to us except as specific revelations of His character augment this general experience of being confronted from beyond ourselves.

In Biblical faith these specific revelations are apprehended in the context of a particular history of salvation in which specific historical events become special revelations of the character of God and of His purposes. Without the principle of interpretation furnished by this "special revelation" the general experience or the general revelation involved in conscience becomes falsified, because it is explained merely as man facing the court of social approval or disapproval or as facing his own "best self." In that case, whatever the provisional verdict, the final verdict always is, "I know nothing against myself" and the conclusion drawn from this verdict must be and is, "I am thereby justified." But this conclusion is at variance with the actual facts of the human situation, for there is no level of moral achievement upon which man can have or actually has an easy conscience.

The fact that a culture which identifies God with some level of human consciousness, either rational or super-rational, or with some order of nature, invariably falsifies the human situation and fails to appreciate either the total stature of freedom in man or the complexity of the problem of evil in him, is the most telling negative proof for the Biblical faith. Man does not know himself truly except as he knows himself confronted by God. Only in that confrontation does he become aware of his full stature and freedom and of the evil in him. It is for this reason that Biblical faith is of such importance for the proper understanding of man, and why it is necessary to correct the interpretations of human nature which underestimate his stature, depreciate his physical existence and fail to deal realistically with the evil in human nature, in terms of Biblical faith.

III

CREATION AS REVELATION

The general revelation of personal human experience, the sense of being confronted with a "wholly other" at the edge of human consciousness, contains three elements, two of which are not too sharply defined, while the third is not defined at all. The first is the sense of reverence for a majesty and of dependence upon an ultimate source of being. The second is the sense of moral obligation laid upon one from beyond oneself and of moral unworthiness before a judge. The third, most problematic of the elements in religious experience, is the longing for forgiveness. All three of these elements become more sharply defined as they gain the support of other forms of revelation. The first, the sense of dependence upon a reality greater and more ultimate than ourselves, gains the support of another form of "general" revelation, the content of which is expressed in the concept of the Creator and the creation. Faith concludes that the same "Thou"

who confronts us in our personal experience is also the source and
Creator of the whole world. The second element in personal religion,
the experience of judgment, gains support from the prophetic-Biblical
concept of judgment in history. The whole of history is seen as
validation of the truth in the personal experience that God stands
over against us as our judge. The third element, the longing for
reconciliation after this judgment (and it must be regarded provisionally as a longing rather than an assurance), becomes the great
issue of the Old Testament interpretation of life. The question is:
is God merciful as well as just? And if He is merciful, how is His
mercy related to His justice? This is the question which hovers over
the whole of Biblical religion. Because Christian faith believes the
final answer to this ultimate question to be given in Christ, it regards the revelation in Christ a final revelation, beyond which there
can be no further essential revelation. For this reason it speaks of
Christ "as the express image of his person." Here the whole depth
and mystery of the divine are finally revealed.

God is Not still Speaking??

In these three types of revelation God becomes specifically defined
as Creator, Judge and Redeemer. It is significant that each term
represents a definition of divine transcendence in increasingly specific
and sharply delineated terms; and yet in each the relation of God
to the world is preserved. They must be studied in order.

To speak of God as Creator of the world, is to regard the world in
its totality as a revelation of His majesty and self-sufficient power.
This revelation still belongs in the category of "general" revelation
though it has been transferred from the inner to the outer world. It
is this transfer which St. Paul effects in his argument that "they are
without excuse" if "they" do not know God, "because," he declares,
"that which may be known of God is manifest *in* them, for God hath
showed it unto them." This God who is manifest *in* them further
establishes Himself, "for the invisible things of him from the creation
of the world are clearly seen, being understood by the things that
are made, even his eternal power and Godhead" (Romans 1:19-20).
The fact that the world is not self-derived and self-explanatory and

self-sufficing but points beyond itself, is used as evidence for the doctrine of Creation and to point to the glory of the Creator. In a sense St. Paul is making use of the cosmological argument at this point, but not in such a way as to be subject to the Kantian criticism. It is not assumed that the reality of God can be proved by the fact that the contingent and dependent character of all finite being implies that the whole of the sensible world "rests upon some intelligible being that is free from all empirical conditions and itself contains the ground of the possibility of all appearances."[1] Rather the creation is contemplated as pointing to a Creator, already known in man's moral experience. Martin Buber accurately describes the process by which Biblical faith arrives at its concept of the Creator. He says: "The polytheist constructs a god out of every divine appearance, that is out of every mystery of the world and of existence; but the monotheist recognizes in all these mysteries the same God whom he experienced in personal confrontation. . . ."[2]

The Biblical doctrine of the Creator, and the world as His creation, is itself not a doctrine of revelation, but it is basic for the doctrine of revelation. It expresses perfectly the basic Biblical idea of both the transcendence of God and His intimate relation to the world. The doctrine is expressed in a "mythical" or supra-rational idea. Genetically the idea of creation is related to primitive concepts in which God is pictured as fashioning the world as the potter moulds his clay. The Bible retains this "primitive" concept because it preserves and protects the idea of the freedom of God and His transcendence. These are lost or imperilled by the more rational concept of "first cause" (which takes the place of God in naturalistic philosophies), and of the concept of a form-giving *nous,* which creates by forming the previously formless stuff or matter (which is the basic conception of divinity in idealistic philosophies).

The doctrine of creation preserves the transcendence and freedom of God without implying that the created world is evil because it

[1]*Cf.* Immanuel Kant, *Critique of Pure Reason,* Book II, Ch. ii, par. 4.
[2]*Koenigtum Gottes,* p. 91.

is not God. On the contrary Biblical religion consistently maintains the goodness of creation precisely on the ground that it is created by God. In this doctrine of the goodness of creation the foundation is laid for the Biblical emphasis upon the meaningfulness of human history. History is not regarded as evil or meaningless because it is involved in the flux of nature, and man is not regarded as evil because he is dependent upon a physical organism. The doctrine of creation escapes the error of the naturalists who, by regarding causality as the principle of meaning, can find no place for human freedom and are forced to reduce man to the level of nature. It escapes the error of the rationalists who make *nous* into the ultimate principle of meaning, and are thereby tempted to divide man into an essentially good reason, which participates in or is identified with the divine, and an essentially evil physical life.

To reject the principle of natural causation as the final principle of interpreting the unity of the world is not to interpret the world merely from the standpoint of man's internal problem or to read psychic attributes of man into nature. The fact is, that the relation of things to each other in the chain of natural causation is not an adequate explanation of their specific givenness. This irrational givenness must be regarded either as merely chance or caprice, or the order of the world must be related to a more ultimate realm of freedom. There is, in other words, a gain for an adequate cosmology, if man uses concepts in his interpretations of the cosmos which he won first of all in measuring the dimension of his own internal reality. Even nature is better understood if it is measured in a dimension of depth which is initially suggested by the structure of human consciousness, and by the experience of a reality more ultimate than his own, which impinges upon his freedom.

In the same manner the doctrine of creation corrects mistakes in rationalistic and idealistic cosmologies. These cosmologies are forced to presuppose some unformed stuff, some realm of chaos, which *nous* fashions into order, and to identify this forming process with creation. The Biblical doctrine of creation derives both the formless stuff and the forming principle from a more ultimate divine source, which it defines as both *logos* and as creative will, as both the principle of form and the principle of vitality. The supra-rational character of this doctrine is proved by the fact that, when pressed logically, it leads to the assertion that God creates *ex nihilo,* the idea at which all logical concepts of derivation must end—and begin.

The only metaphysical system which can be compared with the Biblical idea of Creator and creation, in terms of the dimension of depth which it assigns to the world, is the system of mysticism. One may speak of a mystical metaphysics because there is a remarkable unity and unanimity in mystical interpretations of life and reality, whether they develop in east or west and whether it be Plotinus or Buddha who elaborates the philosophy in detail. In all of them the finite world is regarded as illusory, or evil; in all of them the eternal world is regarded as a realm of undifferentiated unity from which the particularity, individuality and insufficiency of the finite world have been expunged; all of them place *nous, logos,* reason or form, which for the rationalists represents the eternal principle within flux, into the category of the finite, while they seek for a more ultimate and undifferentiated unity than "contrasting thoughts"; all of them seek to arrive at this unity of the divine and eternal by a rigorous discipline of introversion which assumes that the unity of consciousness above the level of sense experience but also above the level of reason, is identical with the divine. Brahman and Atman are one.

Mysticism, which is therefore closest to Biblical religion in measuring the depth of reality and the height of human consciousness, is also in sharpest contrast to the Biblical concept of Creator and creation. The contrast is threefold. (1) In contrast to the creative will and wisdom of the divine in the Biblical conception of God, it defines God in terms of negation.[3] (2) In contrast to the Biblical doc-

[3]Mercer in *Nature Mysticism* describes the mystic process of defining the eternal and divine as follows: "By a ruthless process of abstraction they have abjured the world of sense to vow allegiance to a mode of being about which nothing can be said without denying it ... it embraces everything and remains pure negation—leave us not alone with the abso-

trine of the goodness of creation, the finite, differentiated and particularized world is regarded as either illusory or evil. The human ego, as finite and particularized reality, is evil by virtue of being an ego; and salvation consists essentially in the destruction of individuality. (3) Despite this ultimate destruction of individuality, mysticism makes for a provisional deification of man, since it believes that God is identical with the deepest level of human consciousness. This is in contrast to the Biblical doctrine of the creatureliness of man and to the sharp Biblical distinction between Creator and creature.

The Biblical doctrine of Creator and creation is thus the only ground upon which the full height of the human spirit can be measured, the unity of its life in body and soul be maintained and the essential meaningfulness of its history in the finite world asserted, and a limit set for its freedom, and self-transcendence.

IV

HISTORICAL AND SPECIAL REVELATION

Faith in the transcendent God, as revealed in personal experience and in the character of the whole creation, is the ground upon which the Biblical historical revelation is built up; and this revelation is concerned with the two other attributes of God to man, His judgment and His mercy. This historical revelation is by no means simply the history of man's quest for God or the record of man's increasingly adequate definitions of the person of God, interpretations to which modern liberal thought has sometimes reduced Biblical revelation. It is rather the record of those events in history in which faith discerns the self-disclosure of God. What it discerns are actions of God which clarify the confrontation of man by God in the realm

---

lute of orthodox mysticism lest we perish of inanition." P. 10. Rufus Jones recognizes this tendency in mysticism but, like most Christian mystics, he regards it as an aberration rather than as a constitutional weakness of mysticism. *Studies in Mystical Religion*, Ch. 6.

Not a Hebraic communal understanding

of the personal and individual moral life. In personal life the moral experience consists of the sense of moral obligation as being laid upon man not by himself, nor yet by his society but by God; as a judgment upon man for failing in his obligation; and finally as the need for reconciliation between man and God because of the estrangement resulting from man's rebellion against the divine will.

In the history of revelation the counterpart of the sense of moral obligation is the covenant relation between God and His people. In this covenant we have the basic Biblical idea of the character of human history. It is not regarded as evil by reason of being involved in finiteness. Its ideal possibility is that a particular nation, Israel, should serve not its own purpose but the will of God, according to the covenant between God and His people. But the prophetic consciousness discerns that this ideal possibility is not fulfilled. Israel fails to fulfill its special mission not by reason of any inertia of nature, or any finiteness of mind, or any inability to comprehend the divine mission. On the contrary the basis of the sin of Israel, according to the prophets, lies in the temptation of the nation to identify itself too completely with the divine will of which it is only an historical instrument. Israel makes this mistake particularly; but the prophets discern the same mistake in each of the great empires who become executors of divine judgment upon Israel.

The real evil in the human situation, according to the prophetic interpretation, lies in man's unwillingness to recognize and acknowledge the weakness, finiteness and dependence of his position, in his inclination to grasp after a power and security which transcend the possibilities of human existence, and in his effort to pretend a virtue and knowledge which are beyond the limits of mere creatures. The whole burden of the prophetic message is that there is only one God ("I am the first, and I am the last; and beside me there is no God." Is. 44:6) and that the sin of man consists in the vanity and pride by which he imagines himself, his nations, his cultures, his civilizations to be divine. Sin is thus the unwillingness of man to acknowledge his creatureliness and dependence upon God and his effort to make his

Idolatry

own life independent and secure. It is the "vain imagination" by which man hides the conditioned, contingent and dependent character of his existence and seeks to give it the appearance of unconditioned reality. The second Isaiah laughs at the idol makers who transmute a perishable tree into the image of man and worship this totem as God.[1] The God who protests against this idolatry discloses Himself as the one "who made the earth and created man upon it," who is "the Lord and there is none else beside me" (Is. 45).

In condemning the pride of Babylon the second Isaiah shows a remarkable insight into the fact that the mystery and height of human self-consciousness are among the elements of temptation which betray man into his pride: "thou hast said, None seeth me. Thy wisdom and thy knowledge, it hath perverted thee; and thou hast said in thine heart, I am, and none else beside me" (Is. 47:10). Man, in other words, always transcends the world and contains the world within himself in the process of knowledge. He overestimates the completeness of his knowledge and even more the self-sufficiency of his existence. Ezekiel castigates the pride and self-sufficiency of the various princes and nations of the world in the same vein: "Say unto the prince of Tyrus . . . because thine heart is lifted up, and thou hast said, I am God, I sit in the seat of God in the midst of the seas; yet thou art a man, and not God, though thou set thine heart as the heart of God; . . . Behold, therefore I will bring strangers upon thee, . . . Wilt thou yet say before him that slayeth thee, I am God? but thou shalt be a man, and no God, in the hand of him that slayeth thee" (Ez. 28:2–9).

The catastrophes of history by which God punishes this pride, it

---

[1]The words of the prophet are filled with profound religious insight. He declares: "He heweth him down cedars, and taketh the cypress and the oak—he burneth part thereof in the fire; with part thereof he eateth flesh; he roasteth roast and is satisfied: yea, he warmeth himself, and saith, Aha, I am warm, I have seen the fire: and the residue thereof he maketh a god, even his graven image, he falleth down unto it, and worshippeth it, and prayeth unto it, and saith, Deliver me; for thou art my god" (Is. 44:14–17).

must be observed, are the natural and inevitable consequences of men's effort to transcend their mortal and insecure existence and to establish a security to which man has no right. One aspect of this human pride is man's refusal to acknowledge the dependent character of his life. Thus Egypt exists by the beneficences of nature in terms of the Nile's rhythmic seasons, but, according to Ezekiel, she imagines herself the author of this source of her wealth: "Behold, I am against thee, Pharaoh, king of Egypt, the great dragon that lieth in the midst of his rivers, which hath said, My river is mine own, and I have made it for myself" (Ezek. 29:3). One might write pages on the relevance of this prophetic judgment upon the self-sufficiency of modern man whose technical achievements obscure his dependence upon vast natural processes beyond his control and accentuate the perennial pride of man in his own power and security.

Psalm 49 sees the human problem in terms of this same prophetic insight. It inveighs against those "who trust in their wealth and boast themselves in the multitude of their riches" observing that "none of them can by any means redeem his brother nor give to God a ransom for him," and insisting that no special strength can emancipate man from common human frailty: "Their secret thought is that their houses shall continue forever. . . . Nevertheless man, being in honour, abideth not. He is like a beast that perisheth. Like sheep they are all laid in the grave. . . . Be not afraid when one is made rich and the glory of his house is increased. For when he dieth he shall carry nothing away." Jesus' parable of the rich fool stands squarely in this whole Biblical interpretation of sin. The rich fool imagines himself secure for many years by reason of his filled granaries. He declares: "Soul, thou hast much goods laid up for many years; take thine ease, eat, drink and be merry. But God said unto him, Thou fool, this night thy soul shall be required of thee: then whose shall those things be, which thou hast provided?" (Lk. 12:19–20).

The most classical definition of sin in the New Testament, that of St. Paul, is conceived in terms of perfect consistency with this prophetic interpretation. The sin of man is that he seeks to make himself God: "For the wrath of God is revealed from heaven against all ungodliness and unrighteousness of men, who hold the truth in unrighteousness; . . . because that when they knew God, they glorified him not as God, neither were thankful; but became vain in their imaginations, and their foolish heart was darkened. Professing themselves to be wise, they became fools, and changed the glory of the incorruptible God into an image made like to corruptible man, and to birds, and to four-footed beasts, and creeping things" (Romans 1:18–23).

The serious view which the Bible takes of this sin of man's rebellion against God naturally leads to an interpretation of history in which judgment upon sin becomes the first category of interpretation. The most obvious meaning of history is that every nation, culture and civilization brings destruction upon itself by exceeding the bounds of creatureliness which God has set upon all human enterprises. The prophets discern this fact of judgment most clearly in regard to Israel itself. The first of the great prophets, Amos, transmutes an inchoate Messianic hope into the expectation of doom: "The day of the Lord will be darkness and not light." But Hebraic prophecy soon extends the conception of judgment to apply not only to Israel but to all nations, including those great empires which God used, for the moment, as executors of judgment upon Israel. They all fall prey to the same temptation of pride and all finally face the same doom. Since the prophets were never wholly successful in convincing Israel that this was the right interpretation of history, a good deal of prophetic literature represents the conflict between the sense of impending doom in prophetic thought and the optimism and the complacency of the nation. During and after the exile this prophetic interpretation of history faced, and was deflected by, the complication of a new problem. The question arose why, if God punishes Israel for its sin, does He use, as instruments of judgment, nations which are more wicked than Israel? This problem has its peculiar and poignant relevance to the historical situation of our own day.

While the course of historical events does not inevitably yield the prophetic interpretation of events, it is significant that history does justify such an interpretation, once faith in the God of the prophets is assumed. It is, in fact, impossible to interpret history at all without a principle of interpretation which history as such does not yield. The various principles of interpretation current in modern culture, such as the idea of progress or the Marxist concept of an historical dialectic, are all principles of historical interpretation introduced by faith. They claim to be conclusions about the nature of history at which men arrive after a "scientific" analysis of the course of events; but there can be no such analysis of the course of events which does not make use of some presupposition of faith, as the principle of analysis and interpretation.

For Biblical faith, God is revealed in the catastrophic events of history as being, what each individual heart has already dimly perceived in its sense of being judged: as the structure, the law, the essential character of reality, as the source and centre of the created world against which the pride of man destroys itself in vain rebellion. The God who judges and condemns man is not some capricious tyrant whose will and "law" are irrelevant to the structure of the universe. Yet He is not merely "natural law." It is because He transcends the "laws of nature" in His freedom that He can set a law for man, who in his limited way transcends the "laws of nature" and cannot be bound by them. The relation of the freedom of God to the structure of the universe must be considered more fully later. The important point at the present moment is to record the emphasis of Biblical faith upon history as a revelation of the wrath of God upon the sinful pride of man.

But this interpretation leaves an important and ultimate problem unsolved. The further question is whether there is a resource in the heart of the Divine which can overcome the tragic character of history and which can cure as well as punish the sinful pride in which man inevitably involves himself. The Messianic prophecies of the Old Testament are all concerned with that problem in some form or other. After Amos the prophets all look forward to a final triumph of God over the sinfulness of man. This problem of the relation of mercy to judgment becomes obscured, as we shall see in later chapters, by the subordinate question, why Israel, which has a special historical relation to God, should suffer more than other nations. The Messianic hope was deflected by this issue and finally expressed itself primarily as the hope of Israel's vindication over its foes, or at least the hope of the vindication of the righteous over the unrighteous.

From the standpoint of Christian faith the life and death of Christ become the revelation of God's character with particular reference to the unsolved problem of the relation of His judgment to His mercy, of His wrath to His forgiveness. Christian faith sees in the Cross of Christ the assurance that judgment is not the final word of God to man; but it does not regard the mercy of God as a forgiveness which wipes out the distinctions of good and evil in history and makes judgment meaningless. All the difficult Christian theological dogmas of Atonement and justification are efforts to explicate the ultimate mystery of divine wrath and mercy in its relation to man. The good news of the gospel is that God takes the sinfulness of man into Himself; and overcomes in His own heart what cannot be overcome in human life, since human life remains within the vicious circle of sinful self-glorification on every level of moral advance.

This is rightly regarded as the final revelation of the personality of God. It is final because it is the revelation of God's freedom in the highest reaches of its transcendence. The judgment of God is always partly the effect of the structure of reality upon the vitalities of history which defy that structure. For this reason Greek tragedy can arrive at conclusions about judgment in history so similar to the prophetic interpretation. But Greek tragedy has no word about history to transcend its conception of *nemesis* and its prophecy of doom. In Biblical faith the longing for divine mercy accompanies the expectation of judgment, though Old Testament faith is not clear on just how the mercy of God is to triumph over His wrath, or how the reconciliation between man and God is to be effected, once judgment has taken place.

Christian faith regards the revelation in Christ as final because this ultimate problem is solved by the assurance that God takes man's sin upon Himself and into Himself and that without this divine initiative and this divine sacrifice there could be no reconciliation and no easing of man's uneasy conscience. This revelation is final not only as a category of interpreting the total meaning of history but also as a solution for the problem of the uneasy conscience in each individual. We have previously observed that God as Creator upon whom all life depends and God as Judge who stands over against man is not unknown to each individual in terms of that "general" revelation which is mediated by common human experience. We have also noted that the longing, though not the assurance, of forgiveness and reconciliation is a part of this common experience. The assurance of faith that the nature and character of God are such that He has resources of love and redemption transcending His judgments, is not something which may be known in terms of "general" revelation. It is the most distinctive content of special revelation. It must be observed that, once this character of God is apprehended in terms of special revelation, common human experience can validate it.

There are tentative assurances of divine mercy in the Old Testament. But they do not come to grips with the issue of the relation of mercy to judgment. The characteristic expressions about the mercy of God in the Old Testament are, that He will "cover" our sins, that He will not "remember" them and that He will "blot them out." Sometimes the problem is obscured as in later apocalypse, by the feeling of the righteous that the final revelation of God must consist in His vindication of the righteous rather than in His mercy to sinners.

The difficult conception of the "suffering servant" as the Messiah and messenger of God, suffering for the sins of the guilty though himself guiltless, and revealing thereby not simply the beauty of vicarious suffering in history but the very character of the divine, is thus rightly regarded by Christian faith as the ultimate revelation of God. We shall consider later to what degree Christ himself re-fashioned the Messianic hope and how he disappointed the Messianic dream at certain levels in order to fulfill it at its highest level, at a level at which it was not completely conscious of itself.[2]

It could not be claimed that this interpretation of the Christian revelation is consistently held in Christianity itself. There have al-ways been interpretations of the revelation in Christ, from early Hellenistic Christianity to certain modern forms of Catholic and Anglican thought in which the Incarnation is regarded, not so much as the bearer of the revelation of divine mercy, as the assurance that the gulf between the finite and the eternal, between man and God, between history and superhistory is not unbridgeable. "The word of God became man," said Clement, the early church father, "in order that thou mayest become a god."[3]

This type of Christian faith may be regarded as standing, gen-erally, under the influence of Platonism and Hellenism. For it the problem of human existence is not primarily the problem of sin but the problem of finiteness. Its concern is to prove that God can speak to man and make Himself known, a proposition which Hebraic-Biblical faith has never doubted, since it rests upon the very pre-supposition of such a relationship between God and man. This type of Christianity does not give a Greek or Platonic answer to the prob-lem of time and eternity but it is Greek in regarding this problem as primary. The answer which it gives is a triumph over Greek dual-ism. In Greek thought the tendency is always to regard history as meaningless or evil by reason of its involvement in time and nature. In Hebraic thought it is fully understood that there could be no history at all if human action and existence did not stand in the dimension of eternity as well as of time. For this reason the content of revelation is not primarily the assurance that God can speak to man but rather the assurance that His final word to man is not one of judgment but of forgiveness and mercy. The primary problem of

[2]In Vol. II, Chs. 1, 2.   [3]*Protrepticus*, i.8

human existence is believed to be not man's involvement in nature but the tragic consequence of his effort to extricate himself from nature, finiteness and time by his own effort. This issue must be more fully discussed in the second volume of this study.

The modern liberal Protestant interpretation of Christianity is usually removed one further step from the Biblical faith. In this modern interpretation even the time-eternity issue, which dominates Catholic thought, is not taken seriously; and the problem of sin is not understood at all. This version of Christian faith is obviously informed by, and is an accommodation to, the general presuppositions of modern culture. The optimism of this culture makes the central message of the gospel, dealing with sin, grace, forgiveness and justification, seem totally irrelevant. The naturalism of the culture also reduces the time and eternity problem to meaninglessness.

In consequence the Christology of this type of Christianity is primarily interested in rejecting the rationally absurd orthodox doctrine of the two natures of Christ. Modern liberal Christianity does not understand that this rationally absurd doctrine contains the basic affirmation of the Christian faith in regard to the relation of time and eternity, and that the doctrine is rationally absurd merely because the relevance between time and eternity was stated in terms of Greek philosophy in which it is not possible to state it, since this philosophy assumes an absolute gulf between the "passible" and the "impassible." Since the orthodox doctrine is rejected, the Christ of orthodox faith is transmuted into the "historic Jesus" who "incarnates values worthy of our highest devotion." The whole problem whether there can be anything in the flux of history which is worthy of our highest devotion and by what criterion we are to determine that it has this special eminence and significance is not clearly recognized, because the ethical naturalism, which informs this thought, assumes that nature yields certain ethical values which gradually culminate in human history.

Sometimes modern liberal versions of Christianity become uneasy about the special significance assigned to Jesus. They realize that they are perpetuating an estimate of his significance which is not compatible with their philosophical and theological presuppositions and which is no more than an attenuated form of the orthodox faith. In that case the effort is made to maintain some contact with the traditional faith by affirming simply that Jesus was a very, very, very good man but that of course a better man might appear, at a future date, in which case the loyalty of the faithful would be transferred to him. These moderns do not understand that they cannot transcend the relativities of history by the number of superlatives which they add to their moral estimate of Jesus and that they have not faced the problem of the nature of the criterion by which they judge Jesus to be good and by which they might regard some future character of history to be superior to him. They do not see that all historical judgments are based upon an explicit or implicit assumption about the character of history itself; and that there can be no judgment about the character of history which does not rest upon a further assumption about the relation of history to eternity.

In terms of the study of human nature, the difficulty with all these modern, presumably more credible, interpretations of Christ is that they do not recognize the full stature and freedom of man. Standing in his ultimate freedom and self-transcendence beyond time and nature, he cannot regard anything in the flux of nature and history as his final norm. Man is a creature who cannot find a true norm short of the nature of ultimate reality. This is the significance of the historic doctrine of Christ as the "second Adam." The same Christ who is accepted by faith as the revelation of the character of God is also regarded as the revelation of the true character of man. Christ has this twofold significance because love has this double significance. "God is love," which is to say that the ultimate reality upon which the created world depends and by which it is judged is not an "unmoved mover" or an undifferentiated eternity, but the vital and creative source of life and of the harmony of life with life. But the essence of human nature is also love, which is to say that for man, who is involved in the unities and harmonies of nature but who also transcends them in his freedom, there can be no principle of harmony short of the love in which free personality is united in freedom with other persons. But the coerced unities of nature and the highly relative forms of social cohesion established by historic "laws" are inadequate as final norms of human freedom. The only adequate norm is the historic incarnation of a perfect love which actually transcends history, and can appear in it only to be crucified.[4]

In distinction to modern, and usually covertly naturalistic, versions of Christian revelation the Hellenistic versions (in which the relation of time and eternity in the Incarnation are emphasized) have the merit of insisting upon the true dimension in which human life stands. It stands in the dimension of eternity as well as time. Hellenistic Christianity may be regarded as a partial triumph of the Christian faith over Hellenism. The doctrine of the Incarnation, the belief that God has become man and the hope that man can become divine, is asserted against the dualism of non-Christian and Platonic Hellenism, according to which a great gulf is fixed between the flux of nature and history and the perfection and calm of the eternal order.

But Hellenistic Christianity (and with it the whole of the Catholic tradition insofar as it subordinates all other problems to the time-eternity issue) exhausts itself in maintaining this Biblical emphasis against the dualism and pessimism of Greek thought. It therefore neglects the more basic issue of Biblical religion. This issue is not the finiteness of man but his sin, not his involvement in the flux of nature but his abortive efforts to escape that flux. The issue of Biblical religion is not primarily the problem of how finite man can know God but how sinful man is to be reconciled to God and how history is to overcome the tragic consequences of its "false eternals," its proud and premature efforts to escape finiteness.

It is in answer to this central problem of history, as Biblical faith conceives it, that God speaks to man in the Incarnation; and the content of the revelation is an act of reconciliation in which the judgment of God upon the pride of man is not abrogated, in which

[4]This issue will be dealt with more fully in Vol. II, Ch. 3.

the sin of man becomes the more sharply revealed and defined by the knowledge that God is Himself the victim of man's sin and pride. Nevertheless the final word is not one of judgment but of mercy and forgiveness.

This doctrine of Atonement and justification is the "stone which the builders rejected" and which must be made "the head of the corner." It is an absolutely essential presupposition for the understanding of human nature and human history. It is a doctrine which, as we shall see, was subordinated to the "time-eternity" implications of the doctrine of the Incarnation in patristic Christianity. It was qualified by that same doctrine in medieval Catholicism, so that Catholicism failed to understand the full seriousness of human sin or the full tragedy of human history. It emerged with elemental force in the Protestant Reformation, to become the central truth of the Christian religion. But it quickly lost its central position, so that modern liberal Protestantism knows less of its meaning or significance than the Middle Ages did.

Why this Biblical-Protestant interpretation of human nature should have had such a short life is one of the ancillary problems which must engage our attention. If medieval Catholicism united Biblical and classical Greek interpretations of human nature, and if the modern period begins by the destruction of this synthesis, the Renaissance emphasizing the classical element in the synthesis while the Reformation abstracted the Biblical element from it, the subsequent history of modern culture marks the virtual triumph of the Renaissance viewpoint over Reformation doctrine; and finally the disintegration of the Renaissance viewpoint. In this disintegration the Platonic and idealistic elements in classicism give way to Stoic and finally to Epicurean forms of naturalism.

Thus modern views of man tend to eliminate the very elements in the classical-Renaissance view which are most closely related to the Biblical view. Having eliminated the time-eternity dimension in measuring human nature, they naturally regard with uncomprehending contempt or fury those aspects of the Biblical view which introduce a further complexity into the time-eternity dimension, the complexity of sin.

We shall seek in Volume II of this study to determine how modern culture succeeded so completely in neglecting or destroying those Biblical insights into human nature which the Reformation rescued from the medieval synthesis. Is the pride of modern man a new version of the old human pride which finds the conclusions of Biblical religion too damaging to human self-esteem? Or did the Reformation make a serious error in its transmission of Biblical insights? Before seeking to answer these questions in the second half of this study, we must address ourselves to the task of explicating the meaning of the Biblical doctrine of man.

CHAPTER VI

MAN AS IMAGE OF GOD AND AS CREATURE

THE Christian view of man is sharply distinguished from all alternative views by the manner in which it interprets and relates three aspects of human existence to each other: (1) It emphasizes the height of self-transcendence in man's spiritual stature in its doctrine of "image of God." (2) It insists on man's weakness, dependence, and finiteness, on his involvement in the necessities and contingencies of the natural world, without, however, regarding this finiteness as, of itself, a source of evil in man. In its purest form the Christian view of man regards man as a unity of God-likeness and creatureliness in which he remains a creature even in the highest spiritual dimensions of his existence and may reveal elements of the image of God even in the lowliest aspects of his natural life. (3) It affirms that the evil in man is a consequence of his inevitable though not necessary unwillingness to acknowledge his dependence, to accept his finiteness and to admit his insecurity, an unwillingness which involves him in the vicious circle of accentuating the insecurity from which he seeks escape.

In analysing these three elements in the Christian view of man we shall seek, on the one hand, to trace the various efforts within the Christian faith, to state the logic of this Biblical doctrine clearly against the constant peril of confusing admixtures from other, partially contradictory, views of man. On the other hand we must seek to validate the Christian view by measuring the adequacy of its answer for human problems which other views have obscured and confused.

II

BIBLICAL BASIS OF THE DOCTRINES

The Biblical doctrine that man was made in the image of God and after His likeness is naturally given no precise psychological elaboration in the Bible itself. Nor does Biblical psychology ever achieve the careful distinctions of Greek thought. As in early Greek thought, spirit and soul are not at first carefully distinguished in the Bible. *Ruach* and *nephesh*, both meaning "breath" and "wind," are used interchangeably in the Old Testament and they connote the Hebraic sense of the unity of body and soul rather than any special idea of the transcendence of spirit. It is important for an understanding of this Hebraic sense of man's complete unity that the locus of *nephesh* is believed to be in the blood. Gradually however the term *ruach* becomes the more specific designation of man's organ of relation to God, in distinction to *nephesh* which achieves a connotation identical with "soul" or ψυχή, of the life principle in man (*Vis vitalis*). The prophets for instance are always said to be animated by the *ruach* of God.[1] The New Testament distinction between ψυχή and πνεῦμα is practically identical with that of the later writings in the Old Testament, πνεῦμα expressing the same concept as *ruach*. Thus it is distinguished as spirit from soul, but not absolutely for "spirit is never something separate beside the soul. . . . Spirit and soul are never separated from each other as soul and body. They may be distinguished but not separated: and when distinguished, spirit is the principle of the soul."[2] While the distinction between

[1] *Cf.* H. Wheeler Robinson, *The Christian Doctrine of Man*, pp. 20 and 65; also *Realencyklopaedie fuer Protestantische Theologie und Kirche*, Vol. VI, p. 452.

[2] *Realencyklopaedie*, Vol. VI, p. 453.

soul and spirit is not absolute yet the πνεῦμα, which the New Testament uses almost exclusively to designate spirit in distinction to the more rationalistic νοῦς of Greek philosophy, designates the relative God-likeness of man to such a degree that some commentators advance the plausible, though not conclusive, opinion, that the Pauline psychology assumes no natural πνεῦμα in man but only as a special charismatic gift from God.[3] While St. Paul uses the word πνεῦμα to designate the spirit of man as a natural endowment, it must be admitted that Pauline psychology generally juxtaposes πνεῦμα to σάρξ in terms which are prompted by his doctrine of salvation and in which πνεῦμα means something more than a natural capacity and σάρξ means the principle of sin rather than the body. The Biblical psychology, minus the Genesis doctrine of the image of God in man, does not therefore lay the full foundation for the subsequent Christian view of man but it does fit into the general outline of subsequent emphases by not making too sharp a distinction between body and soul and between soul and spirit, and by not defining spirit in terms of such sharp intellectualistic connotations as are found in Greek philosophy. The Hebraic sense of the unity of body and soul is not destroyed while, on the other hand, spirit is conceived of as primarily a capacity for and affinity with the divine.

This latter emphasis is made explicit through the attempts of Christian theology to define what is meant by the "image of God." These attempts, particularly in the early period of strong Platonic influence and in the latter Middle Ages, when Aristotle shared with Augustine and the Bible the position of ultimate arbiter of theological truth, sometimes define the "imago Dei" in terms which do not advance beyond the limits of the Aristotelian conception of man as a

---

[3] Cf. *inter alia*, Weiss, *The History of Primitive Christianity*, Vol. II, p. 479. Holtzmann held a similar view. The view is not conclusive because St. Paul speaks distinctively of the spirit of man in 1 Cor. 2:11 and 5:3.

For a comprehensive analysis of the Biblical concept of πνεῦμα in the New Testament and for definitions and connotations of "spirit" in Christian thought *see*, Edwyn Bevan, *Symbolism and Belief*, Chs. 7 and 8.

rational creature. Yet even in the most Platonic and Aristotelian forms of Christianity some suggestions of the "imago Dei" as an orientation of man toward God, some hint of the Christian understanding of man's capacity for indeterminate self-transcendence are given.[4]

Augustine is, in this as in other doctrines, the first Christian theologian to comprehend the full implications of the Christian doc-

[4]Gregory of Nyssa defines the image of God in man thus: "The Godhead is mind and word for 'in the beginning was the Word'...humanity too is not far removed from these; you see in yourself word and understanding, an imitation of the very Mind and Word" (Par. V, "On the Making of Man"). And again: "Thus the soul finds its perfection in that which is intellectual and rational; everything which is not may indeed share the name of soul but it is not really soul but a certain vital energy associated with the name of soul" (Par. XV). The implications of this essential Platonism are fully stated: "All the peculiar conditions of brute creation are blended with the intellectual part of the soul. To them belongs anger, to them belongs fear, to them all those opposing activities within us, everything but the faculty of reason and thought. That alone, the choice product, as has been said of all our life, bears the stamp of the Divine image" ("On the Soul and the Resurrection"). Yet Gregory introduces a more Biblical element into this rationalism with the observation: "Again God is love and the fount of love; ... the fashioner of our nature has made this to be our feature too; ... thus if this be absent the whole stamp of the likeness is transformed." Par. XI in the *Nicene and Post-Nicene Fathers, Second Series,* Vol. V, pp. 390–442.

Origen's Platonism completely destroys the Biblical sense of the unity of man. For him the image of God in man, the ψυχή λογική is really a fallen supernal spirit who expiates his pre-existent fall by his life in a physical body.

In Thomas Aquinas intellectualistic and Biblical conceptions of the "image of God" are compounded, with the Aristotelian elements achieving predominance. The image of God is defined as "primarily intellectual nature"; but "secondly we may consider the image of God in man as regards its accidental qualities so far as to observe imitation of God consisting in the fact that man proceeds from man as God from God; and also in the fact that the whole human soul is in the whole human body and again in every part, as God is in regard to the whole world." Nevertheless, this consideration does not shake his dominant rationalism which is strong enough to prompt him to challenge Augustine's assertion that man rather than the angels is made in the image of God. "We must grant," he writes, "that absolutely speaking the angels are

trine of man.[5] Augustine was and remained sufficiently under the influence of neo-Platonism to define the image of God in what seems at first glance to be terms of pure rationalism. He declares: "For not in the body but in the mind was man made in the image of God. In his own similitude let us seek God; in his own image recognize the Creator."[6] Or again: "It is in the soul of man, that is, in his rational or intellectual soul, that we must find that image of the Creator which is immortally implanted in its immortality. . . .

---

more to the image of God than man is, though in some respects man is more like God." *Summa theologiae,* Part I, Question 93, Art. 3.

In regard to the image of God as man's relation of virtuous obedience and love to God, Aquinas holds that this could not have belonged to man's original nature or it could not have been destroyed by the Fall. Since man does not possess it now it must be regarded as a supernatural endowment which man lost in the Fall: "The rectitude [of the primitive state] consisted in his reason being subject to God, the lower powers to reason and the body to the soul; and the first subjection was the cause of both the second and the third. Now it is clear that such a subjection was not from nature; otherwise it would have remained after sin. . . . Hence it is clear that also the primitive subjection by virtue of which reason was subject to God was not merely a natural gift but a supernatural endowment of grace." *Summa,* Part I, Question 95, Art. 1.

This official Catholic doctrine of a *donum superadditum* given to man beyond his natural endowments and lost in the Fall, leaving him thus with his natural virtues unimpaired, is very confusing. Ostensibly it is a supernatural virtue which is destroyed, but the capacity for it is the same as that which leads to sin, namely man's self-transcendent spirit. The structure of man is therefore altered after the Fall. He has become an essentially Aristotelian man. He has a capacity for natural virtue which is subject to the limitations of man immersed in finiteness. He lacks the capacity for the eternal. If this were true he would also lack the capacity for the sinful glorification of himself.

[5]Calvin rightly points to Augustine's profundity in distinction to the inconsistencies and obscurities in the doctrine of man in the early fathers. He says: "Although the Greeks beyond all others and among them particularly Chrysostom have exceeded all bounds in extolling the ability of the human will, yet such are the variations, fluctuations or obscurities of all the fathers, except Augustine, upon this subject that scarcely anything certain can be concluded from their writings." *Institutes,* Book II, Ch. 2, par. 4.

[6]In *Joan. Evang.,* XXIII, 10.

Although reason or intellect be at one time dormant within it, at another appears to be small and at another great, yet the human soul is never anything but rational and intellectual. Hence if it is made after the image of God in respect to this, that it is able to use reason for the understanding and beholding of God, then from the very moment when that nature so marvellous and so great began to be, whether this image be so worn down as to be almost none at all, whether it be obscure and defaced or bright and beautiful, assuredly it always is."[7] But it is immediately apparent that Augustine means by "the rational and intellectual soul" something more than the capacity for discursive reasoning, the ability to form "general concepts." Here his neo-Platonic heritage comes to the aid of his Biblical faith: for the νοῦς of Plotinus represents the capacity for self-knowledge and introspection. Augustine is primarily interested in the capacity of transcendence to the point of self-transcendence in the human spirit. The human memory is of particular importance to him as a symbol of man's capacity to transcend time and finally himself: "When I enter there [the place of memory] I require what I will to be brought forth and something instantly comes; others must be longer sought after, which are fetched as it were out of some inner receptacle. . . . Nor yet do the things themselves enter in; only the images of the things perceived are there in readiness, for thought to recall. . . . For even while I dwell in darkness and silence, in my memory I can produce colours if I will . . . yea I discern the breath of lilies from violets, though smelling nothing. . . . These things I do in the vast court of my memory. . . . There also I meet with myself, and recall myself and when and where and what I have done and under what feelings. . . . Out of the same store do I myself with the past continually combine fresh likenesses of things, which I have experienced, have believed; and thence again infer future actions, events and hopes, and all these again I reflect on, as present. I will do this or that, say I to myself, in that great receptacle of my mind, stored with images of things so many and so great, and this or that might be."

[7]From *De trin.*, XIV, 4, 6.

His description of the capacity to transcend temporal process, and of the ultimate power of self-determination and self-transcendence stir a sense of amazement in Augustine and the conviction that the limits of the self lie finally outside the self. He concludes his hymn of praise to memory with the words: "Great is the force of memory, excessive great, O my God; a large and boundless chamber; who ever sounded the bottom thereof? yet is this a power of mine and belongs to my nature; nor do I myself comprehend all that I am. *Therefore is the mind too strait to contain itself.* And where should that be which it containeth not of itself? Is it without it and not within? and how then does it not comprehend itself? A wonderful admiration surprises me, amazement seizes me upon this." He returns again and again to the power of self-transcendence as the most remarkable aspect of his power of transcendence: "When then I remember memory, memory itself is through itself, present with itself; but when I remember forgetfulness there are present both memory and forgetfulness." . . . "Great is the power of memory, a fearful thing, O my God, a deep and boundless manifoldness; and this thing is the mind and this am I myself. What am I then, O my God? What nature am I?"

The conclusions at which Augustine arrives in the contemplation of this mystery of human self-transcendence are of tremendous importance for the understanding of man's religious nature. He concludes that the power of transcendence places him so much outside of everything else that he can find a home only in God: "I dive on this side and on that, as far as I can and there is no end. So great is the force of memory, so great is the force of life, even in the mortal life of man. What shall I do then, O Thou my true life my God? I will pass beyond this power of mine which is called memory; yea, I will pass beyond it that I may approach unto Thee, O sweet Light. . . . And where shall I find Thee? If I find Thee without my memory then do I not retain Thee in my memory. And how shall I find Thee if I remember Thee not?"[8]

[8]*Confessions*, Book X, par. 7–17.

Those final questions are of particular significance because they mark the watershed between neo-Platonic and Christian thought in Augustine's mind. As a neo-Platonist Augustine sought God in the mystery of self-consciousness; and there are passages in his earlier writings in which he is still close to the deification of self-consciousness: "Descend into thyself; go into the secret chamber of thy mind. If thou be far from thyself, how canst Thou be near to God?"[9] Or again: "If thou dost find that nature is mutable, rise above thyself. But when thou transcendest thyself, remember that thou raisest thyself above the rational soul; strive therefore to reach the place where the very light of reason is lit."[10] Indeed it must be admitted that Augustine's interest in, and emphasis upon, the mysteries and majesties of the human spirit are not derived solely from the insights of the Christian religion. They are so remarkable because he was able to exploit what mysticism and Christianity, at their best, have in common: their understanding that the human spirit in its depth and height reaches into eternity and that this vertical dimension is more important for the understanding of man than merely his rational capacity for forming general concepts. This latter capacity is derived from the former. It is, as it were, a capacity for horizontal perspectives over the wide world, made possible by the height at which the human spirit is able to survey the scene.

However, Augustine's Biblical faith always prompts him finally to stop short of the mystic deification of self-consciousness. Man's powers point to God; but they cannot comprehend him: "Insofar as concerns the nature of man there is in him nothing better than the mind or reason. But he who would live blessedly ought not to live according to them; for then he would live according to man, whereas he ought to live according to God."[11] Or again: "We are speaking of God. Is it any wonder that Thou dost not comprehend? For if Thou dost comprehend, He is not God. . . . To reach God by the mind in any measure is a great blessedness; but to comprehend Him

[9]In *Joan. Evang.*, XXIII, 10.   [10]*De vera relig.*, XXXIX, 72.
[11]*Retract.*, I, i, 2. Quoted by Przywara, *Augustinian Synthesis*, p. 23.

is altogether impossible."[12] At this very point Augustine's strong Christian emphasis upon revelation saves him from the ultimate perils of mysticism. Human life points beyond itself. But it must not make itself into that beyond. That were to commit the basic sin of man. It can, therefore, understand the total dimension in which it stands only by making faith the presupposition of its understanding: "For although, unless he understands somewhat, no man can believe in God, nevertheless by the very faith whereby he believes, he is helped to the understanding of greater things. For there are some things which we do not believe unless we understand them; and there are other things which we do not understand unless we believe them."[13]

When some of Augustine's earlier lapses into neo-Platonism are discounted, it must be recognized that no Christian theologian has ever arrived at a more convincing statement of the relevance and distance between the human and divine than he. All subsequent statements of the essential character of the image of God in man are indebted to him, particularly if they manage to escape the shallows of a too simple rationalism.[14]

Under the influence of Augustinian ideas Christian theology consistently interprets the image of God in terms of the rational faculties of the soul, but includes among these the capacity of rising to the knowledge of God and (when unspoiled by sin) of achieving blessedness and virtue by reason of subjecting its life to the Creator. Calvin writes: "Though the soul is not the whole man yet there is no absurdity in calling him the image of God with relation to the soul: although I retain the principle . . . that the image of God includes all the excellence in which the nature of man surpasses all the other

[12]*Serm. (de script. N. T.)*, CXVII, iii, 5.

[13]In *Ps.* 118, *Serm.* xviii, 3.

[14]It is significant that Karl Barth, who stands, of course, in the general Augustinian tradition but who is interested to prove that revelation from God to man has practically no points of contact with man except those which it itself creates, finds Augustine's definitions of the image of God in man very inconvenient and criticizes them severely. Cf. *Doctrine of the Word of God*, p. 281.

species of animals. This term therefore denotes the integrity which
Adam possessed when he was endued with right understanding,
when he had affections regulated by reason, and all his senses governed in proper order and when in the excellence of his nature he
truly resembled the excellence of his Creator."[15] It will be noted that
here Calvin defines the image of God in terms of both a unique structure of human nature and of an original and now lost perfection of
character. Calvin makes clear that by the reason of the soul he means
capacities which include the self-determination of the will and the
quality of transcendence which Augustine has analysed: "God hath
furnished the soul of man with a mind capable of discerning good
from evil, just from unjust; and of discovering by the light of reason
what ought to be pursued and avoided. . . . To this He hath annexed the will on which depends the choice. The primitive condition
of man was ennobled with those eminent faculties; he possessed
reason, understanding, prudence and judgment not only for the
government of his life upon earth but to enable him to ascend even to
God and eternal felicity."[16] Nor does Calvin omit to do justice to the
Hebraic-Biblical sense of the unity of man in his whole nature, body
and soul: "Though the principal seat of the divine image was in the
mind and heart, or in the soul and its faculties, yet there was no part
of man, not even the body, which was not adorned with some rays
of his glory."[17]

   Though the Protestant Reformation must be regarded, generally,
as a revival of Augustinianism both in its view of the human situa-

---

[15]*Institutes,* Book I, Ch. 15, par. 3.
[16]*Institutes,* Book I, Ch. 15, par. 8.
[17]*Institutes,* Book I, Ch. 15, par. 3. In the same chapter Calvin, following some of the early fathers, points to man's upright position as an
aspect of the image of God in him: "I admit that external form, as it
distinguishes from brutes, also exalts us more nearly to God: nor will I
vehemently contend with any one who would understand by the image
of God that

   'While the mute creation downward bend
   Their sight, and to their earthly mother tend,
   Man looks aloft and with expectant eyes
   Beholds his own hereditary skies.' " (Ovid)

tion and its interpretation of the plan of God to meet that situation, it could hardly be claimed that Martin Luther adds any significant insights to the Augustinian view of the image of God in man. Luther is so concerned to re-establish the Augustinian doctrine of original sin against the semi-Pelagianism of Catholicism that all his interpretations of the image of God are coloured by his eagerness to prove that, whatever the image is, it is now lost: "Wherefore when we now attempt to speak of the image we speak of a thing unknown, an image which we have not only not experienced, but the contrary to which we have experienced all our lives and experience still. Of this image therefore all we now possess are the mere words 'image of God.' . . . But there was in Adam an illumined reason, a true knowledge of God and a will the most upright to love both God and his neighbour."[18] In a sense Luther offers more important indirect than direct, more implicit than explicit, evidence of the fact that some concept of the image of God and of a state of perfection before the Fall is an inevitable consequence of "natural theology," of man's capacity and inclination to transcend his present state of imperfection and sin and posit a state of perfection which must be realized. For, though Luther insists that "the image is so marred and obscured by sin" and is "so utter leprous and unclean" that we cannot even in thought "reach a comprehension of it," he proceeds, nevertheless, to seek to comprehend and define it, largely in terms of contrast to the present state of sin. He declares that though we only "retain the name and the semblance and, as it were, the naked title of an original dominion—the reality of which is now almost

[18] In *Commentary on Genesis*. Luther usually defines the image of God purely in terms of contrast to the present state of sin. He, more than any Reformation theologian, is confused by the mythical aspects of the state of perfection before the Fall, though all of them accepted the historicity of this state. He allows his imagination to run riot in picturing this state of perfection and insists that it included remarkable attributes of physical perfection as well as of mental and spiritual endowments. Adam "had powers of vision exceeding those of a lynx" and "handled lions and bears, being stronger than they, as we handle the young of any animal." (*Ibid.*)

wholly lost . . . still it is good for us to know and to think upon this state of things that we may sigh after that day which shall come." The consequence of his definition by contrast is the conclusion that the image of God is something more than the "powers of the soul, memory and mind or intellect and will." He believes that even the scholastic definition of "man's memory being adorned with hope, his intellect with faith and his will with love" is not enough. "The image of God is something far different from this. . . . The image of God created in Adam was a workmanship, the most beautiful, the most excellent, the most noble, . . . his intellect was most clear, his memory most complete and his will the most sincere, accompanied by a most charming security, without any fear of death and without any care or anxiety whatever."[19] Luther's extravagant descriptions of the state of perfection before the Fall are so obviously prompted by the desire to accentuate man's present state of sin, misery and death, and they are, compared with both Augustine and Calvin, so inexact that his thought is not very helpful in interpreting the real import of the Christian conception of the image of God. They may be regarded rather as evidence of a partial corruption of the paradox that Christianity measures the stature of man more highly and his virtue more severely than any alternative view. In the case of Luther the "uneasy conscience" of Christianity erupts so vehemently and is set so uncompromisingly against the moralism of Catholic scholasticism that it is in danger of obscuring insights into the dimension and structure of the human spirit without which the uneasy conscience of man becomes an absurdity.

Without going into further historical analysis it will suffice to assert by way of summary that the Biblical conception of "image of God" has influenced Christian thought, particularly since Augustine (when not under a too strong Platonic or Aristotelian influence), to interpret human nature in terms which include his rational faculties but which suggest something beyond them. The ablest non-

[19]All quotations from his *Commentary on Genesis*, Part IV, II, V 26 ff

theological analysis of human nature in modern times, by Heidegger, defines this Christian emphasis succinctly as "the idea of 'transcendence,' namely that man is something which reaches beyond itself—that he is more than a rational creature."[20] Max Scheler, following the Biblical tradition, proposes to use the word "spirit" (*Geist*) in distinction to the Greek *nous* to denote this particular quality and capacity in man, because it must be "a word which, though including the concept of reason, must also include, beside the capacity of thinking ideas, a unique type of comprehension for primeval phenomena (*Urphaenomenen*) or concepts of meaning and furthermore a specific class of emotional and volitional capacities for goodness, love, contrition and reverence." "The nature of man," he declares, "and that which could be termed his unique quality transcend that which is usually called intelligence and freedom of choice and would not be reached if his intelligence and freedom could conceivably be raised to the *n*th degree. . . . Between an intelligent monkey and an Edison, merely as technical intelligence, only a difference of degree, though a great degree, exists. It is the quality of the human spirit on the other hand to lift itself above itself as living organism and to make the whole temporal and spatial world, including itself, the object of its knowledge."[21]

The freedom of which Scheler speaks is something more (and in a sense also something less) than the usual "freedom of choice" so important in philosophical and theological theory. Man is self-deter-

[20]Martin Heidegger, *Sein und Zeit,* p. 49.
[21]Max Scheler, *Die Stellung des Menschen im Kosmos,* pp. 46–47. Scheler obviously overstates his case in this statement. The technical intelligence of an Edison depends upon capacities for abstractions and generalizations which are derived from a more ultimate ability "to make the whole temporal and spatial world including itself the object of its knowledge." If this were not so the monkey ought to be able to approximate Edison's technical intelligence in degree. The distinction between the two is qualitative and not merely quantitative. But Scheler is right in his emphasis upon the final dimension of "spirit" in contrast to mere reason. What is ordinarily meant by "reason" does not imply "spirit," but "spirit" does imply "reason."

mining not only in the sense that he transcends natural process in such a way as to be able to choose between various alternatives presented to him by the processes of nature but also in the sense that he transcends himself in such a way that he must choose his total end. In this task of self-determination he is confronted with endless potentialities and he can set no limit to what he ought to be, short of the character of ultimate reality. Yet this same man is a creature whose life is definitely limited by nature and he is unable to choose anything beyond the bounds set by the creation in which he stands. This paradox of human freedom is succinctly stated by Kierkegaard: "Truth [in the human situation] is exactly the identity of choosing and determining and of being chosen and determined. What I choose I do not determine, for if it were not determined I could not choose it; and yet if I did not determine it through my choice I would not really choose it. It is: if it were not I could not choose it. It is not: but becomes reality through my choice, or else my choice were an illusion. . . . I choose the Absolute? What is the Absolute? I am that myself the eternal personality. . . . But what is this myself? . . . It is the most abstract and yet at the same time the most concrete of all realities. It is freedom."[22]

This excellent statement of the paradox by Kierkegaard is partly confused by his identification of the self with the Absolute and with "eternal personality." In Christian faith the place of Christ as both the revelation of the character of God and of the essential nature of man (the "second Adam") does justice to the fact that man can find his true norm only in the character of God but is nevertheless a creature who cannot and must not aspire to be God. The God who is his norm is God as He is revealed in a character of human history, that is, in Christ. Christ is at once an historical character and more than an historical character. His life transcends the possibilities of history but it remains relevant to all historical striving, for all historical goals can be expressed only in supra-historical terms. If stated in purely historical terms they will embody some contingency of

[22]*Entweder Oder Band,* II, p. 182.

nature and history and set a false limit for the human spirit. This aspect of Christian Christology is not understood by naturalistic versions of the Christian faith in which the "Jesus of history" becomes the norm of life. These versions do not understand the total stature of freedom in which human life stands and are therefore not able to appreciate the necessity of a trans-historical norm of historical life.

The perfect love of the life of Christ ends on the Cross, after having existed in history. It is therefore supra-historical, not in the sense of setting up a non-historical eternity as the goal of human life; but in the sense that the love which it embodies is the point where history culminates and ends.[23]

Implicit in the human situation of freedom and in man's capacity to transcend himself and his world is his inability to construct a world of meaning without finding a source and key to the structure of meaning which transcends the world beyond his own capacity to transcend it. The problem of meaning, which is the basic problem of religion, transcends the ordinary rational problem of tracing the relation of things to each other as the freedom of man's spirit transcends his rational faculties.[24]

This problem is not solved without the introduction of a principle of meaning which transcends the world of meaning to be interpreted. If some vitality of existence, or even some subordinate principle of coherence is used as the principle of meaning, man is involved in idolatry. He lifts some finite and contingent element of existence into the eminence of the divine. He uses something which

[23]This problem of the relation of Christology to the Christian conception of human freedom will be considered more fully in Vol. II, Ch. 3.

[24]Max Scheler defines this distinction as follows: "A problem of reason would be the following: 'I have a pain in my arm. Where did it come from and how may I be rid of it?' To determine that is a task of science. But I may use the pain in my arm to reflect upon the fact that the world is tainted with pain, evil and sorrow. Then I will ask: What is pain, evil and sorrow essentially and of what nature is the ground of all existence, making pain as such, without reference to my particular pain, possible?" *Op. cit.*, p 6o.

itself requires explanation as the ultimate principle of coherence and meaning. The most obvious forms of idolatry are those in which the world of meaning is organized around a centre of natural or historical vitality, such as the life of a tribe or nation, which is patently contingent and not ultimate. More covert forms of idolatry are achieved if a subordinate principle of coherence and meaning is regarded as the ultimate principle. The causal sequences of nature represent one such subordinate principle. If the effort is made to comprehend the meaning of the world through the principle of natural causation alone, the world is conceived in terms of a mechanistic coherence which has no place for the freedom which reveals itself in human consciousness. Rational principles of coherence represent another, somewhat higher, and yet inadequate system of meaning. Every effort to identify meaning with rationality implies the deification of reason. That such an identification represents idolatry and that the laws of reason and logic are incapable of fully comprehending the total meaning of the world, is attested by the fact that life and history are full of contradictions which cannot be resolved in terms of rational principles. Furthermore a mind which transcends itself cannot legitimately make itself the ultimate principle of interpretation by which it explains the relation of mind to the world. The fact of self-transcendence leads inevitably to the search for a God who transcends the world. Augustine accurately describes the logic of this procedure in the words: "I dive on this side and on that as far as I can see and there is no end.... I will pass beyond this power of mine which is called memory; yea I will pass beyond it that I may approach unto Thee."

Though the religious faith through which God is apprehended cannot be in contradiction to reason in the sense that the ultimate principle of meaning cannot be in contradiction to the subordinate principle of meaning which is found in rational coherence yet, on the other hand religious faith cannot be simply subordinated to reason or made to stand under its judgment. When this is done the reason which asks the question whether the God of religious faith is plausible has already implied a negative answer in the question because it has made itself God and naturally cannot tolerate another. The usual procedure in purely rational and intellectual judgments upon religion is to find the God of religious faith essentially identical with the god of reason, with the distinction that religious faith is regarded as a somewhat crude form of apprehending what reason apprehends more purely.

The real situation is that man who is made in the image of God is unable, precisely because of those qualities in him which are designated as "image of God," to be satisfied with a god who is made in man's image. By virtue of his capacity for self-transcendence he can look beyond himself sufficiently to know that a projection of himself is not God. This does not mean that he will not commit idolatry and make God in his own image. Man is constantly tempted to the sin of idolatry and constantly succumbs to it because in contemplating the power and dignity of his freedom he forgets the degree of his limitations. Yet the rigorous efforts of mystic religions to escape the sin of idolatry and to overcome the error of defining God in finite and contingent terms attest to a transcendent perspective in the human spirit from which the sin of idolatry is apprehended.

all people or some?

The ability to be conscious of and uneasy about the sin of idolatry, which is revealed in mystic spirituality, does not, of course, solve the problem of man's self-transcendence on the one hand and finiteness on the other. Without the presuppositions of the Christian faith, men run into the Charybdis of life-denial and acosmism in the effort to escape the Scylla of idolatry. Either they make some contingent and relative vitality or coherence into the unconditioned principle of meaning or they negate the whole of temporal and historical existence because it is involved in contingency.

To understand the paradoxical approach of Christian faith to the problem of human freedom and finiteness, it is necessary to set the doctrine of man as creature in juxtaposition to the doctrine of man as *imago Dei*.

III

THE DOCTRINE OF MAN AS CREATURE

The Christian view of the goodness of creation is solidly anchored in a very simple word of Scripture: "And God saw every thing that he had made, and behold, it was very good" (Gen. 1:31). The doctrine does not of course depend merely upon the authority of this estimate of creation in Genesis. The whole Biblical interpretation of life and history rests upon the assumption that the created world, the world of finite, dependent and contingent existence, is not evil by reason of its finiteness.

It must be admitted that sometimes the authority of this simple dictum in Genesis was all that prevented Christian faith from succumbing to dualistic and acosmic doctrines which pressed in upon the Christian church. Nevertheless Christianity has never been completely without some understanding of the genius of its own faith that the world is not evil because it is temporal, that the body is not the source of sin in man, that individuality as separate and particular existence is not evil by reason of being distinguished from undifferentiated totality, and that death is no evil though it is an occasion for evil, namely the fear of death.

The Biblical view is that the finiteness, dependence and the insufficiency of man's mortal life are facts which belong to God's plan of creation and must be accepted with reverence and humility. In one of the most beautiful Biblical expositions of the glory and majesty of God the brevity of man is presented merely as a contrast to and proof of that majesty: "All flesh is grass and all the goodliness thereof is as the flower of the field; The grass withereth, the flower fadeth: . . . but the word of our God shall stand forever." Even man's collective and national life, which so frequently offers him the illusion of an immortality and eternity transcending his individual finiteness, is rightly seen to be involved in the same finiteness: "Behold, the nations are as a drop of a bucket, and are counted as the small dust of the balance: . . . all nations before him are as nothing; and they are counted to him less than nothing" (Is. 40). The fragmentary character of human life is not regarded as evil in Biblical faith because it is seen from the perspective of a centre of life and meaning in which each fragment is related to the plan of the whole, to the will of God. The evil arises when the fragment seeks by its own wisdom to comprehend the whole or attempts by its own power to realize it. All Biblical theism contains the suggestion that God's will and wisdom must be able to transcend any human interpretation of its justice and meaning, or it would be less than the centre of that inclusive meaning which alone can comprehend the seeming chaos of existence into a total harmony. This surely is the significance of the message of the Book of Job. Job seeks to comprehend the justice of God by human standards, is thwarted and baffled and then finally overwhelmed by God's display of all the mysteries and majesties of creation which are obviously beyond human comprehension. These divine arguments are introduced by the challenging question, "Where wast thou when I laid the foundations of the earth?" and they finally reduce Job to contrite submission: "Therefore have I uttered that I understood not; things too wonderful for me, which I knew not. . . . I have heard of thee by the hearing of the ear: but now mine eye seeth thee. Wherefore I abhor myself, and repent in dust and ashes" (Job 42:3, 5, 6).

Jesus compares the impotence and dependence of man to that of the lower creation: "Which of you by taking thought can add one cubit to his stature?" (Mt. 6:27). Significantly this observation is a part of a general analysis of the human situation, the purpose of which is to affirm that both man and the lower creatures have their existence by and in God's providence. It may be observed, by way of anticipating later expositions of the cause of evil in human life, that Jesus' injunction, "Therefore I say unto you be not anxious" contains the whole genius of the Biblical view of the relation of finiteness to sin in man. It is not his finiteness, dependence and weakness but his anxiety about it which tempts him to sin.

The New Testament may contain fewer striking passages on the brevity and impotence of man and the created world than the Old Testament, but there is no change of emphasis with one exception to be noted later. As in the first chapter of Hebrews, the consistent emphasis is upon the brevity and dependence of all temporal existence in contrast to the majesty and eternity of God. But this contrast is never given a moral connotation. The created world is a good world, for God created it.[1]

It is important to recognize how basic the Christian doctrine of the goodness of creation is for a conception of man in which human finiteness is emphasized but not deprecated. In the Biblical view the contrast between the created world and the Creator, between its dependent and insufficient existence and His freedom and self-sufficiency, is absolute. But this contrast never means that the created world is evil by reason of the particularization and individualization of its various types of existence. It is never a corruption of an original divine unity and eternity, as in neo-Platonism; nor is it evil because of the desire and pain which characterize all insufficient and dependent life, as in Buddhism.[2]

The whole import of the Christian doctrine of creation for the

[1]The passage in Hebrews reads: "Thou, Lord, in the beginning hast laid the foundation of the earth; and the heavens are the work of thy hands: They shall perish; but thou remainest; and they all shall wax old as doth a garment; and as a vesture shalt thou fold them up, and they shall be changed: but Thou art the same, and thy years shall not fail" (Hebrews 1:10–12). The passage is a quotation from Ps. 102. The Psalms offer a wide variety of expositions of the same theme.

[2]Augustine strikingly expounds the dialectical emphasis in the Christian doctrine of creation, the emphasis upon both its dependence and goodness: "And what is this? I asked the earth and it answered me 'I am not He'; and whatsoever are in it confessed the same. I asked the sea and the deeps and the living creeping things, and they answered: 'We are not God, seek above us.' . . . I asked the sun, moon, stars. 'Nor (say they) are we the God whom thou seekest.' And I replied to all things that encompass the door of my flesh: 'Ye have told me of my God that ye are not He; tell me something of Him.' And they cried with a loud voice: 'He made us.' . . . I asked the whole frame of the world about my God: and it answered me 'I am not He but He made me.'" *Confessions*, Book X, par. 9.

Christian view of man is really comprehended in the Christian concept of individuality. The individual is conceived of as a creature of infinite possibilities which cannot be fulfilled within terms of this temporal existence. But his salvation never means the complete destruction of his creatureliness and absorption into the divine.[3] On the other hand, though finite individuality is never regarded as of itself evil, its finiteness, including the finiteness of the mind, is never obscured. The self, even in the highest reaches of its self-consciousness, is still the finite self, which must regard the pretensions of universality, to which idealistic philosophies for instance tempt it, as a sin. It is always a self, anxious for its life and its universal perspectives qualified by its "here and now" relation to a particular body. Though it surveys the whole world and is tempted to regard its partial transcendence over its body as proof of its candidature for divinity, it remains in fact a very dependent self. This is not to say that men informed by this interpretation will not commit the same pretensions as other mortals. Half of Christianity has always been influenced by Platonic concepts; but even if this were not the case, the pride of man would express itself even in defiance of a faith which discounted it. Yet it is important to recognize that Christianity in its authentic and Biblical form is not subject to the charge of "idealism" so frequently levelled at it by materialists and naturalists. It knows of the finiteness of the self and of its involvement in all the relativities and contingencies of nature and history. The presuppositions of its faith make it possible to realize that the self in the highest reaches of its self-consciousness is still the mortal and finite self. In this, as in other instances, Kierkegaard has interpreted

[3]Augustine rejects mystic doctrines of the deification of man with the words: "I am of the opinion that the creature will never become equal with God, even when so perfect a holiness is accomplished within us as that it shall be quite incapable of receiving an addition. No, all who maintain that our progress is to be so complete that we shall be changed into the substance of God, and that we shall thus become what He is should look well to it how they build up their opinion; upon myself I must confess that it produces no conviction." *Treatise on Nature and Grace*, Ch. 38. *Anti-Pelagian Works*, Vol. I, p. 266.

the true meaning of human selfhood more accurately than any modern, and possibly than any previous, Christian theologian. He writes: "The determining factor in the self is consciousness, *i.e.* self-consciousness. The more consciousness, the more self; the more consciousness the more will; the more will, the more self. . . . The self is the conscious synthesis of the limited and the unlimited which is related to itself and the task of which is to become a self, a task which can be realized only in relation to God. To become a self means to become concrete. But to become concrete means to be neither limited nor unlimited, for that which must become concrete is a synthesis. Therefore development consists in this: that in the eternalization of the self one escapes the self endlessly and in the temporalization of the self one endlessly returns to the self."[4]

One must not claim that Christian thought and life have consistently preserved the Biblical insights on the basic character and the essential goodness of the finiteness, dependence and insufficiency of the self. On the contrary Christianity from the very beginning incorporated some of the errors of idealism and mysticism, including their mistaken estimates of the human situation, into its own thought; and has never completely expelled them. The greatest of the early Christian theologians, who dominated the centuries before Augustine, Origen, combined Platonism with Christianity by interpreting the myth of the Fall as pointing to a pre-existent defection of man from God, the punishment for which was his involvement in mutability and finiteness. For him therefore sex, as the consequence of this mutability, was the particular symbol of sin. It is interesting to note that, on the whole Greek side of Christianity, sex is regarded as a special symbol and consequence of sin, not only because sexual lust is seen as a vivid form of sensuality, but also because generation is so obviously a necessity of finite existence; because the incompleteness of man and woman, one without the other, is the most striking example of the insufficiency and dependence of one life upon the other and the most vivid illustration of a qualifica-

[4] *Die Krankheit zum Tode* (Diederich Verlag), p. 27.

tion and modification of an abstractly ideal human nature by natural circumstance and necessity. The idea of bi-sexuality as a consequence of the Fall is a frequent doctrine of Hellenistic Christianity, particularly in its more heretical forms.[5] It is interesting to note that the most brilliant modern exponent of Greek orthodox mysticism, Nikolai Berdyaev, clings to this same interpretation of sex.[6] Duns Scotus had the same view of the significance of bi-sexuality.

The identification of sin and evil with the mutability of the temporal world and with the ignorance of the finite mind is very general in the pre-Augustinian period of Christianity. Justin Martyr taught that sin was ignorance; and Clement defined it as "the weakness of matter" and as "the involuntary impulse of ignorance." Gregory of Nyssa tried desperately, though not too successfully, to harmonize Hellenistic and Biblical views of the nature of evil. He wrote: "It is not allowable to ascribe our constitutional liability to passion to that human nature which was fashioned in the divine likeness; but as brute life first entered the world, and man, for the reason already mentioned, took something of their nature (I mean their mode of generation), he accordingly took at the same time a share of the other attributes contemplated in that nature." . . . "Thus our love of pleasure took its beginning from our being made like to the irrational creation." To this Gregory adds the Biblical idea: "and was increased by the transgression of men, becoming the parent of so many varieties of sins, arising from pleasure, as we cannot find among animals."[7] Gregory's thoroughly Platonic conception of the relation of the soul to the body is vividly expressed in his metaphor of the gold and the alloy, a type of metaphor common to dualistic forms

[5]*The Poimandres,* one of the tractates of the Hermetica, has this version of the Fall. Greek thought tends to follow Plato's suggestion in the *Symposium* upon this point. Philo could not conceive of a bi-sexual creature as made in God's image. *Cf.* C. H. Dodd, *The Bible and the Greeks,* p. 165.

[6]*The Destiny of Man,* p. 299.

[7]*On the Making of Man,* XVIII. *Nicene and Post-Nicene Fathers,* Sec. Series. Vol. V.

of Christianity from his day to our own: "Just as those who refine gold from the dross which it contains not only get this base alloy to melt in the fire but are obliged to melt the pure gold along with the alloy and then while this last is being consumed the pure gold remains, so while evil is being consumed in the purgatorial fire, the soul which is welded to this evil must inevitably be in this fire too until the *spurious material alloy* is consumed and annihilated by the fire."[8]

Irenæus' conception of the relation of natural finiteness to the soul is revealed in his belief that the one would be sloughed off to free the other: "We blame Him because He did not make us Gods at the beginning but men first and Gods afterwards. . . . He was aware of the results of human infirmity; but in his love and power He shall subdue the substance of the nature He created. For it was necessary that nature should be exhibited first and afterwards that the mortal part should be subdued by the immortal and finally that man should be made after the image and likeness of God, having received the knowledge of good and evil."[9] On its Hellenistic side, Christianity exhibits many similarities with the Greek cults of immortality and the mystery religions. Salvation is frequently defined as the ultimate deification of man, through Christ's conquest of human mortality.

While it is not Biblical to regard finiteness, as such, as evil it must be admitted that there is strong Biblical support for the conception of death as evil. In Pauline theology death is the consequence of sin. The difference between this idea and the Hellenistic identification of finiteness and sin is trenchantly expressed in the words of Augustine: "It is by sin that we die, and not by death that we sin,"[10] an exposition of the Pauline words in Romans 5:12: "Thus sin came into the world by one man and death came in by sin."

While there is a profound difference between attributing sin to mortality and deriving mortality from sin, the Pauline interpretation of death nevertheless lends itself to dualistic interpretations. It is not

[8]*On the Soul and the Resurrection, op. cit.*
[9]*Treatise Against Heresies*, IV, 38.4. Irenæus was not a Hellenist but yet deeply indebted to the rationalistic Apologists.
[10]*Anti-Pelagian Works*, Vol. I, p. 150.

at all clear that St. Paul consistently regards physical death as the consequence of sin. At any rate he frequently uses the concept of death symbolically to designate spiritual death, as for instance when he speaks of the man who is "dead in trespasses and sins" (Eph. 2:1). Furthermore his classical assertion that the "sting of death is sin" (1 Cor: 15:56) can hardly be interpreted to mean that mortality as such is the consequence of sin. On the contrary, it seems in complete accord with the general Biblical view of the relation of sin to mortality. In this view mortality, insecurity and dependence are not of themselves evil but become the occasion of evil when man seeks in his pride to hide his mortality, to overcome his insecurity by his own power and to establish his independence. The ideal possibility would be that a man of perfect faith would not fear death because of his confidence that "neither life nor death . . . shall be able to separate us from the love of God which is in Christ Jesus our Lord." But since unbelief is the very basis of sin, it is impossible for sinful man to anticipate his end with equanimity. Thus sin is "the sting of death"; and the obvious mark of that sting is fear.

Despite St. Paul's symbolic use of the term death and despite the profound observation in 1 Corinthians 15, it is probable that St. Paul followed the rabbinic teaching of his day in the belief that death was the consequence of Adam's sin.[11] It is frequently assumed that St. Paul merely interpreted the Genesis account of God's curse upon Adam after the Fall. But it must be observed that this account assumes the mortality of man and does not include it as one of the several punishments which Adam must endure.[12]

Certainly the words "for dust thou art" are most naturally re-

[11]The Book of Wisdom asserts: "God created man for incorruption but by the envy of the devil death entered into the world" (ii:23–24).

[12]Gen. 3:17–19: "Cursed is the ground for thy sake; in sorrow shalt thou eat bread all the days of thy life; thorns also and thistles shall it bring forth to thee and thou shalt eat the herb of the field; in the sweat of thy face shalt thou eat bread, till thou return unto the ground; for out of it wast thou taken; for dust thou art, and unto dust shalt thou return."

garded as the statement of a fact and not as the promise of future punishment. The concluding words "and to dust shalt thou return" might be made to yield an implied promise of punishment. If so interpreted they would mean that though man arose from the dust, he would not, but for his sin, have returned to it.

This is precisely the interpretation which became dominant in orthodox Christianity. Athanasius puts this doctrine in classical form: "For man, indeed, is by nature mortal as being made of the things that are not. But yet by reason of the similitude to Him that is, he would have repelled his natural corruption and remained incorruptible, as the Book of Wisdom says: 'The giving heed unto Thy laws is the assurance of incorruption.' But being incorruptible, *i.e.*, immortal, he would have lived for the future as God; for this also the Holy Scripture signifies, I suppose, when it says: 'I said ye are gods and ye are all the sons of the Most Highest; but ye die like men and fall like one of the princes. . . . But men turning away from the things that are eternal, and by the counsel of the devil turning to the things that are corruptible, became to themselves a cause of the corruption which is death; being indeed, as I said before, by nature corruptible yet by grace of the participation of the Word they would have avoided what was according to nature, if they had remained perfect."[13]

This interpretation has the merit of seeking to explain the basic paradox of human existence: man's involvement in finiteness and his transcendence over it. But it confuses the paradox by the belief that, if sin had not intervened, man would have of himself transcended mortality. Such an interpretation obscures man's organic relation to nature and could be made meaningful only if it were assumed that sin had introduced death into the whole of nature. But such an assumption becomes almost identical with the Hellenistic belief that nature and finiteness are themselves evil. The orthodox doctrine, rooted in Pauline theology, therefore has affinities with Hellenistic dualism, despite the important distinction that it regards

[13]*De incarnatione verbi Dei*, Par. 5.

death as the consequence of sin and not sin as the consequence of death.[14]

It can hardly be denied that the Pauline authority, supporting the idea that physical death is a consequence of sin, introduced a note into Christian theology which is not fully in accord with the total Biblical view of the finiteness of man. The dominant note in the Biblical view of death is that it illustrates the difference between the majesty of God and the weakness and dependence of man as creature. This does not mean that physical death is accepted as the final word about the fate of man. We shall have occasion to deal with the

[14]The doctrine that death is the consequence of sin is of course variously stated; but it remains a consistent doctrine of Christian orthodoxy. Irenæus' version is: "But God set a bound to his state of sin by interposing death and thus causing sin to cease, putting an end to it by the dissolution of the flesh, which should take place upon the earth, so that man, ceasing at length to live to sin, and by dying to it, might begin to live to God." *Against Heresies,* Book III, xxiii, 6.

Gregory of Nyssa thinks that God created man as mortal in anticipation of his sin: "But as he perceived in our created nature the bias towards evil and the fact that after its voluntary fall from equality with the angels it would require fellowship with the lower nature, he mingled for this reason with his own image, an element of the irrational—transferring I say to man the special attribute of the irrational formation." *On the Making of Man,* Ch. XXI.

Aquinas' version is: "For man's body was indissoluble not by reason of any intrinsic vigour of immortality but by reason of a supernatural force given by God to the soul whereby it was enabled to preserve the body from corruption so long as it remained itself subject to God. . . . This power of preserving the body was not natural to the soul but was a gift of grace. And though man recovered grace as regards the remission of guilt and the merit of glory; yet he did not recover immortality the loss of which was an effect of sin." *Summa theologiae,* Part I, Question 97, Art. 1.

Martin Luther's view is similar upon this point: "Adam, if he had not sinned, would yet have lived a corporeal life, a life which would have needed meat, drink and rest; a life which would have grown, increased and generated until God would have translated him to that spiritual life in which he would have lived without natural animality if I may so express it. . . . And yet he would have been a man with body and bones and not a pure spirit as angels are." *Commentary on Genesis,* III. 5, 7.

significance of the Biblical hope of the resurrection in the second volume[15] of this treatise. Ideally the hope of the resurrection, this Christian confidence in the fulfillment of life beyond the limitations of temporal existence, does not stand in contradiction to the Biblical interpretation of the temporal order as essentially good and not evil. The Pauline view, even though lacking complete consistency, has the general effect of obscuring the sharp line of demarcation between the classical and the Christian view of the temporal world.

The distinctively Christian doctrine that sin has its source not in temporality but in man's willful refusal to acknowledge the finite and determinate character of his existence is the third element in the Christian doctrine of man and must now be considered more fully.

[15]Vol. II, Chs. 9 and 10.

CHAPTER VII

MAN AS SINNER

"Iɴ ᴇᴠᴇʀʏ religion," declared Albrecht Ritschl, the most authoritative exponent of modern liberal Christianity, "what is sought with the help of the superhuman power reverenced by man is a solution of the contradiction in which man finds himself as both a part of nature and a spiritual personality claiming to dominate nature."[1] It is perfectly true that this problem of finiteness and freedom underlies all religion. But Ritschl does not appreciate that the uniqueness of the Biblical approach to the human problem lies in its subordination of the problem of finiteness to the problem of sin. It is not the contradiction of finiteness and freedom from which Biblical religion seeks emancipation. It seeks redemption from sin; and the sin from which it seeks redemption is occasioned, though not caused, by this contradiction in which man stands. Sin is not caused by the contradiction because, according to Biblical faith, there is no absolute necessity that man should be betrayed into sin by the ambiguity of his position, as standing in and yet above nature. But it cannot be denied that this is the occasion for his sin.

Man is insecure and involved in natural contingency; he seeks to overcome his insecurity by a will-to-power which overreaches the limits of human creatureliness. Man is ignorant and involved in the

[1] *Justification and Reconciliation*, p. 199.

limitations of a finite mind; but he pretends that he is not limited. He assumes that he can gradually transcend finite limitations until his mind becomes identical with universal mind. All of his intellectual and cultural pursuits, therefore, become infected with the sin of pride. Man's pride and will-to-power disturb the harmony of creation. The Bible defines sin in both religious and moral terms. The religious dimension of sin is man's rebellion against God, his effort to usurp the place of God. The moral and social dimension of sin is injustice. The ego which falsely makes itself the centre of existence in its pride and will-to-power inevitably subordinates other life to its will and thus does injustice to other life.

Sometimes man seeks to solve the problem of the contradiction of finiteness and freedom, not by seeking to hide his finiteness and comprehending the world into himself, but by seeking to hide his freedom and by losing himself in some aspect of the world's vitalities. In that case his sin may be defined as sensuality rather than pride. Sensuality is never the mere expression of natural impulse in man. It always betrays some aspect of his abortive effort to solve the problem of finiteness and freedom. Human passions are always characterized by unlimited and demonic potencies of which animal life is innocent. The intricate relation between pride and sensuality must be considered more fully presently. First we must analyse the relation of sin to the contradiction of finiteness and freedom.

II

TEMPTATION AND SIN

While the Bible consistently maintains that sin cannot be excused by, or inevitably derived from, any other element in the human situation it does admit that man was tempted. In the myth of the Fall the temptation arises from the serpent's analysis of the human situation. The serpent depicts God as jealously guarding his prerogatives against the possibility that man might have his eyes opened and become "as God, knowing good and evil." Man is tempted, in other words, to break and transcend the limits which God has set for him. The temptation thus lies in his situation of finiteness and freedom. But the situation would not be a temptation of itself, if it were not falsely interpreted by "the serpent." The story of the Fall is innocent of a fully developed satanology; yet Christian theology has not been wrong in identifying the serpent with, or regarding it as an instrument or symbol of, the devil. To believe that there is a devil is to believe that there is a principle or force of evil antecedent to any evil human action. Before man fell the devil fell. The devil is, in fact, a fallen angel. His sin and fall consists in his effort to transcend his proper state and to become like God. This definition of the devil's fall is implied in Isaiah's condemnation of Babylon, in which the pride of Babylon is compared or identified with "Lucifer's" pride: "How art thou fallen from heaven, O Lucifer, son of the morning! how art thou cut down to the ground. For thou hast said in thine heart, I will ascend into heaven, I will exalt my throne above the stars of God. Yet thou shalt be brought down to hell."[1]

It is not necessary to trace the intricate relation between Old Testament satanology and its source in Babylonian and Persian myths. The importance of Biblical satanology lies in the two facts that: (1) the devil is not thought of as having been created evil. Rather his evil arises from his effort to transgress the bounds set for his life, an effort which places him in rebellion against God. (2) The devil fell before man fell, which is to say that man's rebellion against God is not an act of sheer perversity, nor does it follow inevitably from the situation in which he stands. The situation of finiteness and freedom in which man stands becomes a source of temptation only when it is falsely interpreted. This false interpreta-

---

[1] Is. 14:12, 13, 15. In the Slavonic Enoch the fall of the devil is similarly described: "And one from out of the order of angels, having turned away with the order that was under him, conceived an impossible thought, to place his throne higher than the clouds above the earth that he might become equal in rank with my [God's] power. And I threw him out from the height with his angels, and he was flying continually in the air above the bottomless [abyss]." II Enoch, XXIX, 4.

tion is not purely the product of the human imagination. It is suggested to man by a force of evil which precedes his own sin. Perhaps the best description or definition of this mystery is the statement that sin posits itself, that there is no situation in which it is possible to say that sin is either an inevitable consequence of the situation nor yet that it is an act of sheer and perverse individual defiance of God.

But what is the situation which is the occasion of temptation? Is it not the fact that man is a finite spirit, lacking identity with the whole, but yet a spirit capable in some sense of envisaging the whole, so that he easily commits the error of imagining himself the whole which he envisages? Let us note how quickly a mere analysis of the "situation" yields a definition of sin as error rather than as evil. Sin is not merely the error of overestimating human capacities. St. Paul rightly insists that "their foolish heart was darkened" and that "they became vain in their imagination." Neither the devil nor man is merely betrayed by his greatness to forget his weakness, or by his great knowledge to forget his ignorance. The fact is that man is never unconscious of his weakness, of the limited and dependent character of his existence and knowledge. The occasion for his temptation lies in the two facts, his greatness and his weakness, his unlimited and his limited knowledge, taken together. Man is both strong and weak, both free and bound, both blind and far-seeing. He stands at the juncture of nature and spirit; and is involved in both freedom and necessity. His sin is never the mere ignorance of his ignorance. It is always partly an effort to obscure his blindness by overestimating the degree of his sight and to obscure his insecurity by stretching his power beyond its limits.

This analysis proves the impossibility of either eliminating the element of conscious perversity from sin or of reducing it merely to error. But it also reveals that both freedom and necessity, both man's involvement in nature and his transcendence over it must be regarded as important elements in the situation which tempts to sin. Thus man is, like the animals, involved in the necessities and contingencies of nature; but unlike the animals he sees this situation and anticipates its perils. He seeks to protect himself against nature's contingencies; but he cannot do so without transgressing the limits which have been set for his life. Therefore all human life is involved in the sin of seeking security at the expense of other life. The perils of nature are thereby transmuted into the more grievous perils of human history. Or again: man's knowledge is limited by time and place. Yet it is not as limited as animal knowledge. The proof that it is not so limited is given by the fact that man knows something of these limits, which means that in some sense he transcends them. Man knows more than the immediate natural situation in which he stands and he constantly seeks to understand his immediate situation in terms of a total situation. Yet he is unable to define the total human situation without colouring his definition with finite perspectives drawn from his immediate situation. The realization of the relativity of his knowledge subjects him to the peril of scepticism. The abyss of meaninglessness yawns on the brink of all his mighty spiritual endeavours. Therefore man is tempted to deny the limited character of his knowledge, and the finiteness of his perspectives. He pretends to have achieved a degree of knowledge which is beyond the limit of finite life. This is the "ideological taint" in which all human knowledge is involved and which is always something more than mere human ignorance. It is always partly an effort to hide that ignorance by pretension.

In short, man, being both free and bound, both limited and limitless, is anxious. Anxiety is the inevitable concomitant of the paradox of freedom and finiteness in which man is involved. Anxiety is the internal precondition of sin. It is the inevitable spiritual state of man, standing in the paradoxical situation of freedom and finiteness.[2] Anxiety is the internal description of the state of temptation. It must not be identified with sin because there is always the ideal

[2]Kierkegaard says: "Anxiety is the psychological condition which precedes sin. It is so near, so fearfully near to sin, and yet it is not the explanation for sin." *Der Begriff der Angst*, p. 89. Kierkegaard's analysis of the relation of anxiety to sin is the profoundest in Christian thought.

possibility that faith would purge anxiety of the tendency toward sinful self-assertion. The ideal possibility is that faith in the ultimate security of God's love would overcome all immediate insecurities of nature and history. That is why Christian orthodoxy has consistently defined unbelief as the root of sin, or as the sin which precedes pride.[3] It is significant that Jesus justifies his injunction, "Be not anxious" with the observation, "For your heavenly Father knoweth that ye have need of these things." The freedom from anxiety which he enjoins is a possibility only if perfect trust in divine security has been achieved. Whether such freedom from anxiety and such perfect trust are an actual possibility of historic existence must be considered later. For the present it is enough to observe that no life, even the most saintly, perfectly conforms to the injunction not to be anxious.

Yet anxiety is not sin. It must be distinguished from sin partly because it is its precondition and not its actuality, and partly because it is the basis of all human creativity as well as the precondition of sin. Man is anxious not only because his life is limited and dependent and yet not so limited that he does not know of his limitations. He is also anxious because he does not know the limits of his possibilities. He can do nothing and regard it perfectly done, because higher possibilities are revealed in each achievement. All human actions stand under seemingly limitless possibilities. There are, of course, limits but it is difficult to gauge them from any immediate perspective. There is therefore no limit of achievement in any sphere of activity in which human history can rest with equanimity.[4]

It is not possible to make a simple separation between the creative

[3]Martin Luther, in conformity with the general Christian tradition and quoting Sirach 10: 14, writes in his *Treatise on Christian Liberty:* "The wise man has said: The beginning of all sin is to depart from God and not trust Him." Luther frequently defines the state of perfection before the Fall as being completely free of all anxiety. Here, as frequently in Luther's thought, he overstates the case. Ideally anxiety is overcome by faith but a life totally without anxiety would lack freedom and not require faith.

[4]Heidegger calls attention to the significant double connotation of the word "Care," *Sorge, cura,* that is a double connotation revealed in many

and destructive elements in anxiety; and for that reason it is not possible to purge moral achievement of sin as easily as moralists imagine. The same action may reveal a creative effort to transcend natural limitations, and a sinful effort to give an unconditioned value to contingent and limited factors in human existence. Man may, in the same moment, be anxious because he has not become what he ought to be; and also anxious lest he cease to be at all.

The parent is anxious about his child and this anxiety reaches beyond the grave. Is the effort of the parent to provide for the future of the child creative or destructive? Obviously it is both. It is, on the one hand, an effort to achieve the perfection of love by transcending the limits of finiteness and anticipating the needs of the child beyond the death of the parent. On the other hand, as almost every last will and testament reveals, it betrays something more than the perfection of love. It reveals parental will-to-power reaching beyond the grave and seeking to defy death's annulment of parental authority.

The statesman is anxious about the order and security of the nation. But he cannot express this anxiety without an admixture of anxiety about his prestige as a ruler and without assuming unduly that only the kind of order and security which he establishes is adequate for the nation's health. The philosopher is anxious to arrive at the truth; but he is also anxious to prove that his particular truth is the truth. He is never as completely in possession of the

---

languages. He writes: "The perfection of man, his becoming what in his freedom he can become according to his ultimate possibility, is a capacity of care or anxiety (*Sorge*). But just as basically care points to his being at the mercy of an anxious world, of his contingency (*Geworfenheit*). This double connotation of *cura* points to a basic structure in man of contingency and potentiality" (*geworfenen Entwurfs*). *Sein und Zeit.* p. 199.

This double connotation, according to Heidegger, is clearly revealed if *Sorgfalt* is juxtaposed to *Sorge,* that is care as carefulness to care as anxiety. Unfortunately the English language makes the distinction between *Angst* and *Sorge* impossible. Both of them must be translated as *anxiety.*

truth as he imagines. That may be the error of being ignorant of one's ignorance. But it is never simply that. The pretensions of final truth are always partly an effort to obscure a darkly felt consciousness of the limits of human knowledge. Man is afraid to face the problem of his limited knowledge lest he fall into the abyss of meaninglessness. Thus fanaticism is always a partly conscious, partly unconscious attempt to hide the fact of ignorance and to obscure the problem of scepticism. *Not to say, "I don't know..."*

Anxiety about perfection and about insecurity are thus inexorably bound together in human actions and the errors which are made in the search for perfection are never due merely to the ignorance of not knowing the limits of conditioned values. They always exhibit some tendency of the agent to hide his own limits, which he knows only too well. Obviously the basic source of temptation is, therefore, not the inertia of "matter" or "nature" against the larger and more inclusive ends which reason envisages. It resides in the inclination of man, either to deny the contingent character of his existence (in pride and self-love) or to escape from his freedom (in sensuality). Sensuality represents an effort to escape from the freedom and the infinite possibilities of spirit by becoming lost in the detailed processes, activities and interests of existence, an effort which results inevitably in unlimited devotion to limited values. Sensuality is man "turning inordinately to mutable good" (Aquinas).

Anxiety, as a permanent concomitant of freedom, is thus both the source of creativity and a temptation to sin. It is the condition of the sailor, climbing the mast (to use a simile), with the abyss of the waves beneath him and the "crow's nest" above him. He is anxious about both the end toward which he strives and the abyss of nothingness into which he may fall. The ambition of man to be something is always partly prompted by the fear of meaninglessness which threatens him by reason of the contingent character of his existence. His creativity is therefore always corrupted by some effort to overcome contingency by raising precisely what is contingent to absolute and unlimited dimensions. This effort, though universal, cannot be regarded as normative. It is always destructive. Yet obviously the destructive aspect of anxiety is so intimately involved in the creative aspects that there is no possibility of making a simple separation be-tween them. The two are inextricably bound together by reason of man being anxious both to realize his unlimited possibilities and to overcome and to hide the dependent and contingent character of his existence.

When anxiety has conceived it brings forth both pride and sen-suality. Man falls into pride, when he seeks to raise his contingent existence to unconditioned significance; he falls into sensuality, when he seeks to escape from his unlimited possibilities of freedom, from the perils and responsibilities of self-determination, by immers-ing himself into a "mutable good," by losing himself in some natural vitality.

III

THE SIN OF PRIDE

Biblical and Christian thought has maintained with a fair degree of consistency that pride is more basic than sensuality and that the latter is, in some way, derived from the former. We have pre-viously considered the Biblical definition of basic sin as pride and have suggested that the Pauline exposition of man's self-glorification ("they changed the glory of the incorruptible God into an image made like unto corruptible man") is really an admirable summary of the whole Biblical doctrine of sin.[1]

[1]Again it cannot be claimed that Christian thought is absolutely con-sistent in regarding pride as the basic sin. Wherever the classical view of man predominates, whether in early Greek theology, or medieval or modern liberal thought, the tendency is to equate sin with sensuality. The definition of sin as pride is consistently maintained in the strain of theology generally known as Augustinian.

Augustine defines sin as follows: "What could begin this evil will but pride, that is the beginning of all sin? And what is pride but a perverse desire of height, in forsaking Him to whom the soul ought solely to cleave, as the beginning thereof, to make the self seem the beginning. This is when it likes itself too well. . . ." *De civ. Dei*, Book XII, Ch. 13.

Or again: "What is pride but undue exaltation? And this is undue

This Biblical definition is strictly adhered to in that strain of Christian theology which manages to maintain the Biblical viewpoint against the influence of the rationalist-classical view of man,

exaltation, when the soul abandons Him to whom it ought to cleave as its end and becomes a kind of end in itself." *De civ. Dei*, Book XIV, Ch. 13.

Pascal's definition is: "This I is hateful. . . . In one word it has two qualities: It is essentially unjust in that it makes self the centre of everything and it is troublesome to others in that it seeks to make them subservient; for each I is the enemy and would be the tyrant of all others." Faugère, Vol. I, p. 197.

In Luther, pride and self-love are used synonymously (*Superbia et amor sui*). Original sin is sometimes defined as the lust of the soul in general (*Universa concupiscentia*) (Weimer edition III. 215), which expresses itself in the turning of the soul from God to the creature. Luther's definition of concupiscence is not in opposition to or sharp distinction from sin as pride. Both have their source in *caro*, which for Luther has the exact connotation of the Pauline σάρξ. It is not the "body" as symbol of man's finiteness but "flesh" as symbol of his sinfulness. Stomph defines Luther's conception as follows: "With 'self as flesh' Luther means that the sinner desires himself just as he is, though he does not see himself just as he is and does not expressly will himself as such." M. A. H. Stomph, *Die Anthropologie Martin Luthers*, p. 73.

Thomas Aquinas derives sensuality from a more basic self-love: "The proper and direct cause of sin is to be considered on the part of the adherence to a mutable good, in which respect every sinful act proceeds from inordinate desire for some temporal good. Now the fact that some one desires a temporal good inordinately is due to the fact that he loves himself inordinately." *Summa*, Part I, Third Number, Question 77, Art. 4.

Calvin consistently holds to the Pauline definition of sin given in Romans 1. Sin is pride and not ignorance: "They worship not Him but figments of their own brains instead. This pravity Paul expressly remarks: 'Professing themselves wise they became fools.' He had before said 'they became vain in their imaginations.' But lest any should exculpate them, he adds that they were deservedly blinded, because, not content with the bounds of sobriety, but arrogating themselves more than was right they wilfully darkened and even infatuated themselves with pride, vanity and perverseness. Whence it follows that their folly is inexcusable, which originates not only in a vain curiosity but in false confidence and in immoderate desire to exceed the limits of human knowledge." *Institutes*, Book I, Ch. 4.

in which sin tends to to be identified with ignorance or the passions of the body. The Biblical view colours the definitions of Christian rationalists so that when they define sin primarily as sensuality, they recognize, at least, that this sensuality is not merely the expression of physical impulse but represents an inordinate quality made possible by the freedom of the spirit.[2] We are not at present concerned with the emphasis of Christian theology upon the inexcusable character of this pride and the insistence that sin is rooted in an evil will and not in some antecedent weakness of man.[3] Our present interest is to relate the Biblical and distinctively Christian conception of sin as pride and self-love to the observable behaviour of men. It will be convenient in this analysis to distinguish between three types of pride, which are, however, never completely distinct in actual life: pride of power, pride of knowledge and pride of virtue.[4] The third type, the pride of self-righteousness, rises to a form of spiritual pride, which is at once a fourth type and yet not a specific form of pride at all but pride and self-glorification in its inclusive and quintessential form.

(*a*) "Of the infinite desires of man," declares Bertrand Russell, "the chief are the desires for power and glory. They are not identical though closely allied."[5] Mr. Russell is not quite clear about the relation of the two to each other, and the relation is, as a matter of fact, rather complex. There is a pride of power in which the human ego assumes its self-sufficiency and self-mastery and imagines itself secure against all vicissitudes. It does not recognize the contingent and dependent character of its life and believes itself to be the author of its own existence, the judge of its own values and the master of its own destiny. This proud pretension is present in an

[2]Gregory of Nyssa for instance analyses anger as follows: "Thus the arising of anger in us is indeed akin to the impulses of brutes; but it grows by the alliance of thought." *On the Making of Man,* XVIII, 4.

[3]This aspect of the problem of sin will be considered in Ch. 9.

[4]This is a traditional distinction in Christian thought. *Cf.* Mueller, *On the Christian Doctrine of Sin,* Vol. I, p. 177.

[5]*Power, A New Social Analysis,* p. 11.

inchoate form in all human life but it rises to greater heights among those individuals and classes who have a more than ordinary degree of social power.[6] Closely related to the pride which seems to rest upon the possession of either the ordinary or some extraordinary measure of human freedom and self-mastery, is the lust for power which has pride as its end. The ego does not feel secure and therefore grasps for more power in order to make itself secure. It does not regard itself as sufficiently significant or respected or feared and therefore seeks to enhance its position in nature and in society.

In the one case the ego seems unconscious of the finite and determinate character of its existence. In the other case the lust for power is prompted by a darkly conscious realization of its insecurity.[7] The first form of the pride of power is particularly characteristic of individuals and groups whose position in society is, or seems to be, secure. In Biblical prophecy this security is declared to be bogus and those who rest in it are warned against an impending doom. Thus the second Isaiah describes the pride of Babylon in the words: "Thou saidst, I shall be a lady forever; so that thou dost not lay these things to thy heart." The impending doom is defined as a revelation of the weakness and insecurity of Babylon: "Thy nakedness shall be uncovered; yea, thy shame shall be seen."[8] In the same

[6]"Every man would like to be God," declares Mr. Russell, "if it were possible; some few find it difficult to admit the impossibility." *Ibid.*, p. 11.

[7]In modern international life Great Britain with its too strong a sense of security, which prevented it from taking proper measures of defense in time, and Germany with its maniacal will-to-power, are perfect symbols of the different forms which pride takes among the established and the advancing social forces. The inner stability and external security of Great Britain has been of such long duration that she may be said to have committed the sin of Babylon and declared, "I shall be no widow and I shall never know sorrow." Germany on the other hand suffered from an accentuated form of inferiority long before her defeat in the World War. Her boundless contemporary self-assertion which literally transgresses all bounds previously known in religion, culture and law is a very accentuated form of the power impulse which betrays a marked inner insecurity.

[8]Is. 47:3–7. See also Rev. 18:7; Zeph. 2:15.

way the first Isaiah warns the rulers of Israel who are described as "the crown of pride" that their "glorious beauty is a fading flower." He declares that in the day of judgment the "Lord of hosts" will be vindicated and will be "for a crown of glory and for a diadem of beauty" (Is. 28:1–5). In other words history invariably shatters the illusions of those who overestimate the power of human life and in the day of judgment God is revealed as the true source and end of life as the "crown of glory." In Ezekiel's prophecies of doom upon the nations of the earth, they are constantly accused of having foolishly overestimated their security, independence and self-mastery. Egypt, for instance, is accused of imagining herself the creator of the river Nile and saying, "My river is my own, I have made it for myself." In the doom which overtakes this pride the real source and end of life will be revealed: "They shall know that I am the Lord" (Ez. 30:8).

The second form of the pride of power is more obviously prompted by the sense of insecurity. It is the sin of those, who knowing themselves to be insecure, seek sufficient power to guarantee their security, inevitably of course at the expense of other life. It is particularly the sin of the advancing forces of human society in distinction to the established forces. Among those who are less obviously secure, either in terms of social recognition, or economic stability or even physical health, the temptation arises to overcome or to obscure insecurity by arrogating a greater degree of power to the self. Sometimes this lust for power expresses itself in terms of man's conquest of nature, in which the legitimate freedom and mastery of man in the world of nature[9] is corrupted into a mere exploitation of nature. Man's sense of dependence upon nature and his reverent gratitude toward the miracle of nature's perennial abundance is destroyed by his arrogant sense of independence and his greedy effort to overcome

[9]A legitimate mastery is symbolically expressed in the words of Genesis 1:26: "Let us make man in our image, after our likeness: and let them have dominion over the fish of the sea, and over the fowl of the air, and over the cattle, and over all the earth, and over every creeping thing that creepeth upon the earth."

the insecurity of nature's rhythms and seasons by garnering her stores with excessive zeal and beyond natural requirements. Greed is in short the expression of man's inordinate ambition to hide his insecurity in nature. It is perfectly described in Jesus' parable of the rich fool who assures himself: "Soul, thou hast much goods laid up for many years; take thine ease, eat, drink, and be merry." Significantly this false security is shattered by the prospect of death, a vicissitude of nature which greed cannot master. God said to the rich fool, "This night thy soul shall be required of thee" (Luke 12: 19–20).

Greed as a form of the will-to-power has been a particularly flagrant sin in the modern era because modern technology has tempted contemporary man to overestimate the possibility and the value of eliminating his insecurity in nature. Greed has thus become the besetting sin of a bourgeois culture. This culture is constantly tempted to regard physical comfort and security as life's final good and to hope for its attainment to a degree which is beyond human possibilities. "Modern man," said a cynical doctor, "has forgotten that nature intends to kill man and will succeed in the end."[10]

Since man's insecurity arises not merely from the vicissitudes of

---

[10]Bertrand Russell makes the mistake of assuming that economic desires are never inordinate unless they are the servants of social pride and power. He writes: "The desire for commodities, when separated from power and glory, is finite, and can be fully satisfied by a modest competence. . . . When a moderate degree of comfort is assured, both individuals and communities will pursue power and glory rather than wealth: they may seek wealth as a means to power, or they may forego an increase of wealth to secure an increase of power but in the former as in the latter case the fundamental motive is not economic." *Power*, p. 12.

Mr. Russell rightly criticizes the too simple Marxian interpretation of the primacy of economic motives. But his own interpretation is faulty because he regards the desire for "power and glory" in purely social terms. Greed may indeed be the servant of the desire for social power, since money is one form of "power over men." But the economic motive may be inordinate even when no power over men is sought after. The typical miser seeks absolute security and not social recognition. He wants power over his fate and not over his fellowmen.

nature but from the uncertainties of society and history, it is natural that the ego should seek to overcome social as well as natural in-security and should express the impulse of "power over men" as well as "power over matter." The peril of a competing human will is overcome by subordinating that will to the ego and by using the power of many subordinated wills to ward off the enmity which such subordination creates. The will-to-power is thus inevitably involved in the vicious circle of accentuating the insecurity which it intends to eliminate. "Woe to thee," declares the prophet Isaiah, "that spoil-est, and thou wast not spoiled; and dealest treacherously, and they dealt not treacherously with thee! when thou shalt cease to spoil, thou shalt be spoiled" (Is. 33:1). The will-to-power in short involves the ego in injustice. It seeks a security beyond the limits of human finiteness and this inordinate ambition arouses fears and enmities which the world of pure nature, with its competing impulses of survival, does not know.

The school of modern psychology which regards the will-to-power as the most dominant of human motives has not yet recognized how basically it is related to insecurity. Adler attributes it to specific forms of the sense of inferiority and therefore believes that a correct therapy can eliminate it. Karen Horney relates the will-to-power to a broader anxiety than the specific cases of the sense of inferiority which Adler enumerates. But she thinks that the will-to-power springs from the general insecurities of a competitive civilization and therefore holds out hope for its elimination in a co-operative society.[11] This is still far short of the real truth. The truth is that man is tempted by the basic insecurity of human existence to make himself doubly secure and by the insignificance of his place in the total scheme of life to prove his significance. The will-to-power is in short both a direct form and an indirect instrument of the pride which Christianity regards as sin in its quintessential form.

We have provisionally distinguished between the pride which does not recognize human weakness and the pride which seeks power in

[11] *The Neurotic Personality of Our Time.*

order to overcome or obscure a recognized weakness; and we have
sought to attribute the former to the more established and traditionally respected individuals and groups, while attributing the latter to
the less secure, that is, to the advancing rather than established
groups in society. This distinction is justified only if regarded as
strictly provisional. The fact is that the proudest monarch and the
most secure oligarch is driven to assert himself beyond measure
partly by a sense of insecurity. This is partly due to the fact that the
greater his power and glory, the more the common mortality of
humankind appears to him in the guise of an incongruous fate.
Thus the greatest monarchs of the ancient world, the Pharaohs of
Egypt, exhausted the resources of their realm to build pyramids,
which were intended to establish or to prove their immortality. A
common mortal's fear of death is thus one prompting motive of the
pretensions and ambitions of the greatest lords.[12]

But furthermore, the more man establishes himself in power and
glory, the greater is the fear of tumbling from his eminence, or losing
his treasure, or being discovered in his pretension. Poverty is a peril
to the wealthy but not to the poor. Obscurity is feared, not by those
who are habituated to its twilight but by those who have become

---

[12]Bertrand Russell doubts whether fear or anxiety could be regarded
as the root of the will-to-power among the great leaders of mankind. He
is inclined to believe that a "hereditary position of command" is a more
plausible basis for it. He would, in other words, sharply separate the
pride which does not know its own weakness and the pride which compensates for a recognized weakness. He cites Queen Elizabeth as one
whose will-to-power was prompted by an hereditary position rather than
by fear (*op. cit.*, p. 20). Yet a modern historian makes this interesting
observation upon the fears which harassed Elizabeth: "Strong as was her
sense of public duty, it failed her here [in dealing with the problem
of her succession]. Her egotism blinded her to the dangers to which
her failure to discuss the subject was likely to expose the state. The
thought that her dignities must, by the efflux of time, pass to another
seems only to have suggested to her the insecurity of her own tenure of
them and the coming extinction of her own authority. Such a prospect
she could not nerve herself to face." J. K. Laughton in *The Cambridge
Modern History*, Vol. III, p. 359.

accustomed to public acclaim. Nor is this sense of insecurity of the powerful and the great to be wholly discounted as being concerned with mere vanities. Life's basic securities are involved in the secondary securities of power and glory. The tyrant fears not only the loss of his power but the possible loss of his life. The powerful nation, secure against its individual foes, must fear the possibility that its power may challenge its various foes to make common cause against it. The person accustomed to luxury and ease actually meets a greater danger to life and mere existence in the hardships of poverty than those who have been hardened by its rigours. The will-to-power is thus an expression of insecurity even when it has achieved ends which, from the perspective of an ordinary mortal, would seem to guarantee complete security. The fact that human ambitions know no limits must therefore be attributed not merely to the infinite capacities of the human imagination but to an uneasy recognition of man's finiteness, weakness and dependence, which become the more apparent the more we seek to obscure them, and which generate ultimate perils, the more immediate insecurities are eliminated. Thus man seeks to make himself God because he is betrayed by both his greatness and his weakness; and there is no level of greatness and power in which the lash of fear is not at least one strand in the whip of ambition.

(*b*) The intellectual pride of man is of course a more spiritual sublimation of his pride of power. Sometimes it is so deeply involved in the more brutal and obvious pride of power that the two cannot be distinguished. Every ruling oligarchy of history has found ideological pretensions as important a bulwark of authority as its police power. But intellectual pride is confined neither to the political oligarchs nor to the savants of society. All human knowledge is tainted with an "ideological" taint. It pretends to be more true than it is. It is finite knowledge, gained from a particular perspective; but it pretends to be final and ultimate knowledge. Exactly analogous to the cruder pride of power, the pride of intellect is derived on the one hand from ignorance of the finiteness of the human mind and on the

other hand from an attempt to obscure the known conditioned
character of human knowledge and the taint of self-interest in human truth.

The philosopher who imagines himself capable of stating a final
truth merely because he has sufficient perspective upon past history
to be able to detect previous philosophical errors is clearly the victim
of the ignorance of his ignorance. Standing on a high pinnacle of
history he forgets that this pinnacle also has a particular locus and
that his perspective will seem as partial to posterity as the pathetic
parochialism of previous thinkers. This is a very obvious fact but no
philosophical system has been great enough to take full account of
it. Each great thinker makes the same mistake, in turn, of imagining
himself the final thinker. Descartes, Hegel, Kant, and Comte, to
mention only a few moderns, were so certain of the finality of their
thought that they have become fair sport for any wayfaring cynic.
Not the least pathetic is the certainty of a naturalistic age that its
philosophy is a final philosophy because it rests upon science, a certainty which betrays ignorance of its own prejudices and failure to
recognize the limits of scientific knowledge.

Intellectual pride is thus the pride of reason which forgets that it
is involved in a temporal process and imagines itself in complete
transcendence over history. "It is this appearance of independent
history of state constitutions, systems of law, of ideologies in every
special field which above all has blinded so many people," declares
Friederich Engels.[13] Yet intellectual pride is something more than
the mere ignorance of ignorance. It always involves, besides, a conscious or subconscious effort to obscure a known or partly known
taint of interest. Despite the tremendous contribution of Marxist
thought in the discovery of the ideological taint in all culture, it is
precisely the element of pretense which it fails to understand. Its too
simple theory of human consciousness betrays it here. Thus Engels
declares: "The real driving force which moves it [ideology] remains

[13]From a letter to F. Mehring, quoted by Sidney Hook, *Toward an
Understanding of Karl Marx*, p. 341.

unconscious otherwise it would not be an ideological process."[14] But the real fact is that all pretensions of final knowledge and ultimate truth are partly prompted by the uneasy feeling that the truth is not final and also by an uneasy conscience which realizes that the interests of the ego are compounded with this truth.

Sometimes this root of insecurity in intellectual pride is revealed in the pathetic pretense of an individual thinker; sometimes the thinker hides and exposes not his own insecurity but that of an age, a class or a nation. Descartes' intellectual pride was something more than the ignorance of his ignorance. That was disclosed when he resented the reminder of a friend that his *"Cogito, ergo sum,"* the keystone of his philosophical arch, was derived from Augustinian thought.[15] Schopenhauer's pride was more than the consequence of his inability to measure the limits of his system. It was compensation for his lack of recognition in competition with more widely acclaimed idealistic thinkers. In the case of such men as Hegel and Comte, individual and representative pride is curiously mingled. Hegel not only proclaimed the finality of his own thought but regarded his contemporary Prussian military state as the culmination of human history. Comte believed his philosophy to be final not only as a philosophy but as a religion; and with pathetic national pride he predicted that Paris would be the centre of the new universal culture which he would found.[16]

A particular significant aspect of intellectual pride is the inability of the agent to recognize the same or similar limitations of perspective in himself which he has detected in others. The Marxist detection of ideological taint in the thought of all bourgeois culture is significantly unembarrassed by any scruples about the conditioned character of its own viewpoints. "Socialist thought," declares Karl Mannheim, "which hitherto has unmasked all its adversaries' utopias as ideologies, never raised the problem of determinateness about its

[14]*Ibid.,* p. 341.
[15]*Cf.* Etienne Gilson, *Unity of Philosophical Experience,* p. 157.
[16]Auguste Comte, *Catechism of Positive Religion,* p. 211.

own position. It never applied this method to itself and checked its own desire to be absolute."[17] The fanaticism which springs from this blindness becomes particularly tragic and revealing when it is expressed in conflict between various schools of Marxist thought as for instance between the Stalinists and Trotskyites. Each is forced to prove and to believe that the opponent is really a covert capitalist or fascist, since ideological taint in genuine proletarian thought is inconceivable. The proud achievement of Marxism in discovering the intellectual pride and pretension of previous cultures therefore ends in a pitiful display of the same sin. It has no inkling of the truth of the Pauline observation: "For wherein thou judgest another, thou condemnest thyself; for thou that judgest doest the same things" (Romans 2:1).

The Marxist pride may, as in other instances of similar pride, be regarded as merely the fruit of the ignorance of ignorance. The Marxist has mistakenly confined ideological taint to economic life and therefore erroneously hopes for a universal rational perspective when economic privileges would be equalized. But one has the right to suspect that something more than ignorance is involved. The vehemence with which the foe is accused of errors of which the self regards itself free betrays the usual desperation with which the self seeks to hide the finiteness and determinateness of its own position from itself.

There is in short no manifestation of intellectual pride in which the temptations of both human freedom and human insecurity are not apparent. If man were not a free spirit who transcends every situation in which he is involved he would have no concern for unconditioned truth and he would not be tempted to claim absolute validity for his partial perspectives. If he were completely immersed in the contingencies and necessities of nature he would have only his own truth and would not be tempted to confuse his truth with *the* truth. But in that case he would have no truth at all, for no particular event or value could be related meaningfully to the

[17]*Ideology and Utopia*, p. 225.

whole. If on the other hand man were wholly transcendent he would not be tempted to insinuate the necessities of the moment and the vagaries of the hour into the truth and thus corrupt it. Nor would he be prompted to deny the finiteness of his knowledge in order to escape the despair of scepticism which threatens him upon the admission of such ignorance. Yet the ignorance of ignorance which underlies every attempt at knowledge can never be described as a mere ignorance. The ignorance presupposes pride, for there is always an ideal possibility that man should recognize his own limits. This implicit pride becomes explicit in the conscious efforts to obscure the partiality of the perspective from which the truth is apprehended. The explicit character of this pride is fully revealed in all cases in which the universalistic note in human knowledge becomes the basis of an imperial desire for domination over life which does not conform to it. The modern religious nationalist thus declares in one moment that his culture is not an export article but is valid for his nation alone. In the next moment he declares that he will save the world by destroying inferior forms of culture.

The insecurity which hides behind this pride is not quite as patent as the pride, yet it is also apparent. In the relations of majority and minority racial groups for instance, for which the negro-white relation is a convenient example, the majority group justifies the disabilities which it imposes upon the minority group on the ground that the subject group is not capable of enjoying or profiting from the privileges of culture or civilization. Yet it can never completely hide, and it sometimes frankly expresses the fear that the grant of such privileges would eliminate the inequalities of endowment which supposedly justify the inequalities of privilege.[18] The pretension of pride is thus a weapon against a feared competitor. Sometimes it is intended to save the self from the abyss of self-contempt which always yawns before it.[19]

[18]*Cf.* Paul Levinson, *Race, Class and Party,* for striking examples of this sense of insecurity in the dominant group.

[19]An interesting example of pride as defense against self-contempt is offered by an historian of the French Directory. He writes: "These

(c) All elements of moral pride are involved in the intellectual pride which we have sought to analyse. In all but the most abstract philosophical debates the pretension of possessing an unconditioned truth is meant primarily to establish "my good" as unconditioned moral value. Moral pride is revealed in all "self-righteous" judgments in which the other is condemned because he fails to conform to the highly arbitrary standards of the self. Since the self judges itself by its own standards it finds itself good. It judges others by its own standards and finds them evil, when their standards fail to conform to its own. This is the secret of the relationship between cruelty and self-righteousness. When the self mistakes its standards for God's standards it is naturally inclined to attribute the very essence of evil to non-conformists. The character of moral pride is perfectly described in the words of St. Paul: "For I bear them record that they have the zeal of God, but not according to knowledge. For they, being ignorant of God's righteousness and going about to establish their own righteousness, have not submitted themselves unto the righteousness of God" (Romans 10:2–3). Moral pride is the pretension of finite man that his highly conditioned virtue is the final righteousness and that his very relative moral standards are absolute. Moral pride thus makes virtue the very vehicle of sin, a fact which explains why the New Testament is so critical of the righteous in comparison with "publicans and sinners." This note in the Bible distinguishes Biblical moral theory from all simple moralism, including Christian moralism. It is the meaning of Jesus' struggle with the pharisees, of St. Paul's insistence that man is saved "not by works

---

profiteers were also doctrinaires and they clung to their doctrines with the greater tenacity because only thus could they escape the self-contempt which otherwise they would have felt in their secret hearts. They were under no illusion as to the life they were leading, the system of government they had established or the persons they employed to maintain it. But sunk though they were in foulness they cling to the shadow of an ideal aim. . . . They asked nothing better than to be stigmatized as sectaries, illuminati and fanatics, for in that case people would forget to call them 'rotten.'" Pierre Gaxotte, *The French Revolution,* p. 390.

lest any man should boast," in fact of the whole Pauline polemic against the "righteousness of works"; and it is the primary issue in the Protestant Reformation. Luther rightly insisted that the unwillingness of the sinner to be regarded as a sinner was the final form of sin.[20] The final proof that man no longer knows God is that he does not know his own sin.[21] The sinner who justifies himself does not know God as judge and does not need God as Saviour. One might add that the sin of self-righteousness is not only the final sin in the subjective sense but also in the objective sense. It involves us in the greatest guilt. It is responsible for our most serious cruelties, injustices and defamations against our fellowmen. The whole history of racial, national, religious and other social struggles is a commentary on the objective wickedness and social miseries which result from self-righteousness.

(*d*) The sin of moral pride, when it has conceived, brings forth spiritual pride. The ultimate sin is the religious sin of making the self-deification implied in moral pride explicit. This is done when our partial standards and relative attainments are explicitly related to the unconditioned good, and claim divine sanction. For this reason religion is not simply as is generally supposed an inherently virtuous human quest for God. It is merely a final battleground between God and man's self-esteem. In that battle even the most pious practices may be instruments of human pride. The same man may in one moment regard Christ as his judge and in the next moment seek to prove that the figure, the standards and the righteousness of Christ bear a greater similarity to his own righteousness than to that of his enemy. The worst form of class domination is religious class domination in which, as for instance in the Indian caste system, a dominant priestly class not only subjects subordinate classes to social disabilities but finally excludes them from participation in any universe of meaning. The worst form of intolerance is religious in-

[20]*Superbus primo est excusator sui ac defensor, justificator,* Weimar ed. of *Works,* Vol. 3, p. 288.

[21]*Nescimus, quid Deus, quid justitia, denique quid ipsum peccatum sit.* ibid., Vol. 2, p. 106.

tolerance, in which the particular interests of the contestants hide behind religious absolutes.[22] The worst form of self-assertion is religious self-assertion in which under the guise of contrition before God, He is claimed as the exclusive ally of our contingent self. "What goes by the name of 'religion' in the modern world," declares a modern missionary, "is to a great extent unbridled human self-assertion in religious disguise."[23]

Christianity rightly regards itself as a religion, not so much of man's search for God, in the process of which he may make himself God; but as a religion of revelation in which a holy and loving God is revealed to man as the source and end of all finite existence against whom the self-will of man is shattered and his pride abased. But as soon as the Christian assumes that he is, by virtue of possessing this revelation, more righteous, because more contrite, than other men, he increases the sin of self-righteousness and makes the forms of a religion of contrition the tool of his pride.

Protestantism is right in insisting that Catholicism identifies the church too simply with the Kingdom of God. This identification, which allows a religious institution, involved in all the relativities of history, to claim unconditioned truth for its doctrines and un-

---

[22]One example is worth quoting, the manifesto of Philip of Spain against William of Nassau: "Philip by the grace of God, King of Castile . . . whereas William of Nassau, a foreigner in our realm once honoured and promoted by the late emperor and ourselves, has by sinister practices and arts gained over malcontents, lawless men, insolvents, innovators, and especially those whose religion was suspected, and has instigated these heretics to rebel, to destroy sacred images and churches and to profane the sacraments of God . . . with a view of exterminating by impieties our Holy Catholic faith . . . whereas the country can have no peace with this wretched hypocrite . . . we empower all and every to seize the person and property of this William of Nassau as an enemy of the human race and hereby on the word of a king and minister of God promise any one . . . who will deliver him dead or alive . . . the sum of 25,000 crowns in gold . . . and we will pardon him of any crime if he has been guilty and give him a patent of nobility."

[23]Henrik Kraemer, *The Christian Message in the Non-Christian World*, p. 212.

conditioned moral authority for its standards, makes it just another tool of human pride. For this reason Luther's insistence that the pope is Anti-Christ was religiously correct. A vicar of Christ on earth is bound to be, in a sense, Anti-Christ. The whole contemporary political situation yields evidence of the perils of the Catholic doctrine of the church. Everywhere the church claims to be fighting the enemies of God without realizing to what degree these enemies are merely the rebels against a corrupt feudal civilization.

But as soon as the Protestant assumes that his more prophetic statement and interpretation of the Christian gospel guarantees him a superior virtue, he is also lost in the sin of self-righteousness. The fact is that the Protestant doctrine of the priesthood of all believers may result in an individual self-deification against which Catholic doctrine has more adequate checks. The modern revival of Reformation theology may be right in regarding the simple moralism of Christian liberalism as just another form of pharisaism. But the final mystery of human sin cannot be understood if it is not recognized that the greatest teachers of this Reformation doctrine of the sinfulness of all men used it on occasion as the instrument of an arrogant will-to-power against theological opponents.[24] There is no final guarantee against the spiritual pride of man. Even the recognition in the sight of God that he is a sinner can be used as a vehicle of that very sin.[25] If that final mystery of the sin of pride is not recognized the meaning of the Christian gospel cannot be understood.

It must be added that it is not necessary to be explicitly religious in order to raise moral pride to explicit religious proportions. Stalin

[24]Luther's attitude toward Schwenkfeld for instance and Calvin's against Castellio and Servetus. It may not be amiss to call attention to the fact that Karl Barth engaged in theological controversy with Emil Brunner some years ago on the theological issues raised in this chapter. He feared that Brunner's pamphlet on "Nature and Grace" conceded too much to the natural goodness of men. His own answer, entitled *Nein,* is informed by a peculiar quality of personal arrogance and disrespect for the opponent.

[25]"Discourses on humility are a source of pride to the vain," declares Pascal, "and of humility in the humble." *Pensées,* 377.

can be as explicit in making unconditioned claims as the pope; and a French revolutionist of the eighteenth century can be as cruel in his religious fervour as the "God-ordained" feudal system which he seeks to destroy. We have previously dwelt upon the fallacious hope of modern culture, that the elimination of religion might result in the elimination of religious intolerance. Religion, by whatever name, is the inevitable fruit of the spiritual stature of man; and religious intolerance and pride is the final expression of his sinfulness. A religion of revelation is grounded in the faith that God speaks to man from beyond the highest pinnacle of the human spirit; and that this voice of God will discover man's highest not only to be short of the highest but involved in the dishonesty of claiming that it is the highest.

IV

THE RELATION OF DISHONESTY TO PRIDE

Our analysis of man's sin of pride and self-love has consistently assumed that an element of deceit is involved in this self-glorification. This dishonesty must be regarded as a concomitant, and not as the basis, of self-love. Man loves himself inordinately. Since his determinate existence does not deserve the devotion lavished upon it, it is obviously necessary to practice some deception in order to justify such excessive devotion. While such deception is constantly directed against competing wills, seeking to secure their acceptance and validation of the self's too generous opinion of itself, its primary purpose is to deceive, not others, but the self. The self must at any rate deceive itself first. Its deception of others is partly an effort to convince itself against itself. The fact that this necessity exists is an important indication of the vestige of truth which abides with the self in all its confusion and which it must placate before it can act. The dishonesty of man is thus an interesting refutation of the doctrine of man's total depravity.

The Biblical analysis of sin is filled with references to the function of deception in the economy of sin. Jesus speaks of the devil as the father of lies (John 8:44). St. Paul declares that the self-glorification of man is a process of changing "the truth of God into a lie" (Romans 1:25) and, with psychological astuteness, he regards the blindness of self-deception not as the consequence of ignorance but ignorance as the consequence of sin. They "became vain in their imaginations and their foolish heart was darkened." They "hold the truth in unrighteousness."[1]

The dishonesty which is an inevitable concomitant of sin must be regarded neither as purely ignorance, nor yet as involving a conscious lie in each individual instance. The mechanism of deception is too complicated to fit into the category of either pure ignorance or pure dishonesty.[2]

A certain degree of inevitable ignorance may be said to constitute the temptation to deception. This natural illusion may be defined as the tendency of the self as knower, finding its self-consciousness at the very centre of the world which it beholds, to believe itself to be the whole world, an error of solipsism which philosophy finds difficulty in avoiding. Yet the self as a determinate existence is obviously not the centre of the world. Furthermore, the self as self-knower may mistake its capacity for self-transcendence as the proof of having a position as ultimate judge, transcending all things.[3] Yet the self,

[1]Other Biblical passages which deal with the deceptions of sin are: Hebrews 3:13; Romans 7:11; Rev. 12:9; II Cor. 11:3 and Gen. 3:13, in which the deception of the serpent in the myth of the Fall is recorded.

[2]Philip Leon, in an invaluable study of human egotism, analyses self-deception as follows: "The self-deceiver does not believe . . . what he says or he would not be a deceiver. He does believe what he says or he would not be deceived. He both believes and does not believe . . . or he would not be self-deceived." *The Ethics of Power*, p. 258.

[3]In Isaiah 47 the sin of Babylon is defined as consisting in the two claims: "I am and none else beside me" and "None seeth me," which may be regarded as succinct definitions of the illusions of the self as centre of the world and of the self as transcending the world, in the one case leading to the denial of the existence of other life and in the other case to a denial of a higher court of judgment. Significantly these illusions are attributed on the one hand to the very greatness of the human mind: "Thy wisdom and thy knowledge, it hath perverted thee," and on the other to dishonesty: "Thou hast trusted thy wickedness."

though standing outside itself and the world, is obviously a finite existence within the world. The pretensions of the self therefore can be maintained only by wilful deception, for which Tertullian had the very accurate description of "willing ignorance."[4] This deception does not require a conscious act of dishonesty in each individual instance. The deception of sin is rather a general state of confusion from which individual acts of deception arise. Yet the deception never becomes so completely a part of the self that it could be regarded as a condition of ignorance. In moments of crisis the true situation may be vividly revealed to the self, prompting it to despairing remorse or possibly to a more creative contrition. The despair of remorse is essentially the recognition of the lie involved in sin without any recognition of either the truth or the grace by which the confusion of dishonesty might be overcome.

Modern psychology and Marxist social analyses have fully substantiated the Christian doctrine of the lie involved in sin, up to a certain point. Marxism cannot see the whole truth about the lie because its materialist conception of consciousness prevents it from understanding the self in all the complexities of its self-transcendence.[5] The psychologists also have had a great deal to say about "ra-

[4]"Such is the power of earthly pleasures, that to retain the opportunity of still partaking of them it [the self] contrives to prolong a willing ignorance and bribes knowledge to play a dishonest part." *De spectaculis,* Ch. 1.

[5]Harold Laski, for instance, declares: "I fully admit that statesmen at any given time are likely to be as sincere as their critics in the belief that they devote the machinery of state to the highest ends they know. My point is the wholly different one that what they can know is set by the economic relationships which the state exists to maintain. . . . The history of British exploitation in Africa is sufficient proof of that. We have set up admirable principles of stewardship through which to guard the interests of the native races there; but immediately gold is discovered on native reserves we can exhaust the resources of human reason to discover grounds on which to invade those preserves. We can even persuade ourselves to believe that the native ought to accept our view that it is for his benefit that we are above all concerned. . . . But these men are sincere; they are seeking to do their best; they genuinely will the good of the whole community. Of course they are and do; this book will have

tionalization" defined by a recent psychologist as "an attempt to make conduct appear sensible and in conformity with custom and social expectation."[6] Their difficulty is usually that they cannot imagine any but a social norm to which the self pretends to conform. They consequently regard deception as primarily intent on social approval; and derive self-deception from this prior social deception.[7]

The real nature of the lie involved in all sinful self-love can be fully understood only in terms of the Christian understanding of the self-transcendent and yet determinate self; and the Christian distinction between the sinful state of the self which denies its limitations and an essential self, whose knowledge of the truth can never be so completely obscured as to make the lies, in which the sinful self involves itself in the process of its self-glorification, either superfluous or wholly convincing. The sinful self needs these deceptions because it cannot pursue its own determinate ends without paying tribute to the truth. This truth, which the self, even in its sin, never wholly obscures, is that the self, as finite and determinate, does not deserve unconditioned devotion. But though the deceptions are needed they are never wholly convincing because the self is the only ego fully privy to the dishonesties by which it has hidden its own interests behind a façade of general interest.

The desperate effort to deceive others must, therefore, be regarded as, on the whole, an attempt to aid the self in believing a pretension it cannot easily believe because it was itself the author of the decep-

---

been written wholly in vain if it suggests that I cast any doubt on the motives of statesmen." *The State in Theory and Practice*, pp. 101–164.

Mr. Laski is a very astute social analyst, who is evidently trying to maintain his convictions within the bounds of Marxist presuppositions. But he does not quite succeed. "Are likely to be as sincere as their critics." How sincere is that? Such a qualified sincerity is adequate ground for casting suspicion upon the motives of statesmen.

[6] L. F. Shaffer, *The Psychology of Adjustment*, p. 168.

[7] Thus the quoted author continues: "Not only are they [drives regarded as inferior or blameworthy] not acknowledged in polite society but the individual becomes so conditioned that he will not admit them to himself." *Ibid.*, p. 169.

tion. If others will only accept what the self cannot quite accept, the self as deceiver is given an ally against the self as deceived. All efforts to impress our fellowmen, our vanity, our display of power or of goodness must, therefore, be regarded as revelations of the fact that sin increases the insecurity of the self by veiling its weakness with veils which may be torn aside. The self is afraid of being discovered in its nakedness behind these veils and of being recognized as the author of the veiling deceptions. Thus sin compounds the insecurity of nature with a fresh insecurity of spirit.

CHAPTER VIII

MAN AS SINNER (*Continued*)

THE egotism of man has been defined and illustrated thus far without a careful discrimination between group pride and the pride and egotism of individuals. This lack of discrimination is provisionally justified by the fact that, strictly speaking, only individuals are moral agents, and group pride is therefore merely an aspect of the pride and arrogance of individuals. It is the fruit of the undue claims which they make for their various social groups. Nevertheless some distinctions must be made between the collective behaviour of men and their individual attitudes. This is necessary in part because group pride, though having its source in individual attitudes, actually achieves a certain authority over the individual and results in unconditioned demands by the group upon the individual. Whenever the group develops organs of will, as in the apparatus of the state, it seems to the individual to have become an independent centre of moral life. He will be inclined to bow to its pretensions and to acquiesce in its claims of authority, even when these do not coincide with his moral scruples or inclinations.

A distinction between group pride and the egotism of individuals is necessary, furthermore, because the pretensions and claims of a collective or social self exceed those of the individual ego. The group is more arrogant, hypocritical, self-centred and more ruthless in the pursuit of its ends than the individual. An inevitable moral tension between individual and group morality is therefore created. "If," said the great Italian statesman, Cavour, "we did for ourselves what we do for our country, what rascals we would be." This tension is naturally most apparent in the conscience of responsible statesmen, who are bound to feel the disparity between the canons of ordinary morality and the accepted habits of collective and political behaviour. Frederick the Great was not, as statesmen go, a man of unique moral sensitivity. His confession of a sense of this tension is therefore the more significant. "I hope," said he, "that posterity will distinguish the philosopher from the monarch in me and the decent man from the politician. I must admit that when drawn into the vortex of European politics it is difficult to preserve decency and integrity. One feels oneself in constant danger of being betrayed by one's allies and abandoned by one's friends, of being suffocated by envy and jealousy, and is thus finally driven to the terrible alternative of being false either to one's country or to one's word."[1]

The egotism of racial, national and socio-economic groups is most consistently expressed by the national state because the state gives the collective impulses of the nation such instruments of power and presents the imagination of individuals with such obvious symbols of its discrete collective identity that the national state is most able to make absolute claims for itself, to enforce those claims by power and to give them plausibility and credibility by the majesty and panoply of its apparatus. In the life of every political group, whether nation or empire, which articulates itself through the instrument of a state, obedience is prompted by the fear of power on the one hand and by reverence for majesty on the other. The temptation to idolatry is implicit in the state's majesty. Rationalists, with their simple ideas of government resting purely upon the consent of the governed, have never appreciated to what degree religious reverence for majesty is implicit in this consent. The political history of man begins with tribal polytheism, can be traced through the religious pretensions of empires with their inevitable concomitants of imperial religions and

[1] Quoted by F. Meinecke, *Die Idee der Staatsraison*, p. 377.

their priest-kings and god-kings, and ends with the immoderate and idolatrous claims of the modern fascist state. No politically crystallized social group has, therefore, ever existed without entertaining, or succumbing to, the temptation of making idolatrous claims for itself. Frequently the organs of this group pride, the state and the ruling oligarchy which bears the authority of the state, seek to detach themselves from the group pride of which their majesty is a symbol and to become independent sources of majesty. But this inversion is possible only because the original source of their majesty lies in something which transcends their individual power and prestige, namely the pride and greatness of the group itself.

Sinful pride and idolatrous pretension are thus an inevitable concomitant of the cohesion of large political groups. This is why it is impossible to regard the lower morality of groups, in comparison with individuals, as the consequence of the inertia of "nature" against the higher demands of individual reason. It is true of course that the group possesses only an inchoate "mind" and that its organs of self-transcendence and self-criticism are very unstable and ephemeral compared to its organs of will. A shifting and unstable "prophetic minority" is the instrument of this self-transcendence, while the state is the organ of the group's will. For this reason the immorality of nations is frequently regarded as in effect their unmorality, as the consequence of their existence in the realm of "nature" rather than the realm of reason. "I treat government not as a conscious contrivance," wrote Professor Seeley in a sentiment which expresses the conviction of many modern political scientists, "but as an half-instinctive product of the effort of human beings to ward off from themselves certain evils to which they are exposed."[2]

[2]*Political Science*, p. 129. I have interpreted the behaviour of nations primarily from this viewpoint in a previous work, declaring: "Since there can be no ethical action without self-criticism and no self-criticism without the rational capacity for self-transcendence, it is natural that national attitudes can hardly approximate the ethical. . . . The nation is a unity held together much more by force and emotion than by mind." *Moral Man and Immoral Society*, p. 88.

Such an interpretation has a measure of validity but it certainly does not do justice to the "spiritual" character of national pride, nor to the contribution which individuals, with all their rational and spiritual faculties, make to pride of groups and the self-deification of nations. The most conducive proof that the egotism of nations is a characteristic of the spiritual life, and not merely an expression of the natural impulse of survival, is the fact that its most typical expressions are the lust-for-power, pride (comprising considerations of prestige and "honour"), contempt toward the other (the reverse side of pride and its necessary concomitant in a world in which self-esteem is constantly challenged by the achievements of others); hypocrisy (the inevitable pretension of conforming to a higher norm than self-interest); and finally the claim of moral autonomy by which the self-deification of the social group is made explicit by its presentation of itself as the source and end of existence.

It cannot be denied that the instinct of survival is involved in all these spiritual manifestations of egotism; but that is equally true of individual life. We have previously noted that the fear of death is a basic motive of all human pretensions. Every human self-assertion, whether individual or collective, is therefore involved in the inconsistency of claiming, on the one hand, that it is justified by the primary right of survival and, on the other hand, that it is the bearer of interests and values larger than its own and that these more inclusive values are the justification of its conflict with competing social wills. No modern nation can ever quite make up its mind whether to insist that its struggle is a fight for survival or a selfless effort to maintain transcendent and universal values. In the World War both claims were constantly made; and it is significant that even modern Germany, though it has constructed a primitive tribal religion which makes the power and pride of the nation a self-justifying end, nevertheless feels constrained to pretend that its expected victory in Europe is desired as a triumph of a high type of (Aryan) culture over an allegedly inferior and decadent form of (Jewish or liberal) culture. The nation claims (or the claim is made for it) that it is the instrument of a value more universal than its contingent self, because, like the individual, the determinateness of its life is too obvious to be denied, at least by modern man. But the claim that it is itself the final and ultimate value, the cause which gives human existence meaning, is one which no individual can plausibly make for himself. It is plausible, though hardly credible, only because the social unit, particularly the nation, to which the individual belongs, transcends the individual life to such a degree in power, majesty, and pseudo-immortality that the claim of unconditioned value can be made for it with a degree of plausibility.

The significance of this claim is that through it human pride and self-assertion reach their ultimate form and seek to break all bounds of finiteness. The nation pretends to be God. A certain ambiguity which envelops this claim has already been noted. It is on the one hand a demand of a collective will and mind upon the individual. The social group asks for the individual's unconditioned loyalty, asserting that its necessities are the ultimate law of the individual's existence. But on the other hand it is a pretension which the individual makes for himself, not as an individual but as a member of his group. Collective egotism does indeed offer the individual an opportunity to lose himself in a larger whole; but it also offers him possibilities of self-aggrandizement beside which mere individual pretensions are implausible and incredible. Individuals "join to set up a god whom each then severally and tacitly identifies with himself, to swell the chorus of praise which each then severally and tacitly arrogates to himself."[3] It may be that such group pride represents a particular temptation to individuals who suffer from specific forms of the sense of inferiority. The relation of modern fascist nationalism to the insecurity and sense of inferiority of the lower middle classes is therefore significant. But it hardly can be denied that extravagant forms of modern nationalism only accentuate a general character of group life and collective egotism; and that specific forms of inferiority feeling for which this pride compensates

[3]Philip Leon, *The Ethics of Power,* p. 140.

only accentuate the general sense of inferiority from which all men suffer. Collective pride is thus man's last, and in some respects most pathetic, effort to deny the determinate and contingent character of his existence. The very essence of human sin is in it. It can hardly be surprising that this form of human sin is also most fruitful of human guilt, that is of objective social and historical evil. In its whole range from pride of family to pride of nation, collective egotism and group pride are a more pregnant source of injustice and conflict than purely individual pride.

The pride of nations is, of course, not wholly spurious. Their claim to embody values which transcend their mere existence has foundations in fact. It is the very character of human life, whether individual or collective, that it incarnates values which transcend its immediate interests. A particular nation or group of nations may actually be the bearers of a "democratic civilization" or of a communist one. Men are not animals and never fight merely for existence, because they do not have a mere animal existence. Their physical life is always the base for a superstructure of values which transcends physical life.

The pride of nations consists in the tendency to make unconditioned claims for their conditioned values. The unconditioned character of these claims has two aspects. The nation claims a more absolute devotion to values which transcend its life than the facts warrant; and it regards the values to which it is loyal as more absolute than they really are. Nations may fight for "liberty" and "democracy" but they do not do so until their vital interests are imperiled. They may refuse to fight and claim that their refusal is prompted by their desire to "preserve civilization." Neutral nations are not less sinful than belligerent ones in their effort to hide their partial interests behind their devotion to "civilization." Furthermore the civilization to which they claim loyalty does not deserve such absolute devotion as the nation asks for it.

This does not mean that men may not have to make fateful decisions between types of civilization in mortal combat. The moralists who contend that the imperfection of all civilizations negates every obligation to preserve any of them suffer from a naive cynicism. Relative distinctions must always be made in history. But these necessary distinctions do not invalidate the general judgment upon the collective life of man, that it is invariably involved in the sin of pride.

Prophetic religion had its very inception in a conflict with national self-deification. Beginning with Amos, all the great Hebrew prophets challenged the simple identification between God and the nation, or the naive confidence of the nation in its exclusive relation to God. The prophets prophesied in the name of a holy God who spoke judgment upon the nation; and the basic sin against which this judgment was directed was the sin of claiming that Israel and God were one or that God was the exclusive possession of Israel.[4] Judgment would overtake not only Israel but every nation, including the great nations who were used for the moment to execute divine judgment upon Israel but were also equally guilty of exalting themselves beyond measure (Is. 47; Jer. 25:15; Ez. 24-39).

This insight of Biblical religion stands in sharpest contrast to the simple identification of morals and politics in the thought of Plato and Aristotle and their inability to find any perspective from which to judge the relative character and contingent achievements of their Greek city-state. In this realm of thought Greek philosophy must be regarded as no more than a rationalized form of tribal religion. It does not achieve a vantage point from which to criticize the most pretentious and the most plausible form of human pride. This is natural enough, because there is no such vantage point in man himself. The conviction that collective pride is the final form of sin is possible only within terms of a religion of revelation in the faith of which a voice of God is heard from beyond all human majesties

----

[4]*Cf.* Amos 7:16, 17: "Hear thou the word of the Lord: Thou sayest prophesy not against Israel, and drop not thy word against the house of Isaac. Therefore thus saith the Lord: Thy wife shall be an harlot in the city, and thy sons and thy daughters shall fall by the sword, etc."

and a divine power is revealed in comparison with which the "nations are as a drop of a bucket" (Is. 40:15).[5]

This genius of prophetic faith enables Augustine in the Christian era to view the destruction of the Roman Empire without despair and to answer the charge that Christianity was responsible for its downfall with the assertion that, on the contrary, destruction is the very law of life of the "city of this world" and that pride is the cause of its destruction. "But because it [the earthly city] is not a good which acquits the possessors of all troubles, therefore this city is divided in itself into wars, altercations and appetites of bloody and deadly victories. For any part of it that wars against another desires to be the world's conqueror, whereas indeed it is vice's slave. And if it conquer it extols itself and so becomes its own destruction."[6] There are suggestions of a similar perspective upon national pride in Stoic universalism. But the presuppositions of its pantheism betray Stoicism into a doctrine of ἀπάθεια which condemns human vitality indiscriminately and renders it incapable of a discriminate judgment upon the pride and self-will of man. With the exception of Stoicism, prophetic Christianity and qualifiedly Judaism[7] have alone been able

[5]There are of course universalistic notes in both Aristotle and Plato (particularly in the *Timæus*) and Stoic universalism will be considered presently. However none of the classical philosophers conceive of the universal value as standing in contradiction to particular values of Greek culture and civilization, which seem to them final. They think of the universal as the extension of their particular viewpoint, just as a modern communist is a universalist in his hope that communism may become the basis of a world civilization.

The first word to be spoken against a nation and its rulers from within that nation was spoken by a prophet, Amos. He pronounced the judgment of the "Holy One of Israel" against Israel. The difference between the prophetic faith in a God who transcends the nation and whose judgments may condemn a nation and its rulers and the universalistic overtones in high philosophies is very considerable. This difference makes nonsense of the claims of the rationalists that only reason is able to emancipate men of excesive devotion to the parochial and the partial.

[6]*De civ. Dei,* Book XV, Ch. 4.

[7]One must say "qualifiedly Judaism" because post-exilic Judaism exhausted its spiritual resources in maintaining the integrity of a nation,

to find a certain and secure vantage point from which to oppose the self-glorification of nations. This does not, of course, prevent many forms of historic Christianity from playing the part of the court chaplain to the pride of nations. Yet the word of Augustine against the pretensions of empire is one which is possible only in terms of the presuppositions of the Christian faith: "Set justice aside and what are kingdoms but large robber bands, and what are robber bands but little kingdoms? . . . Excellent and elegant was the pirate's answer to the great Macedonian Alexander, who had taken him. The king asking him how he durst molest the seas so, he replied with a free spirit 'How darest thou molest the whole world? But because I do it with a little ship only I am called a thief; thou doing it with a great navy art called a conqueror.' "[8]

Unfortunately this prophetic insight of Augustine's was partially obscured by his identification, however qualified, of the city of God with the historic church, an identification which was later to be stripped of all its Augustinian reservations to become the instrument of the spiritual pride of a universal church in its conflict with the political pride of an empire. This identification had the merit of introducing a religio-political institution into the world which actually placed a check upon the autonomy of nations; but at the price of developing in that institution dangerous similarities with the old Roman Empire, and of establishing the pope as a kind of spiritualized Cæsar. The conflict between Papacy and Empire therefore revealed a curiously ironic quality from beginning to end. The pot called the kettle black. Pope and emperor levelled the charge of

---

scattered among the nations of the earth. Its historic faith became too much a necessity of its racial existence to maintain the prophetic words, spoken against the nation, at their full vigour. Judaism has frequently elaborated moral ideals of relatively universal value, in cooperation with the general tendencies of a liberal culture, more successfully than historic Christianity. It has been "prophetic" in its passion for justice but not usually "prophetic" in its understanding of the basic character of collective pride as a cause of injustice.

[8]*De civ. Dei,* Book IV, Ch. 4.

Anti-Christ at each other; and both were justified in doing so because each saw in the other the sin of pretension, the exaltation above his measure, which defines the Anti-Christ.[9] This was a struggle between two political forces one of which had distilled political power from the principle of sanctity while the other had exalted power to the proportions of sanctity.

The fact that human pride insinuated itself into the struggle of the Christian religion against the pride and self-will of nations merely proves how easily the pride of men can avail itself of the very instruments intended to mitigate it. The church, as well as the state, can become the vehicle of collective egotism. Every truth can be made the servant of sinful arrogance, including the prophetic truth that all men fall short of the truth. This particular truth can come to mean that, since all men fall short of the truth and since the church is a repository of a revelation which transcends the finiteness and sinfulness of men, it therefore has the absolute truth which other men lack.

The element of sinful human pretension which entered into the medieval Christian opposition to the pride of nations made the rise of the new nation, beginning with the Renaissance and Reformation, appear in the light of emancipation from religious tyranny. Even so pious a Catholic as Dante had foreshadowed this interpretation by his opposition to the political ambitions of the papacy. Thus the Renaissance ushered in a period in which not only individuals but

[9]Gregory VII, the founder of the medieval political papacy, indicted Emperor Henry IV as Anti-Christ, and was in turn accused by the German bishops of megalomania. And who is to determine how much personal and clerical pride and how much genuine passion for the "city of God" was mixed into the compound of motives which actuated Gregory's policies?

At the very end of the medieval period Gregory IX and Frederick II charged each other with being Anti-Christ. The emperor insisted that the pope was a false vicar of Christ and therefore the Anti-Christ and the pope made the same charge against the emperor; and not without reason because the emperor proclaimed himself a new Messiah, as the primeval norm of all good, as the ideal man. *Cf.* Alois Demph, *Sacrum Imperium,* pp. 190 and 324 ff.

also nations were to defy all bounds of creatureliness in the name of liberty. Machiavelli fashioned the doctrine of the moral autonomy for the state as Bruno and others conceived it for the individual. Significantly Luther, through the exigencies of religious warfare, was more intent upon challenging the pride of the pope than the arrogance of kings. The pope for him was Anti-Christ but kings ruled by divine right. Thus Protestantism, in spite of its more prophetic conception of the inevitability of sinful pride in all the activities of mankind, allowed a vent for political arrogance of which the rising nation was to take full advantage.

As a consequence a culture, schooled by the Renaissance on the one hand and the Reformation on the other, has resulted in a contemporary period of decadence in which the collective will of man, particularly as embodied in the nation, has achieved heights of sinful pretension never before equalled. The nation is god. The naive polytheism of early empires and their consequent unconscious glorification of themselves as the centre and end of existence has given way to a sophisticated self-glorification of the nation which consciously defies the obvious fact that it is not the whole of existence. This net result is partly a reaction to the error and sin which had crept into Christianity's testimony against the nations, that is, its deification of the historic church. But the very extravagence of modern nationalism must be regarded as partly a reaction to the truth in Christianity rather than the error of the church. It is only within terms of a Christian civilization, though a decadent one, that collective egotism can reach such desperate proportions. For conscious defiance of a known law is bound to be desperate. Here, in the realm of collective behaviour, is a striking commentary on the truth of the Pauline observation: "For I had not known lust, except the law had said, thou shalt not covet. But sin, taking occasion by the commandment, wrought in me all manner of concupiscence. For without the law sin was dead" (Romans 7:7–8).

The pride of nations and the arrogance of self-deification of collective man are the more extravagant for being expressed in and against a Christian culture in which it must consciously negate and defy the highest insights of the faith which formed the culture of the western world.

The most dæmonic form of nationalism today is expressed against rather than in a Christian culture. The German Nazis were quite right in regarding the Christian faith as incompatible with their boundless national egoism. While Christianity may itself be made the tool of nationalism, the Christian faith, if it retains any vitality, is bound to mediate some word of divine judgment upon the nation, which the Nazis find intolerable. No nation is free of the sin of pride, just as no individual is free of it. Nevertheless it is important to recognize that there are "Christian" nations, who prove themselves so because they are still receptive to prophetic words of judgment spoken against the nation. It may be that only a prophetic minority feels this judgment keenly. But there is a genuine difference between nations which do not officially destroy the religious-prophetic judgment against the nation and those which do. While all modern nations, and indeed all nations of history, have been involved in the sin of pride, one must realize, in this as in other estimates of human sinfulness, that it is just as important to recognize differences in the degree of pride and self-will expressed by men and nations, as it is to know that all men and nations are sinful in the sight of God. Here, as in individual life, the final sin is the unwillingness to hear the word of judgment spoken against our sin. By that criterion, the modern fascist nations have achieved a dæmonic form of national self-assertion which is more dangerous even than that of the ancient religious empires because it is expressed within and against the insights of a Christian culture.

II

THE EQUALITY OF SIN AND THE INEQUALITY OF GUILT

Orthodox Christianity has held fairly consistently to the Biblical proposition that all men are equally sinners in the sight of God. The Pauline assertion: "For there is no difference: for all have sinned, and come short of the glory of God" (Romans 3:22, 23) is an indispensable expression of the Christian understanding of sin. Yet it is quite apparent that this assertion imperils and seems to weaken all moral judgments which deal with the "nicely calculated less and more" of justice and goodness as revealed in the relativities of history. It seems to inhibit preferences between the oppressor and his victim, between the congenital liar and the moderately truthful man, between the debauched sensualist and the self-disciplined worker, and between the egotist who drives egocentricity to the point of sickness and the moderately "unselfish" devotee of the general welfare. Though it is quite necessary and proper that these distinctions should disappear at the ultimate religious level of judgment, yet it is obviously important to draw them provisionally in all historic judgments. The difference between a little more and a little less justice in a social system and between a little more and a little less selfishness in the individual may represent differences between sickness and health, between misery and happiness in particular situations. Theologies, such as that of Barth, which threaten to destroy all relative moral judgments by their exclusive emphasis upon the ultimate religious fact of the sinfulness of all men, are rightly suspected of imperilling relative moral achievements of history. In this connection it is significant that Germany, with its Augustinian-Lutheran theological inheritance, has had greater difficulty in achieving a measure of political sanity and justice than the more Pelagian, more self-righteous and religiously less profound Anglo-Saxon world.

Orthodox Catholicism answered this problem of relative moral judgments by incorporating into its system of ethics the whole Stoic concept of the natural law, including its distinction between a relative and an absolute natural law, by which rational norms of justice were made definitive for the Christian conception of virtue and vice. The difficulty with this impressive structure of Catholic ethics, finally elaborated into a detailed casuistic application of general moral standards to every conceivable particular situation, is that it constantly insinuates religious absolutes into highly contingent and historical moral judgments. Thus the whole imposing structure of Thomistic ethics is, in one of its aspects, no more than a religious sanctification of the relativities of the feudal social system as it flowered in the thirteenth century. The confusion between ultimate religious perspectives and relative historical ones in Catholic thought accounts for the fury and self-righteousness into which Catholicism is betrayed when it defends feudal types of civilization in contemporary history as in Spain for instance.

Orthodox Protestantism, both Calvinistic and Lutheran, rightly discerned the perils of moralism and self-righteousness in the rigidities of the natural law; and therefore allowed natural law theories an only subordinate place in its system of thought. In one instance it was prompted by Biblical authority (the Pauline doctrine of the divine ordinance of government in Romans 13) to qualify its aversion to absolute moral judgments in the field of historical relativity. It gave government and the principle of order an absolute preference over rebellion and political chaos. This one exception had morally catastrophic consequences. It tended to ally the Christian church too uncritically with the centres of power in political life and tempted it to forget that government is frequently the primary source of injustice and oppression. Happily Calvin in his later years, and more particularly the later Calvinists, discovered that it was as important to place the ruler under the judgment of God as to regard him as an instrument of God for checking individual sin. This important Calvinistic discovery bore rich consequences in the relation of Calvinistic piety to the democratic movements toward social justice in the seventeenth and eighteenth centuries.

The mistake of Catholic moral casuistry to derive relative moral judgments too simply from the presuppositions of its natural law and the opposite tendency of orthodox Protestantism to efface all moral distinctions of history in the light of a religious conviction of the undifferentiated sinfulness of all men persuade us to walk warily in relating the Biblical truth that all men are sinners to the other truth that there is nevertheless an ascertainable inequality of guilt among men in the actualities of history. Guilt is distinguished from sin in that it represents the objective and historical consequences of sin, for which the sinner must be held responsible. It is the guilt of the sinner that his self-love results in the consequence of broken or unhappy homes, of children made unhappy by the tyranny of their parents, of peoples destroyed by wars which were prompted by the vanity of their rulers, of the poverty of the victims of greed and the unhappiness of the victims of jealousy and envy. Guilt is the objective consequence of sin, the actual corruption of the plan of creation and providence in the historical world.

Obviously men who are equally sinful in the sight of God may also be equally guilty in a specific situation. The equality of their sin must, in fact, lead to the general assumption that their guilt is more equal than it will seem to be upon cursory analysis. Two nations involved in perennial war may thus be equally guilty, even though only one was responsible for the latest act of provocation. A ruthless father may be more equally guilty of the waywardness of his son than a superficial analysis would reveal. An abandoned wife may share equal guilt with her faithless husband though the overt act of desertion was his alone. The Christian doctrine of the sinfulness of all men is thus a constant challenge to re-examine superficial moral judgments, particularly those which self-righteously give the moral advantage to the one who makes the judgment. There is no moral situation in which the Pauline word does not apply: "Therefore thou art inexcusable, O man, whosoever thou art that judgest: for wherein thou judgest another, thou condemnest thyself; for thou that judgest doest the same things" (Romans 2:1).

Yet men who are equally sinners in the sight of God need not be equally guilty of a specific act of wrong-doing in which they are involved. It is important to recognize that Biblical religion has emphasized this inequality of guilt just as much as the equality of sin. A primary source of orthodox Lutheranism's inability to deal effectively with specific moral issues in history is its blindness to the prophetic note in Scriptures in which those who are particularly guilty of moral wrong-doing are constantly singled out. Specially severe judgments fall upon the rich and the powerful, the mighty and the noble, the wise and the righteous (that is, those who are tempted to spiritual pride by their attainment of some relative, socially approved standard of righteousness, the Pharisees). The strictures of the prophets against the mighty, accusing them of pride and injustice, of both the religious and the social dimensions of sin, are consistently partial. Prophetic judgment is levelled at those "which oppress the poor, which crush the needy" (Amos 4:1), those who "lie upon beds of ivory, and stretch themselves upon their couches, and eat the lambs out of the flock, and the calves out of the midst of the stall" (Amos 6:4), who "swallow up the needy, even to make the poor of the land to fail" (Amos 8:4).

The simple religious insight which underlies these prophetic judgments is that the men who are tempted by their eminence and by the possession of undue power become more guilty of pride and of injustice than those who lack power and position. The injustice of the powerful and the pride of the eminent are assumed as a matter of course and they are threatened with judgment: "For the day of the Lord of hosts shall be upon every one that is proud and lofty, and upon every one that is lifted up . . . and the loftiness of man shall be bowed down, and the haughtiness of men shall be made low: and the Lord alone shall be exalted in that day" (Is. 2:12, 17, also Is. 26:5). While the religious dimension of sin, pride, is always the primary concern of the prophets, they see much more clearly than most historic Christianity has seen, that an inevitable concomitant of pride is injustice. The pride which makes itself the source and end of existence subordinates other life to its will and despoils it of its rightful inheritance. Therefore Isaiah continues: "The Lord will enter into judgment with the ancients of his people, and the princes thereof; for ye have eaten up the vineyard; the spoil of the poor is in your houses. What mean ye that ye beat my people to pieces, and grind the faces of the poor? saith the Lord God of hosts" (Is. 3:14, 15). Nor do the prophets hesitate to draw the conclusion that the poor shall be exalted as the powerful are abased: "The meek also shall increase their joy in the Lord, and the poor among men shall rejoice in the Holy One of Israel" (Is. 29:19). The judgment upon the powerful and proud and the promise to the poor and needy is not only an ultimate judgment in the sight of God. The promised judgment is one which reveals itself in history: "Thus saith the Lord, Even the captives of the mighty shall be taken away, and the prey of the terrible shall be delivered: for I will contend with him that contendeth with thee, and I will save thy children" (Is. 49:25).

The prophetic note of moral discrimination between rich and poor, between the powerful and the weak, the proud and the meek is maintained in the New Testament, beginning with Mary's *Magnificat:* "He hath put down the mighty from their seats, and exalted them of low degree. He hath filled the hungry with good things; and the rich he hath sent empty away" (Lk. 1:52 ff.). St. Paul's judgment that "not many wise men after the flesh, not many mighty, not many noble, are called" (1 Cor. 1:26) stands in this same prophetic tradition; and significantly it adds the wise to the mighty and the noble, as standing particularly under the judgment of God. And rightly so; for the pride of the wise and the pretensions of the spiritual leaders of culture and civilization may be more productive of evil than the simpler will-to-power of the mighty and the noble. In the teachings of Jesus this prophetic note of moral discrimination is maintained without reservation. His blessings upon the poor and his woes upon the rich in the beatitudes, as recorded in St. Luke, have sometimes been found inconvenient, and commentators have been happy to prefer the seemingly less rigorous and more ambiguous blessings upon the "poor in spirit" in the version of the beatitudes as recorded in St. Matthew. But the Aramaic word which Jesus probably used had a highly significant double connotation. It meant both "poor" and "humble."[1] The very use of the word therefore would have given support to the anti-aristocratic tradition which fashioned the word. The "poor of the land" were unable to maintain

[1] The Hebrew word *amē ha-ares.*

the meticulous observances of Pharisaic righteousness. They were therefore outcastes by the rules which the moral aristocracy had fash-ioned and which had become instruments of their power and social prestige rather than guides to good conduct. To prefer these poor and humble men to the conventionally good and self-righteous men was to strengthen rather than weaken the prophetic anti-aristocratic tradition. The good are added to the mighty, noble and wise as standing particularly under the judgment of God.

If one realizes to what degree every civilization, as a system of power, idealizes and rationalizes its equilibrium of power and how these rationalizations invariably include standards of morals which serve the moral and spiritual pride of the ruling oligarchy, it is apparent that an attack upon Pharisaism is really an attack upon the final and most confusing and dishonest pretension of power.

The anti-aristocratic emphasis of the Bible has been interpreted by certain types of sectarian Christianity and by modern secular radicalism in too simple politico-moral terms. Jesus is reduced in this type of thought to the stature of a leader of a proletarian revolt against the rich. The same emphasis has, on the other hand, been too simply obscured by most types of conventional Christianity. These have been anxious to regard the humility of spirit which Jesus extolled as a spiritual grace which transcended all social, political and economic circumstances and might be absent or present among rich or poor alike. Biblical religion is too concerned with the ultimate and perennial human situation to permit a simple political inter-pretation of its anti-aristocratic tendencies. It is on the other hand too realistic to obscure the fact that socio-economic conditions ac-tually determine to a large degree that some men are tempted to pride and injustice, while others are encouraged to humility.

This Biblical analysis agrees with the known facts of history. Capitalists are not greater sinners than poor labourers by any natural depravity. But it is a fact that those who hold great economic and political power are more guilty of pride against God and of injustice against the weak than those who lack power and prestige. Gentiles

are not naturally more sinful than Jews. But Gentiles, holding the
dominant power in their several nations, sin against Semitic minority
groups more than the latter sin against them. White men sin against
Negroes in Africa and America more than Negroes sin against white
men. Wherever the fortunes of nature, the accidents of history or
even the virtues of the possessors of power, endow an individual or
a group with power, social prestige, intellectual eminence or moral
approval above their fellows, there an ego is allowed to expand. It
expands both vertically and horizontally. Its vertical expansion, its
pride, involves it in sin against God. Its horizontal expansion involves it in an unjust effort to gain security and prestige at the expense of its fellows. The two forms of expansion cannot be sharply
distinguished because, as previously noted, spiritual pretension can
be made an instrument of power in social conflict, and dominant
power, measured socially, inevitably seeks to complete its structure
by spiritual pretensions.

A too simple social radicalism does not recognize how quickly the
poor, the weak, the despised of yesterday, may, on gaining a social
victory over their detractors, exhibit the same arrogance and the
same will-to-power which they abhorred in their opponents and
which they were inclined to regard as a congenital sin of their
enemies. Every victim of injustice makes the mistake of supposing
that the sin from which he suffers is a peculiar vice of his oppressor.
This is the self-righteousness of the weak in distinction to the self-
righteousness of the powerful; and it cannot be denied, as Nietzsche
observed, that it is a vehicle of vindictive passions. Such a form of
moral pride among the weak will accentuate their arrogance when
the fortunes of history transmute their weakness into strength. This
fact explains the unique fury and the insufferable moral and spiritual
arrogance of the new Russian oligarchy, which believes that the very
sins of power which it exemplifies by its arrogance are the peculiar
vices of capitalism. But the mistakes of a too simple social radicalism
must not obscure the fact that in a given historical situation the
powerful man or class is actually more guilty of injustice and pride
than those who lack power.

The fact that men of intellectual, spiritual and moral eminence should fall under the same judgment as the men of power according to the Bible will seem particularly offensive to most moralists. It is at this point that the anti-aristocratic tendencies of Biblical religion stand in sharpest contrast to all forms of rationalism which assume that the intelligent man is also the good man, and which do not recognize to what degree reason may be the servant of passion; and that the genuine achievements of mind and conscience may also be new occasions for expressing the pride of sinful man. "If any man stand, let him take heed lest he fall" is a warning which is as relevant to bishops, professors, artists, saints and holy men as to capitalists, dictators and all men of power. Every one who stands is inclined to imagine that he stands by divine right. Every one who has achieved a high form of culture imagines that it is a necessary and final form of culture. It is the man who stands, who has achieved, who is honoured and approved by his fellowmen who mistakes the relative achievements and approvals of history for a final and ultimate approval.

It is at this point that the Biblical insight into the sinfulness of all human nature actually supports rather than contradicts the prophetic strictures against the wise, the mighty, the noble and the good. For without understanding the sinfulness of the human heart in general it is not possible to penetrate through the illusions and pretensions of the successful classes of every age. If one did not know that all men are guilty in the sight of God it would not be easy to discern the particular measure of guilt with which those are covered who are able to obscure the weakness and insecurity of man so successfully by their power, and the sinfulness of man by their good works. Aristotelian and Platonic thought, with all of its derivatives, will continue to persuade kings that they are philosophers and philosophers that they are kings; and will tempt them to hide their will-to-power behind their virtues and to obscure their injustices behind their generosities. It is only by an ultimate analysis from beyond all human standards that the particular guilt of the great and the good men of history is revealed.

III

SIN AS SENSUALITY

Without question Biblical religion defines sin as primarily pride and self-love and classical Christian theology remains fairly true to this conception, though on its Hellenistic side Christianity is always tempted to regard sin as basically lust and sensuality. But this definition of sin as pride, which history and experience have amply verified, raises the problem of the relation of sensuality to selfishness. Is it merely a form of selfishness? Or a consequence of selfishness? Or does it betray characteristics which must prompt the conclusion that sensuality is a distinctive form of sin, to be sharply distinguished from self-love?

A provisional distinction must certainly be made. If selfishness is the destruction of life's harmony by the self's attempt to centre life around itself, sensuality would seem to be the destruction of harmony within the self, by the self's undue identification with and devotion to particular impulses and desires within itself. The sins of sensuality, as expressed for instance in sexual license, gluttony, extravagance, drunkenness and abandonment to various forms of physical desire, have always been subject to a sharper and readier social disapproval than the more basic sin of self-love. Very frequently the judge, who condemns the profligate, has achieved the eminence in church or state from which he judges his dissolute brethren, by the force of a selfish ambition which must be judged more grievously sinful than the sins of the culprit. Yet Christian cultures have usually not deviated from the severer condemnations which non-Christian cultures have visited upon the sins of sensuality. The reason for this aberration is obviously the fact that sensuality is a more apparent and discernible form of anarchy than selfishness.

The compliance of conventional Christian morality with this essential identification of sin and sensuality has given modern critics of Christianity a partial justification for their belief that Christianity encourages prurience in its judgment of sexual problems and a cruel self-righteousness on the part of the self-possessed and respectable members of the community toward those who have fallen into obvious forms of sin. Yet the fact is that only the more Hellenistic and rationalistic forms of Christianity, with which modern critics of Christianity have more kinship than with the main body of Christian tradition, have ever defined sin as primarily sensuality or been inclined to identify sensuality particularly with sexual license.

Origen, the greatest of Hellenistic theologians, had beside his theory of a pre-historic Fall which resulted in man's involvement in the material world another theory of an actual historic Fall in which the serpent is represented as having seduced Eve and as having physically infected her, and in which original sin is defined as an inclination "to ignominy and wantonness."[1] As a consequence Origen consistently regarded all sex activity as inherently wrong and as the ground and origin of all actual sins. Clement of Alexandria defined the Fall as a falling "under the power of pleasure, for by the serpent pleasure creeping on its belly is in a figure signified."[2] Gregory of Nyssa, as noted in another chapter, not only identifies sin with the love of pleasure but derives it from "our being made like unto the irrational creation" though he admits that something is added to animal passion in human life, for it (the love of pleasure) "was increased by the transgression of man becoming the parent of so many varieties of sins arising from pleasure as we can not find among animals."[3] Gregory, following the general views of Platonism in regard to sex, attributed the bi-sexuality of man to the Fall. Such an interpretation is obviously unscriptural since the Genesis account of creation regards bi-sexuality as a part of the original creation: "Male and female created he them." Gregory overcame this difficulty by suggesting that God created man bi-sexually in anticipation of the Fall. Gregory's morbid attitude toward sex is expressed in extrava-

[1] *Cf.* N. P. Williams, *The Ideas of the Fall and Original Sin,* p. 227.
[2] *Protrepticus,* XI. iii.
[3] *On the Making of Man,* XVIII, 4.

gant terms in his treatise *De Virginitate*. It is unnecessary to make an exhaustive analysis of the writings of the Greek Fathers to establish the conclusion that the tendency of Greek thought to attribute evil to animal passion has tempted Hellenistic Christianity to a fairly consistent identification of sin with the love of pleasure, with sensuality and lust and prompted it to make sexual life the particular symbol of this lust.[4]

The Pauline-Augustinian theological tradition interprets the relation of sensuality to sin fairly consistently in the light of the first chapter of Paul's epistle to the Romans. Here lust, particularly unnatural lust, is described as a consequence of and punishment for the more basic sin of pride and self-deification. Because men changed the glory of the incorruptible God into the image of corruptible man, and because they "worshipped and served the creature rather than the Creator," therefore "God gave them up unto vile passions, for their women changed the natural use into that which is against nature . . . and even as they refused to have God in their knowledge God gave them up unto a reprobate mind, to do those things which are not fitting, being filled with all unrighteousness, fornication, wickedness, covetousness, maliciousness, etc." (Romans 1:26–30). In enumerating the various forms of sin, St. Paul makes no clear distinction between anti-social vices (selfishness) and lust, but in this instance his thought obviously is that the sins of lust (more particularly unnatural lust) are fruits of the more primal sin of rebellion against God.[5]

Augustine follows the Pauline interpretation literally and, quoting

[4] N. P. Williams, an Anglo-Catholic theologian, curiously seeks to establish the implausible thesis that a morbid attitude toward sex is a characteristic of the Pauline-Augustinian, or in his terms, of the "African" or "twice-born" theology and that it is inconsistent with the "Hellenic" viewpoint. Cf. *The Ideas of the Fall and of Original Sin*, p. 273.

[5] In cataloguing the various vices and sins, St. Paul sometimes enumerates anti-social and sensual sins separately and sometimes lists them indiscriminately, without a clear distinction between them. *Cf.* I Cor. 5:10–11; II Cor. 12:20; Gal. 5:19–21; Eph. 5:3–5; Col. 3:5–8.

from the first chapter of Romans the words "and receiving in themselves that recompense of their error which was due" (v. 27), declares that "these things were not only sins in themselves but punishment for sins." He continues. "Here now let our opponents say: 'Sin ought not to have been punished in this way that the sinner through his punishment should commit more sins.' Perhaps he may say in answer: God does not compel men to do these things; He only leaves those alone who deserve to be forsaken."[6]

Sensuality as a secondary consequence of man's rebellion against God is explained in more explicit terms by Augustine in the following words: "When the first man transgressed the law of God, he began to have another law in his members which was repugnant to his mind; then he felt evil of disobedience when he experienced in the rebellion of his own flesh a most righteous retribution recoiling on himself.—For it certainly was not just and right that obedience should be rendered by his servant, that is, his body to him who had not obeyed his own Lord and Master."[7] Whatever Augustine may say about the passions of the flesh and however morbidly he may use sex as the primary symbol of such passions, his analyses always remain within terms of this general statement. He never regards sensuality as a natural fruit of the man's animal nature: "We should therefore wrong our Creator in imputing our vices to our flesh: the flesh is good, but to leave the Creator and live according to this created good is mischief."[8]

The Thomistic version of the Pauline-Augustinian interpretation

[6]*Treatise on the Nature of Grace,* Chs. 24 and 25.
[7]*On Marriage and Concupiscence,* Ch. 7.
[8]*De civ. Dei,* Book XIV, Ch. v. Or again: "If any man say that flesh is the cause of the viciousness of the soul, he is ignorant of man's nature, for the corruptible body does not burden the soul.—For this corruption that is so burdensome to the soul is the punishment for the first sin and not the cause. The corruptible flesh made not the soul to sin, but the sinning soul made the flesh corruptible; from which corruption although there arise some incitements to sin, and some vicious desires, yet are not all sins of an evil life to be laid to the flesh, otherwise we shall make the devil, who has no flesh. sinless." *De civ. Dei,* Book XIV, Ch. 3

ot sensuality as the consequence of and punishment for sin is fairly true to the original. St. Thomas writes: "God bestowed this favour upon man in his primitive state, that as long as his mind was subject to God, the lower powers of his soul would be subject to his rational mind, and his body to his soul. But inasmuch as through sin man's mind withdrew from subjection to God, the result was that neither were his lower powers wholly subject to his reason; and from this there followed so great a rebellion of carnal appetite against reason that neither was the body subject to the soul; whence arose death and other bodily defects."[9] Though St. Thomas defines original sin as concupiscence he still insists that concupiscence is a consequence of self-love: "Every sinful act proceeds from inordinate desire of a mutable good. Now the fact that some one desires a temporal good inordinately is due to the fact he loves himself inordinately."[10]

The Lutheran interpretation does not differ materially from the Thomistic one, except that Luther eliminates the implicit Aristotelian emphasis upon reason as the master of the body. For Luther, as for St. Thomas, sin is essentially lust (*concupiscentia* or *cupiditas*) but he does not mean by this the natural desires and impulses of physical life. Lust is the consequence of man's turning from God, which results in the corruption of his heart and will with evil desire.[11] This evil desire includes both self-love and sensuality. It is the preference of the self and that which pertains to the self (*se et quae sua*) instead of God. Thus while Luther, as St. Thomas, uses the word lust as the inclusive term for sin, he follows the general tradition in regarding lust, in the narrower sense of sinful pleasure, as a consequence of man's turning from God, of his disobedience and pride. Sensuality is, in effect, the inordinate love for all creaturely and mutable values which results from the primal love of self, rather than love of God.

If we discount Hellenistic theology with its inclination to make

[9]*Summa theologiae*, Part II (Second Part), Question 164, Art. 1.

[10]*Summa*, Part II (First Part), Question 77, Art. 4.

[11]*Mala inclinatio cordis, inordinatio in volunte.*" Werke, *Weimarausgabe*, Vol. III, 453.

sensuality the primary sin and to derive it from the natural inclinations of the physical life, we must arrive at the conclusion that Christian theology in both its Augustinian and semi-Augustinian (Thomistic) forms, regards sensuality (even when it uses the words *concupiscentia* or *cupiditas* to denote sin in general) as a derivative of
the more primal sin of self-love. Sensuality represents a further
confusion consequent upon the original confusion of substituting the
self for God as the centre of existence. Man, having lost the true
centre of his life, is no longer able to maintain his own will as the
centre of himself. While we accept this general analysis it must be
pointed out that the explanations of the relation of sensuality to
self-love are unsatisfactory, partly because they are too vague and
partly because they are partially contradictory. They do not give a
precise or psychologically convincing account of how self-love results
in the further consequence of sensuality. Inasfar as the explanation
is precise it suffers from the contradiction that on the one hand the
self is said to have lost control over the impulses of the body while
on the other hand its undue gratification of these impulses is regarded as merely a further form of self-love. This inconsistency raises
an interesting question.

The question is: does the drunkard or the glutton merely press
self-love to the limit and lose all control over himself by his effort to
gratify a particular physical desire so unreservedly that its gratification comes in conflict with other desires? Or is lack of moderation
an effort to escape from the self? And does sexual license mean
merely the subordination of another person to the ego's self-love,
expressed in this case in an inordinate physical desire; or does un-
disciplined sex life represent an effort on the part of a disquieted and
disorganized self to escape from itself? Is sensuality, in other words,
a form of idolatry which makes the self god; or is it an alternative
idolatry in which the self, conscious of the inadequacy of its self-
worship, seeks escape by finding some other god?

The probable reason for the ambiguous and equivocal answers to
this question in the whole course of Christian theology is that there

is a little of both in sensuality. An analysis of various forms of sensuality may prove the point. Luxurious and extravagant living, the gratification of various sensual desires without limit, is on the one hand a form of self-love. Sometimes its purpose is to display power and to enhance prestige.[12] Sometimes it is not so much the servant of pride as the consequence of the freedom which power secures. Freed of the restraints, which poverty places upon all forms of expansive desires, the powerful individual indulges these desires without restraint. But sometimes luxurious living is not so much an advertisement of the ego's pride or even a simple and soft acquiescence with the various impulses of the physical life, as it is a frantic effort to escape from self. It betrays an uneasy conscience. The self is seeking to escape from itself and throws itself into any pursuit which will allow it to forget for a moment the inner tension of an uneasy conscience. The self, finding itself to be inadequate as the centre of its existence, seeks for another god amidst the various forces, processes and impulses of nature over which it ostensibly presides.

Drunkenness exhibits the same ambivalence of purpose. The drunkard sometimes seeks the abnormal stimulus of intoxicating drink in order to experience a sense of power and importance which normal life denies him. This type of intoxication represents a pathetic effort to make the self the centre of the world to a degree which normal reason with its consciousness of the ego's insignificance makes impossible. But drunkenness may have a quite different purpose. It may be desired not in order to enhance the ego but to escape from it.[13] It would not be inaccurate to define the first purpose of

[12]*Cf.* Thorstein Veblen, *Theory of the Leisure Class.*

[13]A modern psychoanalyst explains this twofold function of addiction to alcohol as follows: " 'Alcoholics' are almost invariably jolly, sociable, talkative fellows—who indeed seem obliged to make themselves well liked and are skillful in doing so. It takes very little penetration to discover, however, that this inordinate wish to be loved which compels them to be at so much pains to be charming . . . bespeaks a great underlying feeling of insecurity, a feeling which must constantly be denied, compensated for or anesthetized. . . . Such feelings of insecurity and inferiority

intoxication as the sinful ego-assertion which is rooted in anxiety and unduly compensates for the sense of inferiority and insecurity; while the second purpose of intoxication springs from the sense of guilt, or a state of perplexity in which a sense of guilt has been compounded with the previous sense of insecurity. The tension of this perplexity is too great to bear and results in an effort to escape consciousness completely. Thus drunkenness is merely a vivid form of the logic of sin which every heart reveals: Anxiety tempts the self to sin; the sin increases the insecurity which it was intended to alleviate until some escape from the whole tension of life is sought.

It has been previously noted that in all forms of Christian thought sexual passion is regarded as a particularly vivid form of, or at least occasion for, sensuality. The modern fashion is to deride this characteristic of Christian thought as morbid and as leading to an accentuation of sexual passion by its prurient repression. While it must be admitted that Christian thought on sex has frequently been unduly morbid and that dualistic forms of Christianity have regarded sex as evil of itself, there are nevertheless profound insights into the problem of sex in the Christian interpretation of sin, which modern thought has missed completely.

Both modern and traditional Christian thought would agree that sexual passion is a particularly powerful impulse which has expressed itself more vigorously throughout human history than the physical function of procreation requires. The usual modern explanation for this hypertrophy of the impulse is that it has been accentuated by repression.[14] This explanation fails to take account of

depend less upon actual reality comparisons than upon unconscious 'irrational' reasons, generally feelings of great frustration and rage and the fear and guilt which the rage induces. . . . A supplementary function of alcohol drinking is the further repression of such feelings and memories, which threaten to emerge and become again conscious." Karl A. Menninger, *Man Against Himself*, p. 169.

[14]Thus a modern psychologist writes: "In the lower animals in a state of nature, and natively in man, the sex drive is a glandular and physiological one, satisfied by direct (though learned) mechanisms when it arises. In civilized man the direct satisfaction of the sexual urges is

the fact that the social disciplines, which civilized society has thrown about the satisfaction of the sex impulse, are made necessary by the very fact that the impulse has exceeded the necessities of the preservation of the species, from the very beginning; and that even in primitive man sex has never been merely "glandular and physiological." The sexual, as every other physical, impulse in man is subject to and compounded with the freedom of man's spirit. It is not something which man could conceivably leave imbedded in some natural harmony of animal impulses. Its force reaches up into the highest pinnacles of human spirituality; and the insecurity of man in the heights of his freedom reaches down to the sex impulse as an instrument of compensation and as an avenue of escape.

From the standpoint of "pure nature" the sex impulse is a natural basis of "alteregoism"; for it is the method by which nature insures that the individual shall look beyond himself to the preservation of the species. The fact that upon the purely instinctive basis both the self and the other are involved in sexual passion makes it possible for spirit to use the natural stuff of sex for both the assertion of the ego and the flight of the ego into another. The sexual act thus becomes, in human life, a drama in which the domination of one life over the desires of another and the self-abnegation of the same life in favour of another are in bewildering conflict, and also in baffling intermixture. Furthermore these corruptions are complexly interlaced and compounded with a creative discovery of the self through its giving of itself to another. Thus the climax of sexual union is also a climax of creativity and sinfulness. The element of sin in the experience is not due to the fact that sex is in any sense sinful as such. But once sin is presupposed, that is, once the original harmony of nature is disturbed by man's self-love, the instincts of sex are

---

thwarted at their appearance in infancy and at their strengthening in the glandular changes of adolescence by social conventions and economic obstacles. This thwarting directs attention to the drive and attaches it to many substitute stimuli and substitute responses." L. F. Shaffer, *The Psychology of Adjustment,* p. 105.

particularly effective tools for both the assertion of the self and the flight from the self. This is what gives man's sex life the quality of uneasiness. It is both a vehicle of the primal sin of self-deification and the expression of an uneasy conscience, seeking to escape from self by the deification of another. The deification of the other is almost a literal description of many romantic sentiments in which attributes of perfection are assigned to the partner of love, beyond the capacities of any human being to bear, and therefore the cause of inevitable disillusionment.[15] While the more active part of the male and the more passive part of the female in the relation of the sexes may seem to point to self-deification as the particular sin of the male and the idolatry of the other as the particular temptation of the woman in the sexual act, yet both elements of sin are undoubtedly involved in both sexes.

An analysis of sexual passion thus verifies the correctness of the seemingly contradictory Christian interpretation of the relation of sensuality to self-love. It contains both a further extension of the sin of self-love and an effort to escape from it, an effort which results in the futility of worshipping the "creature rather than the Creator." To complete the analysis it must be mentioned that sexuality is subject to the development of one further degree of sensuality. Sexual passion may, by the very power it develops in the spiritual confusion of human sin, serve exactly the same purpose as drunkenness. It may serve as an anodyne. The ego, having found the worship both of self and of the other abortive, may use the passion of sex, without reference to self and the other, as a form of escape from the tension of life. The most corrupt forms of sensuality, as for instance in commercialized vice, have exactly this characteristic, that personal considerations are excluded from the satisfaction of the sexual impulse. It is a flight not to a false god but to nothingness. The strength of the passion which makes this momentary escape possible is itself a consequence of sin primarily and of an uneasy conscience consequent

---

[15]*Cf.*, for a convincing analysis of this aspect of sexual attachment, Emil Brunner, *Man in Revolt*, Ch. 15.

upon sin secondarily. If this analysis be correct it verifies the Augustinian conception of sensuality as a further sin which is also a punishment for the more primary sin; and justifies his conclusion: "God does not compel men to do these things; He only leaves those alone who deserve to be forsaken."[16]

The proof that sex is a very crucial point in the spirituality of sinful man is that shame is so universally attached to the performance of the sexual function. The profundity of the account of the Fall in Genesis cannot be overestimated. For though the account describes sin as primarily disobedience to God through the temptation of pride and not as sensual passion, it understands that guilt becomes involved in sensual passion after the Fall, for man becomes suddenly conscious of his sexuality: "And the eyes of them both were opened, and they knew that they were naked; and they sewed fig leaves together, and made themselves aprons" (Gen. 3:7).

The idea of modern psychology, particularly Freudian psychology, that this sense of guilt is abnormal, unnecessary and entirely due to the repressions of civilization, is a consequence of a too superficial view of the complexities of the relationship of spirit to nature. The sense of shame in relation to sex antedates the conventions of civilized society, just as the inordinate expression of sexual passion is the cause and not the consequence of the social disciplines and restraints which society has set around this area of life. A sophisti-

[16]The flight of the self into the other and the escape into oblivion are recurring themes in D. H. Lawrence's analysis of sex. Thus for instance he describes the experience of a man and woman in *Sons and Lovers:* "To know their own nothingness, to know the tremendous living flood which carried them always, gave them rest within themselves. If so great a magnificent power could overwhelm them, identify them altogether with itself, so that they knew that they were only grains in the tremendous heave that lifted every grass blade its little height and living thing, then why fret about themselves? They could let themselves be carried by life and they felt a sort of peace each in the other" (p. 436). It will be noted that the motif of escape into subconscious nature is more dominant than the sense of loss in the other.

Sometimes Lawrence explicitly identifies the sex impulse with the longing for death.

cated effort to destroy modesty and the sense of shame by the simple device of making the function of sex more public is therefore bound to aggravate rather than alleviate the difficulties of man's sex life.[17]

On the other hand it must be admitted that Christian puritanism and asceticism have usually been just as much in error in their effort to eliminate the sin attached to and expressed in sex by undue repressions. Such efforts have not only aggravated the sexual problem but have contributed to the self-righteous fury of those who sin covertly in matters of sex against those who sin overtly.[18]

The problem of sex, sensuality and sin is very complex and for that reason a constant source of confusion. Since sin is inevitably attached to sex, the dualist and ascetic is tempted to regard it as sinful *per se*. The anti-ascetic on the other hand, viewing the difficulties which arise from morbidity and undue prurience, imagines he can solve the problem by relaxing all restraints and by regarding minimal restraints only from the standpoint of social utility. The real situation is that man, granted his "fallen" nature, sins in his sex life but not because sex is essentially sinful. Or in other words, man, having lost the true centre of his life in God, falls into sensuality; and sex is the most obvious occasion for the expression of sensuality and the most vivid expression of it. Thus sex reveals sensuality to be first another and final form of self-love, secondly an effort to escape self-love by the deification of another and finally as an escape from the futilities of both forms of idolatry by a plunge into unconsciousness.

What sex reveals in regard to sensuality is not unique but typical in regard to the problem of sensuality in general. Whether in drunk-

[17]The criticism of Augustine, directed against the Cynics, is strikingly applicable to these modern theories: "It was against the modesty of natural shame that the Cynic philosophers struggled so hard in the error of their astonishing shamelessness; they thought that the intercourse between husband and wife was indeed honourable and that therefore it should be done in public. Such barefaced obscenity deserved to receive a doggish name; and so they went by the title of 'Cynics'" (Κῠνικοί— doglike). From *On Marriage and Concupiscence*, Book I, Ch. 25.

[18]This is the point of criticism, for instance, in Ibsen's *The Wild Duck* and Hawthorne's *The Scarlet Letter*.

enness, gluttony, sexual license, love of luxury, or any inordinate devotion to a mutable good, sensuality is always: (1) an extension of self-love to the point where it defeats its own ends; (2) an effort to escape the prison house of self by finding a god in a process or person outside the self; and (3) finally an effort to escape from the confusion which sin has created into some form of subconscious existence.

CHAPTER IX

ORIGINAL SIN AND MAN'S RESPONSIBILITY

T HE Christian doctrine of sin in its classical form offends both rationalists and moralists by maintaining the seemingly absurd position that man sins inevitably and by a fateful necessity but that he is nevertheless to be held responsible for actions which are prompted by an ineluctable fate. The explicit Scriptural foundation for the doctrine is given in Pauline teaching. On the one hand St. Paul insists that man's sinful glorification of himself is without excuse: "So that they are without excuse: because that, when they knew God, they glorified him not as God" (Romans 1:20-21). And on the other hand he regards human sin as an inevitable defect, involved in or derived from the sin of the first man: "Wherefore, as by one man sin entered into the world, and death by sin; and so death passed upon all men, for that all have sinned" (Romans 5:12). Augustine manages to compress both of these assertions of inevitability and of responsibility into one statement when he writes: "Man's nature was indeed at first created faultless and without sin; but nature as man now has it into which every one who is born from Adam, wants the Physician, being no longer in a healthy state. All good qualities which it still possesses . . . it has from the most High God, its Creator and Maker. But the flaw which darkens and weakens all these natural goods, it has not contracted from its blame-

241

less Creator . . . but from that *original sin* which it committed *of its own free will*."[1]

Here is the absurdity in a nutshell. Original sin, which is by definition an inherited corruption, or at least an inevitable one, is nevertheless not to be regarded as belonging to his essential nature and therefore is not outside the realm of his responsibility. Sin is natural for man in the sense that it is universal but not in the sense that it is necessary. Calvin makes this distinction very carefully: "We say therefore that man is corrupted by natural pravity but which did not originate from nature. We deny that it proceeded from nature to signify that it is rather an adventitious quality or accident, than a substantial quality originally innate." But again: "We call it natural that no one may suppose it to be contracted by every individual from corrupt habit, whereas it prevails over all by hereditary right."[2]

Sin is to be regarded as neither a necessity of man's nature nor yet as a pure caprice of his will. It proceeds rather from a defect of the will, for which reason it is not completely deliberate; but since it is the will in which the defect is found and the will presupposes freedom the defect cannot be attributed to a taint in man's nature. Here again Calvin is most precise: "Wherefore as Plato has been deservedly censured for imputing all sins to ignorance, so also we must reject the opinion of those who maintain that all sins proceed from deliberate malice and pravity. For we too much experience how frequently we fall into error even when our intentions are good. Our reason is overwhelmed with deceptions in so many forms. . . ."[3] The doctrine of original sin never escapes the logical absurdities in which these words of Calvin abound. Calvin remains within speaking terms of logic by insisting that sin is "an adventitious quality or accident" rather than a necessity. But if this were true it could not be as inevitable as Calvin's own doctrine assumes. Kierkegaard

[1] *Treatise on Nature and Grace*, Ch. 3. *Anti-Pelagian Works*, Vol. I, p. 238.
[2] *Institutes*, Book II, Ch. 1, par. 11.
[3] *Institutes*, Book II, Ch. 2, par. 25.

is more correct in his assertion that "sin comes as neither necessity nor accident."[4] Naturally a position which seems so untenable from a logical standpoint has been derided and scorned not only by non-Christian philosophers but by many Christian theologians.[5]

The whole crux of the doctrine of original sin lies in the seeming absurdity of the conception of free-will which underlies it. The Pauline doctrine, as elaborated by Augustine and the Reformers, insists on the one hand that the will of man is enslaved to sin and is incapable of fulfilling God's law. It may be free, declares Augustine, only it is not free to do good. "How then do miserable men dare to be proud of free-will before they are liberated or of their own strength after they are liberated?" Yet on the other hand the same Augustine insists upon the reality of free-will whenever he has cause to fear that the concept of original sin might threaten the idea of human responsibility: "Only let no man dare so to deny the freedom of the will as to desire to excuse sin." Calvin is willing to accept Augustine's emphasis upon free-will when it is intended to emphasize human responsibility and yet he rejects Peter Lombard's definition, which is practically identical with Augustine's, because he suspects that it contains the Catholic heresy of belief in some native

[4]*Begriff der Angst,* p. 95. He advances psychological reasons for this assertion which are not immediately relevant but yet important. He believes that the anomaly of something which is neither necessity nor accident can be explained by the relation of sin to anxiety.

[5]Consider Pascal's frank acceptance of the logical absurdity of the doctrine of original sin:

"In fact if man had never been corrupt, he would enjoy in his innocence both truth and happiness with assurance; and if man had always been corrupt he would have no idea of truth and bliss. But wretched as we are, and more so than if there were no greatness in our condition, we have an idea of happiness and cannot reach it. We perceive an image of truth and possess only a lie. . . . For it is beyond doubt that there is nothing which more shocks our reason than to say that the sin of the first man has rendered guilty those who, being so removed from its source, seem incapable of participating in it. . . . Certainly nothing offends us more rudely than this doctrine, and yet without this mystery, the most incomprehensible of all, we are incomprehensible to ourselves." *Pensées,* 434.

endowment of man, which remains untainted by sin. Lombard's assertion that man is free not in the sense that he has an equal choice between good and evil but in the sense that he does evil voluntarily and not by constraint is accepted by Calvin sneeringly: "That indeed is very true; but what end could it answer to decorate a thing so diminutive with a title so superb?"[6]

One could multiply examples in the thought of theologians of the Pauline tradition in which logical consistency is sacrificed in order to maintain on the one hand that the will is free in the sense that man is responsible for his sin, and is not free in the sense that he can, of his own will, do nothing but evil. Sometimes, as in Luther, the vehemence of the attack upon doctrines of free-will which seem to deny the inevitability of sin, is such that the inconsistency is eliminated in favour of a position which retains nothing of the doctrine of free-will but the term. In the words of Luther, "Free-will lies prostrate . . . for it must either be that the Kingdom of Satan in man is nothing at all and thus Christ will be made to lie; or if the Kingdom be such as Christ describes, free-will must be nothing but a beast of burden, the captive of Satan, which cannot be liberated unless the devil be first cast out by the finger of God."[7] In this, as in other instances, Luther seems to heighten the Augustinian doctrine in the interest of a greater consistency but at the price of imperiling one element in the paradox, the element of human responsibility. Free-will is denied to the point of offering man an excuse for his sin. It is obviously not easy to state the doctrine of original sin without falling into logical pitfalls on the one hand and without obscuring factors in man's moral experience on the other. Before considering the conformity of the doctrine to actual experience it is, therefore, important to ascertain whether alternative doctrines, which may boast the virtue of a higher consistency, may also be regarded as more consonant with the facts of human experience.

[6]*Institutes,* Vol. I, Book II, Ch. 2, par. 7
[7]*On the Bondage of the Will,* trans. by Reverend Henry Cole, London, p. 298.

II

PELAGIAN DOCTRINES

The various alternative doctrines all may be regarded as variants of what has become known in the history of Christian thought as Pelagianism. The essential characteristic of Pelagianism is its insistence that actual sins cannot be regarded as sinful or as involving guilt if they do not proceed from a will which is essentially free. The bias toward evil, that is, that aspect of sin which is designated as "original" in the classic doctrine is found not in man's will but in the inertia of nature. It is in other words not sin at all. Actual sin is on the other hand regarded as more unqualifiedly a conscious defiance of God's will and an explicit preference of evil, despite the knowledge of the good, than in the classical doctrine. While traditional Pelagianism is not sharply defined until it takes form in the classic debates between Augustine and his critics, it is not unfair to regard all Christian thinkers before Augustine as more or less Pelagian. They may not define actual sin so explicitly as a perverse choice of the will as does Pelagius but they do define original sin as essentially some force of inertia in nature and history. They are in other words sufficiently under Platonic influence to find no real place for the myth of the Fall in their thought, though of course they seek to incorporate the Biblical story in their system. Kierkegaard thinks it significant that the Greek church defines original sin to this day as "the sin of the forefather" (ἀμάρτημα προπᾰτορικόν),[1] a concept which refers merely to an historical occurrence and has no other connotation. There is according to J. B. Mozeley no suggestion of an enslaved will in any Christian theology before Augustine.[2] Essentially Platonic doctrines of human nature could be brought into ostensible conformity with Pauline thought by the simple and natural expedient of stripping the Pauline *sarx* of its special connotation as

[1] *Begriff der Angst*, p. 21.
[2] *The Augustinian Doctrine of Predestination*, p. 125.

the principle of sinfulness in man and accepting merely the literal meaning of "the flesh" which wars against the spirit.

It is not surprising that wherever essentially classical views of man prevail, as for instance in both secular and Christian modern liberalism, the bias toward evil should be defined as residing not in man's will but in some sloth of nature which man has inherited from his relation to the brute creation. This remains true even when, as in the thought of men like Schleiermacher and in the theology of the social gospel, this sloth is attributed to the institutions and traditions of history rather than purely to sensual passion or to the finiteness of the mind.[3] By thus placing the inherited sloth in history rather than in each man's own sensual nature, some justice is done to the actual historical continuum in which every human action takes place, but the bias toward evil is always outside and never inside a particular will. The theory is thus virtually identical with the modern secular idea of the "cultural lag" as the explanation of evil in human actions.

Frequently the explicit purpose and always the inevitable consequence of this denial of individual responsibility for the bias toward evil is to increase the sense of responsibility for an individual evil

[3]Schleiermacher's explanation of original sin is: "Just as the Ego, with reference to each later generation, is due to the action of the one before it, so the sinful self-assertiveness of sense, proceeding as it does from its earlier development, has a more remote source than the individual's own life. But once God consciousness has emerged as a definite and effective agency and capable of growth, then every moment in which it does not manifest itself in comparison with earlier moments is an arrest originating in the doer himself and is veritable sin." Schleiermacher admits that this explanation destroys the connotation of "sin" and leaves only the idea of "original" (*Erb*) in the concept of original sin. *The Christian Faith*, par. 69. Walter Rauschenbusch places the primary emphasis on the transmission of sin through social institutions. He writes: "Theology has done considerable harm in concentrating the attention of religious minds on the biological transmission of evil. It has diverted our minds from the power of social transmission, from the authority of the social group in justifying, urging, and idealizing wrong, and from the decisive influence of economic profit in the defense and propagation of evil." *A Theology for the Social Gospel*, p. 67.

act. The argument by which this is done has not varied from the day of Augustine's critics. Every modern criticism of the Augustinian doctrine has been anticipated by Augustine's contemporaries. The logical inconsistency of the doctrine is emphasized. It is insisted that man cannot be held responsible for keeping a law or achieving an ideal if he lacks the capacity to do so. Thus the Kantian "I ought, therefore I can" is neatly anticipated in the argument of Cœlestius: "We have to inquire whether a man is commanded to be without sin; for either he is unable so to live and then there is no such commandment; or else if there be such a commandment he has the ability."[4]

The effect of such an effort to increase the sense of responsibility for individual sinful acts by emphasizing the freedom in which they are committed, is to make every sinful act appear as a conscious choice of evil in defiance of a known good. It is precisely to such acts of sheer perversity that F. R. Tennant confines the idea of sin in the most elaborate of modern Pelagian treatises.[5] Schleiermacher significantly makes no distinction between sin and the consciousness of sin. "We must insist on the fact," he writes, "that sin in general exists only insofar as there is consciousness of it."[6] Pelagianism in short ascribes all sins to "deliberate malice and pravity," to use Calvin's phrase.

The official Catholic doctrine of original sin, usually regarded as "Semi-Pelagian," does not greatly vary the emphasis of Pelagianism.

[4]Augustine, *Anti-Pelagian Works*, Vol. I, *Treatise on Man's Perfection in Righteousness*, p. 317. The logical difficulty in the doctrine of original sin is succinctly stated in Cœlestius' words: "We must ask whether sin comes from necessity or from choice. If from necessity then it is not sin; if from choice then it can be avoided." *Ibid.*, p. 315. Or again: "We must ask any one who denies man's ability to live without sin of what sort sin is. Is it such as can be avoided? Or is it unavoidable? If it is unavoidable then it is not sin; if it can be avoided then man can live without the sin which can be avoided." *Ibid.*, p. 315.

[5]*Cf.* F. R. Tennant, *The Concept of Sin*, and *The Origin and Propagation of Sin*.

[6]*Op. cit.*, par. 68.

The doctrine presupposes a distinction between the *pura naturalia,* the essential character of man as man and a "further gift" (*donum superadditum*) which God bestowed upon man in addition to his natural creation. This distinction, first suggested by Athanasius and achieving its final definition in the system of Aquinas, enables Catholic theology to incorporate the Biblical idea of the Fall without disturbing the concept of original sin as an inertia of nature. For in the Fall, the *donum superadditum* is lost and, until restored by sacramental grace, man is subject to the natural limitations of his finite nature.[7] Original sin is thus described negatively. It is the privation of something which does not belong to man essentially and, therefore, cannot be regarded as a corruption of his essential nature. As in Pelagianism a basic purpose of the doctrine is to guard against conceptions of total depravity which destroy the idea of responsibility and thereby vitiate the very meaning of sin.[8] The logical difficulties of the Augustinian doctrine are thus avoided, and the peril of denying the structure of freedom in the assertion of its corruption is averted, as in Pelagianism. But the question remains whether either Pelagianism or Semi-Pelagianism is true to the psychological and moral facts in human wrong-doing.

III

AUGUSTINIAN DOCTRINES

The truth is that, absurd as the classical Pauline doctrine of original sin may seem to be at first blush, its prestige as a part of the Christian

[7]Thomas Aquinas writes: "The privation of original justice whereby the will is made subject to God, is the formal element in original sin, while every other disorder of the soul's powers is a kind of material element in respect to original sin. . . . Hence original sin is concupiscence materially and privation of original justice formally." *Summa theol.* Part Two (First Part), Second Number, Question 83, Art. I.

[8]Aquinas declares: "Sin cannot take away entirely from man the fact that he is a rational being, for then he would no longer be capable of sin. Wherefore it is not possible for this good of nature to be destroyed entirely." *Ibid.* Question 85, Art. 2.

truth is preserved, and perennially re-established, against the attacks of rationalists and simple moralists by its ability to throw light upon complex factors in human behaviour which constantly escape the moralists. It may be valuable to use a simple example of contemporary history to prove the point. Modern religious nationalism is obviously a highly explicit expression of the collective pride in which all human behaviour is involved and which Christian faith regards as the quintessence of sin. Inasfar as this pride issues in specific acts of cruelty, such as the persecution of the Jews, these acts obviously cannot be defined as proceeding from a deliberate and malicious preference for evil in defiance of the good. It is true of course that a modern devotee of the religion of race and nation regards his nation as the final good more deliberately than a primitive tribalist, who merely assumed that his collective life was the end of existence. Yet it would be fallacious to assume that a Nazi gives unqualified devotion to the qualified and conditioned value of his race and nation by a consciously perverse choice of the lesser against the higher good. But it would be equally erroneous to absolve the religious nationalist of responsibility merely because his choice is not consciously perverse.

He is obviously tempted to his attitude of self-glorification by feelings of inferiority which he shares with all mankind as a common fate but which in his case have been accentuated by historical vicissitudes to which his class and nation have been subjected. To understand this may prompt forgiveness but it cannot eliminate responsibility. For the general insecurity of man and the special sense of inferiority of his class and nation do not lead necessarily to the excessive self-assertion in which he is involved. They do not lead to sin unless sin is first presupposed. In other words actual sin is involved in the bias toward sin which issues in specific acts of cruelty.

If the sin of self-glorification is not an inevitable consequence of anxiety and insecurity it is even less the natural consequence of a primitive herd impulse which has not yet yielded to higher and more universal loyalties. The "cultural lag" theory of human evil is completely irrelevant to the analysis of his sin. For the sin of the religious nationalist represents a "conscious" defiance of more universal standards of loyalty which had been consciously established. In that sense it conforms perfectly to the Pauline doctrine of the relation of law to sin. Law makes sin more explicit: "I had not known lust, except the law had said, Thou shalt not covet." Sin is thus both unconscious and conscious. The degree of conscious choice may vary in specific instances of course. Yet even the more conscious choices do not come completely into the category of conscious perversity. Even particular acts of cruelty are probably not the consequence of a conscious love of evil, nor do they find an obvious satisfaction in inflicting pain upon others. They are, rather, the consequence of sin's pathetic vicious circle. The attempt to maintain one's own pride and self-respect by holding others in contempt adds an uneasy conscience to the general insecurity which the attitude of contempt is meant to alleviate. Stronger and stronger measures must therefore be taken to ward off the final breakdown. Here the Pauline psychology is more clarifying than any alternative analysis. The specific act of sin is the consequence of blindness: "Their foolish heart was darkened." But this blindness is not merely the blindness of man's natural ignorance. It is derived from a "vain imagination." It was because they "professed themselves wise" that they "became fools."

It is clear from such analysis of religious nationalism in terms of Pauline psychology that the distinction between original sin and actual sin cannot be made as clearly as is assumed in moralistic treatises on sin. The actual sin follows more inevitably from the bias toward sin than is usually assumed. On the other hand the bias toward sin is something more than a mere lag of nature or physical impulse or historical circumstance. There is, in other words, less freedom in the actual sin and more responsibility for the bias toward sin (original sin) than moralistic interpretations can understand.

The actual sin is the consequence of the temptation of anxiety in which all life stands. But anxiety alone is neither actual nor original sin. Sin does not flow necessarily from it. Consequently the bias toward sin from which actual sin-flows is anxiety plus sin. Or, in the words of Kierkegaard, sin presupposes itself. Man could not be tempted if he had not already sinned.

IV

TEMPTATION AND INEVITABILITY OF SIN

The full complexity of the psychological facts which validate the doctrine of original sin must be analysed, first in terms of the relation of temptation to the inevitability of sin. Such an analysis may make it plain why man sins inevitably, yet without escaping responsibility for his sin. The temptation to sin lies, as previously observed, in the human situation itself. This situation is that man as spirit transcends the temporal and natural process in which he is involved and also transcends himself. Thus his freedom is the basis of his creativity but it is also his temptation. Since he is involved in the contingencies and necessities of the natural process on the one hand and since, on the other, he stands outside of them and foresees their caprices and perils, he is anxious. In his anxiety he seeks to transmute his finiteness into infinity, his weakness into strength, his dependence into independence. He seeks in other words to escape finiteness and weakness by a quantitative rather than qualitative development of his life. The quantitative antithesis of finiteness is infinity. The qualitative possibility of human life is its obedient subjection to the will of God. This possibility is expressed in the words of Jesus: "He that loseth his life for my sake shall find it." (Mt. 10:39).

It will be noted that the Christian statement of the ideal possibility does not involve self-negation but self-realization. The self is, in other words, not evil by reason of being a particular self and its salvation does not consist in absorption into the eternal. Neither is the self divided, as in Hegelianism, into a particular or empirical and a universal self; and salvation does not consist in sloughing off its particularity and achieving universality. The Christian view of the self is only possible from the standpoint of Christian theism in which God is not merely the *x* of the unconditioned or the undifferentiated eternal. God is revealed as loving will; and His will is active in creation, judgment and redemption. The highest self-realization for the self is therefore not the destruction of its particularity but the subjection of its particular will to the universal will.

But the self lacks the faith and trust to subject itself to God. It seeks to establish itself independently. It seeks to find its life and thereby loses it. For the self which it asserts is less than the true self. It is the self in all the contingent and arbitrary factors of its immediate situation. By asserting these contingent and arbitrary factors of an immediate situation, the self loses its true self. It increases its insecurity because it gives its immediate necessities a consideration which they do not deserve and which they cannot have without disturbing the harmony of creation. By giving life a false centre, the self then destroys the real possibilities for itself and others. Hence the relation of injustice to pride, and the vicious circle of injustice, increasing as it does the insecurity which pride was intended to overcome.

The sin of the inordinate self-love thus points to the prior sin of lack of trust in God. The anxiety of unbelief is not merely the fear which comes from ignorance of God. "Anxiety," declares Kierkegaard, "is the dizziness of freedom,"[1] but it is significant that the same freedom which tempts to anxiety also contains the ideal possibility of knowing God. Here the Pauline psychology is penetrating and significant. St. Paul declares that man is without excuse because "the invisible things of him from the creation of the world are clearly seen, being understood by the things that are made, even his eternal power and Godhead" (Romans 1:20). The anxiety of freedom leads to sin only if the prior sin of unbelief is assumed. This is the meaning of Kierkegaard's assertion that sin posits itself.[2]

The sin of man's excessive and inordinate love of self is thus

[1]*Begriff der Angst*, p. 57.
[2]*Ibid.*, p. 27.

neither merely the drag of man's animal nature upon his more universal loyalties, nor yet the necessary consequence of human freedom and self-transcendence. It is more plausibly the consequence of the latter than of the former because the survival impulse of animal nature lacks precisely those boundless and limitless tendencies of human desires. Inordinate self-love is occasioned by the introduction of the perspective of the eternal into natural and human finiteness. But it is a false eternal. It consists in the transmutation of "mutable good" into infinity. This boundless character of human desires is an unnatural rather than natural fruit of man's relation to the temporal process on the one hand and to eternity on the other. If man knew, loved and obeyed God as the author and end of his existence, a proper limit would be set for his desires including the natural impulse of survival.[3]

The fact that the lie is so deeply involved in the sin of self-glorification and that man cannot love himself inordinately without pretending that it is not his, but a universal, interest which he is supporting, is a further proof that sin presupposes itself and that it is neither ignorance nor yet the ignorance of ignorance which forces the self to sin. Rather it "holds the truth in unrighteousness."

The idea that the inevitability of sin is not due merely to the strength of the temptation in which man stands by reason of his relation to both the temporal process and eternity, is most perfectly expressed in the scriptural words: "Let no man say when he is tempted, I am tempted of God: for God cannot be tempted with evil, neither tempteth he any man: But every man is tempted, when

[3]Failure to understand the difference between a natural and an unnatural though inevitable characteristic of human behaviour confuses otherwise clear analyses such as that of Bertrand Russell's: He declares: "Between man and other animals there are various differences some intellectual and some emotional. One chief emotional difference is that human desires, unlike those of animals, are essentially boundless and incapable of complete satisfaction." *Power,* p. 9.
Thus Mr. Russell is forced to regard the boundless will-to-power as natural in his analysis of human nature and as the very principle of evil in his analysis of society.

he is drawn away of his own lust, and enticed. Then when lust hath conceived, it bringeth forth sin: and sin, when it is finished, bringeth forth death."[4] But on the other hand the idea that the situation of finiteness and freedom is a temptation once evil has entered it and that evil does enter it prior to any human action is expressed in Biblical thought by the conception of the devil. The devil is a fallen angel, who fell because he sought to lift himself above his measure and who in turn insinuates temptation into human life. The sin of each individual is preceded by Adam's sin: but even this first sin of history is not the first sin. One may, in other words, go farther back than human history and still not escape the paradoxical conclusion that the situation of finiteness and freedom would not lead to sin if sin were not already introduced into the situation. This is, in the words of Kierkegaard, the "qualitative leap" of sin and reveals the paradoxical relation of inevitability and responsibility. Sin can never be traced merely to the temptation arising from a particular situation or condition in which man as man finds himself or in which particular men find themselves. Nor can the temptation which is compounded of a situation of finiteness and freedom, plus the fact of sin, be regarded as leading necessarily to sin in the life of each individual, if again sin is not first presupposed in that life. For this reason even the knowledge of inevitability does not extinguish the sense of responsibility.

[4]James 1: 13–15.
This word succinctly expresses a general attitude of the Bible which places it in opposition to all philosophical explanations which attribute the inevitability of sin to the power of temptation. One of the most ingenious of these is the theory of Schelling, who, borrowing from the mystic system of Jacob Boehme, declares that God has a "foundation that He may be"; only this is not outside himself but within him and he has within him a nature which though it belongs to himself is nevertheless different from him. In God this foundation, this "dark ground," is not in conflict with His love, but in man it "operates incessantly and arouses egotism and a particularized will, just in order that the will to love may arise in contrast to it." Schelling, *Human Freedom*, trans. by J. Gutman, pp. 51–53. Thus in this view sin is not only a prerequisite of virtue but a consequence of the divine nature.

V

RESPONSIBILITY DESPITE INEVITABILITY

The fact of responsibility is attested by the feeling of remorse or repentance which follows the sinful action. From an exterior view not only sin in general but any particular sin may seem to be the necessary consequence of previous temptations. A simple determinism is thus a natural characteristic of all social interpretations of human actions. But the interior view does not allow this interpretation. The self, which is privy to the rationalizations and processes of self-deception which accompanied and must accompany the sinful act, cannot accept and does not accept the simple determinism of the exterior view. Its contemplation of its act involves both the discovery and the reassertion of its freedom. It discovers that some degree of conscious dishonesty accompanied the act, which means that the self was not deterministically and blindly involved in it. Its discovery of that fact in contemplation is a further degree of the assertion of freedom than is possible in the moment of action.

The remorse and repentance which are consequent upon such contemplation are similar in their acknowledgment of freedom and responsibility and their implied assertion of it. They differ in the fact that repentance is the expression of freedom and faith while remorse is the expression of freedom without faith. The one is the "Godly sorrow" of which St. Paul speaks, and the other is "the sorrow of this world which worketh death." It is, in other words, the despair into which sin transmutes the anxiety which precedes sin.

There are of course many cases in which the self seems so deeply involved in its own deceptions and so habituated to standards of action which may have once been regarded as sinful that it seems capable of neither repentance nor remorse. This complacency is possible on many levels of life from that of a natural paganism in which the freedom of spirit is not fully developed, to refined forms of Pharisaism in which pride as self-righteousness obscures the sin of pride itself. It is not true, however, that habitual sin can ever destroy the uneasy conscience so completely as to remove the individual from the realm of moral responsibility to the realm of unmoral nature.[5]

The religious sacrifices of nature religions, in which primitive peoples express an uneasy conscience and assume that natural catastrophe is the expression of their god's anger against their sins, is a proof of the reality of some degree of freedom even in primitive life.[6] The brutality with which a Pharisee of every age resists those who puncture his pretensions proves the uneasiness of his conscience. The insecurity of sin is always a double insecurity. It must seek to hide not only the original finiteness of perspective and relativity of value which it is the purpose of sin to hide, but also the dishonesty by which it has sought to obscure these. The fury with which oligarchs, dictators, priest-kings, ancient and modern, and ideological pretenders turn upon their critics and foes is clearly the fury of an uneasy conscience, though it must not be assumed that such a conscience is always fully conscious of itself.

An uneasy conscience which is not fully conscious of itself is the root of further sin, because the self strives desperately to ward off the *dénouement* of either remorse or repentance by accusing others, seeking either to make them responsible for the sins of the self, or attributing worse sins to them. There is a certain plausibility in this self-defense, because social sources of particular sins may always be

[5]James Martineau erroneously regards the state of habitual sin as a reversion to natural necessity. He writes: "The forfeiture of freedom, the relapse into automatic necessity, is doubtless a most fearful penalty for persistent unfaithfulness; but once incurred it alters the complexion of all subsequent acts. They no longer form fresh constituents in the aggregate of guilt but stand outside in a separate record after its account is closed. . . . The first impulse of the prophets of righteousness when they see him thus is, 'he cannot cease from sin' and perhaps to predict for him eternal retribution; but looking a little deeper, they will rather say, 'he has lost the privilege of sin and sunk away from the rank of persons into the destiny of things." *A Study of Religion*, II, 108.

[6]*Cf.* W. E. Hocking, *The Meaning of God in Human Experience*, p. 235.

found and even the worst criminal can gain a certain temporary self-respect by finding some one who seems more deeply involved in disaster than he is. On the other hand such social comparisons always increase the force of sin, for they are efforts to hide a transaction between the self and God, even though God is not explicitly known to the sinner. While all particular sins have both social sources and social consequences, the real essence of sin can be understood only in the vertical dimension of the soul's relation to God because the freedom of the self stands outside all relations, and therefore has no other judge but God.[7] It is for this reason that a profound insight into the character of sin must lead to the confession, "Against thee, thee only, have I sinned, and done this evil in thy sight" (Ps. 51). All experiences of an uneasy conscience, of remorse and of repentance, are therefore religious experiences, though they are not always explicitly or consciously religious. Experiences of repentance, in distinction to remorse, presuppose some knowledge of God. They may not be consciously related to Biblical revelation but yet they do presuppose some, at least dim, awareness of God as redeemer as well as God as judge. For without the knowledge of divine love remorse cannot be transmuted into repentance. If man recognizes only judgment and knows only that his sin is discovered, he cannot rise above the despair of remorse to the hope of repentance.

The vertical dimension of the experience of remorse and repentance explains why there is no level of moral goodness upon which the sense of guilt can be eliminated. In fact the sense of guilt rises with moral sensitivity: "There are only two kinds of men," declares Pascal, "the righteous who believe themselves sinners; the rest, sinners, who believe themselves righteous." Pascal does not fully appreciate, at least as far as this statement is concerned, how infinite may be the shades of awareness of guilt from the complacency of those

---

[7]*Cf.* 1 Cor. 4:3f.: "But with me it is a very small thing that I should be judged of you, or of man's judgement: yea, I judge not mine own self. For I know nothing against myself; yet am I not hereby justified: but he that judgeth me is the Lord."

who are spiritually blind to the sensitivity of the saint who knows that he is not a saint. Yet it is obviously true that awareness of guilt arises with spiritual sensitivity and that such an awareness will be regarded as morbid only by moralists who have no true knowledge of the soul and God. The saint's awareness of guilt is no illusion. The fact is that sin expresses itself most terribly in its most subtle forms. The sinful identification of the contingent self with God is less crass on the higher levels of the spiritual life but it may be the more dangerous for being the more plausible. An example from the realm of political life may explain why this is true. The inevitable partiality of even the most impartial court is more dangerous to justice than the obvious partiality of contending political factions in society, which the impartiality of the court is intended to resolve. The partiality of the contending forces is so obvious that it can be discounted. The partiality of the court, on the other hand, is obscured by its prestige of impartiality. Relative degrees of impartiality in judicial tribunals are important achievements in political life. But without a judgment upon even the best judicial process from a higher level of judgment, the best becomes the worst.[8]

The fact that the sense of guilt rises vertically with all moral achievement and is, therefore, not assuaged by it nor subject to diminution or addition by favourable and unfavourable social opinion, throws a significant light on the relation of freedom to sin. The ultimate proof of the freedom of the human spirit is its own recognition that its will is not free to choose between good and evil. For in the highest reaches of the freedom of the spirit, the self discovers in contemplation and retrospect that previous actions have invariably confused the ultimate reality and value, which the self as spirit senses, with the immediate necessities of the self. If the self assumes that

[8]Surely this is the significance of the words of Isaiah: "He maketh the judges of the earth as vanity" (Is. 40:23). In one of the great documents of social protest in Egypt, "The Eloquent Peasant," the accused peasant standing in the court of the Grand Visier declares: "Thou hast been set as a dam to save the poor man from drowning, but behold thou art thyself the flood." Cf. J. H. Breasted, *The Dawn of Conscience*, p. 190.

because it realizes this fact in past actions it will be able to avoid the corruption in future actions, it will merely fall prey to the Pharisaic fallacy.

This difference between the self in contemplation and the self in action must not be regarded as synonymous with the distinction between the self as spirit and the self as natural vitality. To regard the two distinctions as identical is a plausible error, and one which lies at the root of all idealistic interpretations of man. But we have already discovered that the sins of the self in action are possible only because the freedom of spirit opens up the deterministic causal chains of the self in nature and tempts the self to assume dignities, to grasp after securities and to claim sanctities which do not belong to it. The contemplating self which becomes conscious of its sins does not therefore view some other empirical self which is not, properly speaking, its true self. There is only one self. Sometimes the self acts and sometimes it contemplates its actions. When it acts it falsely claims ultimate value for its relative necessities and falsely identifies its life with the claims of life *per se*. In contemplation it has a clearer view of the total human situation and becomes conscious, in some degree, of the confusion and dishonesty involved in its action. It must not be assumed, however, that the contemplating self is the universal self, judging the finite and empirical self. At its best the contemplating self is the finite self which has become conscious of its finiteness and its relation to God as the limit and the fulfillment of its finiteness. When the self in contemplation becomes contritely aware of its guilt in action it may transmute this realization into a higher degree of honesty in subsequent actions. Repentance may lead to "fruits meet for repentance"; and differences between the moral quality in the lives of complacent and of contrite individuals are bound to be discovered by observers. But the self cannot make too much of them; for its real standard is not what others do or fail to do. Its real standard is its own essential self and this in turn has only God's will as norm. It must know that judged by that standard, the experience of contrition does not prevent the self from new dishonesties in subsequent actions. The self, even in contemplation, remains the finite self. In one moment it may measure its situation and discover its sin. In the next moment it will be betrayed by anxiety into sin. Even the distinction between contemplation and action must, therefore, not be taken too literally. For any contemplation which is concerned with the interests, hopes, fears and ambitions of this anxious finite self belongs properly in the field of action; for it is a preparation for a false identification of the immediate and the ultimate of which no action is free.

We cannot, therefore, escape the ultimate paradox that the final exercise of freedom in the transcendent human spirit is its recognition of the false use of that freedom in action. Man is most free in the discovery that he is not free. This paradox has been obscured by most Pelagians and by many Augustinians. The Pelagians have been too intent to assert the integrity of man's freedom to realize that the discovery of this freedom also involves the discovery of man's guilt. The Augustinians on the other hand have been so concerned to prove that the freedom of man is corrupted by sin that they have not fully understood that the discovery of this sinful taint is an achievement of freedom.

VI

LITERALISTIC ERRORS

The paradox that human freedom is most perfectly discovered and asserted in the realization of the bondage of the will is easily obscured. Unfortunately the confusion revealed in the debate between Pelagians and Augustinians has been further aggravated by the literalism of the Augustinians. In countering the simple moralism of the Pelagians they insisted on interpreting original sin as an inherited taint. Thus they converted the doctrine of the inevitability of sin into a dogma which asserted that sin had a natural history. Thereby they gave their Pelagian critics an unnecessary advantage in the debate, which the latter have never been slow to seize.[1]

[1]One can never be certain whether Pelagian and Semi-Pelagian criticisms of the Pauline doctrine are primarily directed against the literalistic

While Augustinian theology abounds in doctrines of original sin which equate it with the idea of an inherited corruption and which frequently make concupiscence in generation the agent of this inheritance, it is significant that Christian thought has always had some suggestions of the representative rather than historical character of Adam's sin. The idea of Adam as representative man allowed it to escape the historical-literalistic illusion. The very fountain-source of the doctrine of original sin, the thought of St. Paul, expresses the idea of original sin in terms which allow, and which possibly compel the conclusion that St. Paul believed each man to be related to Adam's sin in terms of "seminal identity" rather than historical inheritance. The Pauline words are: "Wherefore as by one man sin entered the world and death by sin; and so death passed to all men *for that all have sinned.*"[2] The idea of a mystical identity between Adam and all men is found in Irenæus and is explicitly formulated in Ambrose.[3] Even Augustine, who insists on the theory of an inherited corruption, inserts an interesting qualification which points in the same direction when he quotes the Pauline passage, Romans 3:23, so that it reads: " 'For all have sinned'—*whether in Adam or in themselves*—'and come short of the glory of God.' " The same idea struggles for, and achieves partial, expressions in some of the explana-

---

corruptions of it or against its basic absurd but profound insights. A good instance of such a criticism is to be found in a modern Anglo-Catholic treatise on the subject: "Nor is it necessary to do more than point out the absurdity of the theory of 'original guilt,' which asserts that human beings are held responsible to an all-just Judge for an act which they did not commit and for physiological and psychological facts which they cannot help. . . . Those (if there be any such) who demand formal disproof of the belief that what is *ex hypothesi* an inherited psychological malady is regarded by God in the light of a voluntarily committed crime, may be referred to the scathing satire of Samuel Butler's *Erewhon.*" N. P. Williams, *Ideas of the Fall and Original Sin*, p. 381.

[2]*Cf.* C. H. Dodd, *Epistle to the Romans*, p. 79.

[3]He writes: "So then Adam is in each one of us, for in him human nature itself sinned." *Apol. David altera*, 71.

tions of original sin in Calvin, even while he insists on the idea of inheritance.[4]

It is obviously necessary to eliminate the literalistic illusions in the doctrine of original sin if the paradox of inevitability and responsibility is to be fully understood; for the theory of an inherited second nature is as clearly destructive of the idea of responsibility for sin as rationalistic and dualistic theories which attribute human evil to the inertia of nature.[5] When this literalistic confusion is eliminated the truth of the doctrine of original sin is more clearly revealed; but it must be understood that even in this form the doctrine remains absurd from the standpoint of a pure rationalism, for it expresses a relation between fate and freedom which cannot be fully rationalized, unless the paradox be accepted as a rational understanding of the limits of rationality and as an expression of faith that a rationally irresolvable contradiction may point to a truth which logic cannot contain. Formally there can be of course no conflict between logic

[4] *Cf. Institutes,* Book II, Ch. i, par. 7. "We ought to be satisfied with this, that the Lord deposited with Adam the endowments he chose to confer on human nature; and therefore that when he lost the favours he had received *he lost them not only for himself* but for us all. Who will be solicitous about a transmission of the soul when he hears that Adam received the ornaments that he lost, *no less for us* than for himself? That they were given, not to one man only, *but to the whole human nature.*" It must be admitted that Calvin confines Adam's identity with human nature to the original endowments. The loss of these endowments is conceived in terms of an hereditary relation between Adam and subsequent men, for Calvin continues: "For the children were so vitiated in their parent that they became contagious to their descendants; there was in Adam such a spring of corruption that it is transfused from parents to children in a perpetual stream."

[5] Harnack declares: "The doctrine of original sin leads to Manichean dualism, which Augustine never surmounted, and is accordingly an impious and foolish dogma. . . . His doctrine of concupiscence conduces the same view." *History of Dogma,* Vol. V, p. 217. Harnack's criticisms must of course be discounted, as those of other Christian moralists, because he is as unable to understand the doctrine of original sin, when stripped of its literalistic errors, as when stated in its crude form. His assertion that "turn as he will, Augustine affirms an evil nature and therefore a diabolical creator of the world" is simply not true.

and truth. The laws of logic are reason's guard against chaos in the realm of truth. They eliminate contradictory assertions. But there is no resource in logical rules to help us understand complex phenomena, exhibiting characteristics which seem to require that they be placed into contradictory categories of reason. Loyalty to all the facts may require a provisional defiance of logic, lest complexity in the facts of experience be denied for the sake of a premature logical consistency. Hegel's "dialectic" is a logic invented for the purpose of doing justice to the fact of "becoming" as a phenomenon which belongs into the category of neither "being" nor "nonbeing."

The Christian doctrine of original sin with its seemingly contradictory assertions about the inevitability of sin and man's responsibility for sin is a dialectical truth which does justice to the fact that man's self-love and self-centredness is inevitable, but not in such a way as to fit into the the category of natural necessity. It is within and by his freedom that man sins. The final paradox is that the discovery of the inevitability of sin is man's highest assertion of freedom. The fact that the discovery of sin invariably leads to the Pharisaic illusion that such a discovery guarantees sinlessness in subsequent actions is a revelation of the way in which freedom becomes an accomplice of sin. It is at this point that the final battle between humility and human self-esteem is fought.

Kierkegaard's explanation of the dialectical relation of freedom and fate in sin is one of the profoundest in Christian thought. He writes: "The concept of sin and guilt does not emerge in its profoundest sense in paganism. If it did paganism would be destroyed by the contradiction that man becomes guilty by fate. . . . Christianity is born in this very contradiction. The concept of sin and guilt presupposes the individual as individual. There is no concern for his relation to any cosmic or past totality. The only concern is that he is guilty; and yet he is supposed to become guilty through fate, the very fate about which there is no concern. And thereby he becomes something which resolves the concept of fate, and to become that through fate! If this contradiction is wrongly understood it leads to false concepts of original sin. Rightly understood it leads to a true concept, to the idea namely that every individual is itself and the race and that the later individual is not significantly differentiated from the first man. In the possibility of anxiety freedom is lost, for it is overwhelmed by fate. Yet now it arises in reality but with the explanation that it has become guilty."[6]

[6]*Begriff der Angst,* p. 105.

CHAPTER X

JUSTITIA ORIGINALIS

"THE greatness of man," declares Pascal, "is so evident that it is even proved by his wretchedness. For what in animals is called nature we call wretchedness in man; by which we recognize that, his nature now being like that of animals, he has fallen from a better nature which once was his. For who is unhappy at not being a king except a deposed king? . . . Who is unhappy at having only one mouth? And who is not unhappy at having only one eye? Probably no man ever ventured to mourn at not having three eyes. But any one is inconsolable at having none."[1] No man, however deeply involved in sin, is able to regard the misery of sin as normal. Some memory of a previous condition of blessedness seems to linger in his soul; some echo of the law which he has violated seems to resound in his conscience. Every effort to give the habits of sin the appearance of normality betrays something of the frenzy of an uneasy conscience. The contrast between what man is truly and essentially and what he has become is apparent even to those who do not understand that this contrast is to be found in every human being and has its seat in the will of man himself. Those who do not understand the real nature of sin sometimes portray the contrast in terms of various levels of human culture. "The superman built the aeroplane," de-

[1] Pascal, *Pensées*, par. 409.

clared a modern scientist recently, "but the ape-man got ahold of it."
Or sometimes they regard the contrast as one between the good man
and his lagging and imperfect institutions.[2] The sense of a conflict
between what man is and ought to be finds universal expression,
even though the explanations of the conflict are usually contradictory
and confused.

This universal testimony of human experience is the most persua-
sive refutation of any theory of human depravity which denies that
man has any knowledge of the good which sin has destroyed. It is
true of course, as Christian faith declares, that any human statement
of the blessedness and perfection which are man's proper state and
nature, are themselves coloured by sin, so that Christ, as the second
Adam, is required to restore the image of the first Adam as he was
before the Fall. The reason why there is a heightened sense of sin
in Christianity is that the vision of Christ heightens the contrast
between what man is truly and what he has become; and destroys
the prestige of normality which sinful forms of life periodically
achieve in the world. Yet faith in Christ could find no lodging place
in the human soul, were it not uneasy about the contrast between
its true and its present state; though this same faith in Christ also
clarifies that contrast. Men who have fallen deeply into the wretchedness of sin are never easy in their minds; but their uneasiness is frequently increased by some vivid reminder of the innocency of their
childhood or the aspirations of their youth.

There are no forms of disease or corruption, short of death, which
do not reveal something of the healthful structure which they have
corrupted. The blind eye is still an eye, though it may be completely
sightless. The aberrations of an insane mind betray coherences in
the very welter of incoherences which only a human and not an
animal mind could conceive. The disorder of war would not be an
evil did it not operate within and against some kind of harmony
and interdependence of nations; and it could not be evil if it could
not avail itself of the good of internal and domestic peace, from

[2] *Cf.* Robert Briffault, *Breakdown*

which it draws the capacity of conquest. "Even the thieves themselves that molest the world beside them," declared Augustine, "are at peace amongst themselves."[3]

Though Christian theology has frequently expressed the idea of the total depravity of man in extravagant terms, it has never been without witnesses to the fact that human sin cannot destroy the essential character of man to such a degree that it would cease being implied in, and furnishing a contrast to, what he had become. It is not surprising to find this emphasis in Thomas Aquinas, who does not hold to the doctrine of total depravity.[4] Yet even Luther, who believes that nothing but the name of the "image of God" is left to sinful man, animadverts upon the significance of man's uneasy conscience, a phenomenon which can be understood only as the protest of man's essential nature against his present state. Augustine is very explicit in his affirmation that the evil of sin cannot completely destroy the goodness of what God has created in man: "And it was manifested unto me that those things be good, which yet are corrupted; which neither were they sovereignly good nor unless they were good could be corrupted: for if sovereignly good, they were incorruptible, if not good at all there is nothing in them to be corrupted. . . . But if they be deprived of all good they would cease to be. . . . So long therefore as they are, they are good: therefore whatsoever is, is good."[5]

The problem of the relation of man's essential nature to his sinful state unfortunately has been confused in the history of Christian thought by a difficulty which we have previously observed in the doctrine of original sin: Christian theology has found it difficult to refute the rationalistic rejection of the myth of the Fall without falling into the literalistic error of insisting upon the Fall as an his-

[3] *De civ. Dei*, Book IV, Ch. 12.
[4] Aquinas writes: "Sin cannot take away entirely from man the fact that he is a rational being, for then he would no longer be capable of sin. Wherefore it is not possible for this good of nature to be destroyed entirely." *Summa*, First Part, Third Number, Question 85, Art. 1.
[5] *Confessions*, Book VII. Ch. 12.

torical event. One of the consequences of this literalism, which has seriously affected the thought of the church upon the problem of man's essential nature, is the assumption that the perfection from which man fell is to be assigned to a particular historical period, *i.e.* the paradisical period before the Fall. This chronological interpretation of a relation which cannot be expressed in terms of time without being falsified must not be attributed to the authority of the Biblical myth alone. The Stoics, after all, also believed in a golden age of innocency at the beginning of the world, and thought that the equality and liberty which their natural law enjoined, but which were beyond the possibilities of actual history, were realities of that blessed period. Furthermore every individual is inclined to give a chronological and historical version of the contrast between what he is and what he ought to be; for he regards the innocency of his childhood as a symbol and a reminder of his true nature. Yet the Biblical myth must be regarded as the primary source of the Christian belief in a chronological period in which man had a perfection which he has since lost.

The effect of this literalism has been to bring confusion into Christian thought on the relation of man's essential nature to his sinful condition. In Protestant thought it aggravated the tendency toward extravagant statements of man's depravity[6] and confused the effort to moderate such statements by the admission that some little power of justice remained to man. For the remnant of original perfection which was conceded to man was falsely identified with the capacity for "civil justice,"[7] a capacity which is as obviously corrupted by sin as any other human capacity. In Catholic thought, chronological literalism encouraged the definition of the state of original righteousness as a special supernatural gift, a DONUM SUPER-

[6]The most extreme statement of the doctrine of total depravity is probably found in the Lutheran Formulary of Concord, in which we read: "They are also likewise repudiated and rejected who teach that our nature has indeed been greatly weakened but nevertheless has not altogether lost all goodness relating to divine and spiritual things."

[7]Cf. *Augsburg Confession,* Art. 18.

NATURALE which was added to the PURA NATURALIA, that is to the essential humanity which Adam had as man. In consequence the paradox, that sin is a corruption of man's true essence but not its destruction, is obscured in both Protestant and Catholic thought. In Catholicism the Fall means the loss of something which is not essential to man and does not therefore represent a corruption of his essence. In radical Protestantism the very image of God in man is believed to be destroyed.[8] And when Protestant thought recoils from such extravagance, it looks for the remnant of man's .original goodness in insignificant aspects of human behaviour.

The relation of man's essential nature to his sinful state cannot be solved within terms of the chronological version of the perfection before the Fall. It is, as it were, a vertical rather than horizontal relation. When the Fall is made an event in history rather than a symbol of an aspect of every historical moment in the life of man, the relation of evil to goodness in that moment is obscured.

II

ESSENTIAL NATURE AND ORIGINAL RIGHTEOUSNESS

It is impossible to do justice to the concept of the image of God and to the perfection of that image before the Fall without making a distinction between the essential nature of man and the virtue of conformity to that nature. Nothing can change the essential nature and structure, just as blindness of the eye does not remove the eye from the human anatomy. Not even the destruction of the eye can change the fact that the human anatomy requires two eyes. On the other hand the freedom of man creates the possibility of actions which are contrary to and in defiance of the requirements of this essential nature. This fact justifies the distinction between the essential structure and nature, and the virtue of conformity to it. Man may lose this virtue and destroy the proper function of his

[8]Karl Barth concedes only "that man is man and not a cat," when describing the sinful state of man. *Cf.* his brochure *Nein,* p. 27.

nature but he can do so only by availing himself of one of the elements in that nature, namely his freedom.

This fact prompted Irenæus to distinguish between the image and the likeness of God upon the basis of Genesis 1:26, a distinction which persisted in Christian tradition until the Reformation questioned its exegetical validity.[1] According to Irenæus the Fall destroyed the likeness but not the image of God. (In Greek the ὁμοίωσις but not the εἰκών: in Latin the *similitudo* but not the *imago*.) Luther was quite right in rejecting the theory from the standpoint of exegesis. The original text: "Let us make man in our image and after our likeness," represents no more than a common Hebraic parallelism. It certainly does not justify the later Catholic distinction between the *pura naturalia* and a *donum supernaturale*, the latter a special gift which God gave to man in addition to his natural endowment, a distinction which was reared upon Irenæus' original differentiation. Nevertheless, the distinction, properly limited and safeguarded, is helpful and even necessary.

It is important to distinguish between the essential nature of man and the virtue and perfection which would represent the normal expression of that nature. The essential nature of man contains two elements; and there are correspondingly two elements in the original perfection of man. To the essential nature of man belong, on the one hand, all his natural endowments, and determinations, his physical and social impulses, his sexual and racial differentiations, in short his character as a creature imbedded in the natural order. On the other hand, his essential nature also includes the freedom of his spirit, his transcendence over natural process and finally his self-transcendence.

The virtue and perfection which corresponds to the first element of his nature is usually designated as the natural law. It is the law which defines the proper performance of his functions, the normal harmony of his impulses and the normal social relation between himself and his fellows within the limitations of the natural order.

[1] *Cf.* Harnack, *History of Dogma*, II, p. 171.

Since every natural function of man is qualified by his freedom and since a "law" defining normality is necessary only because of his freedom, there is always an element of confusion in thus outlining a law of nature. It has nevertheless a tentative validity; for it distinguishes the obvious requirements of his nature as a creature in the natural order from the special requirements of his nature as free spirit.

The virtues which correspond to the second element in his nature, that is, to the freedom of his spirit, are analogous to the "theological virtues" of Catholic thought, namely faith, hope and love. They must be analysed at greater length presently. For the moment it is necessary to identify and validate them only provisionally as basic requirements of freedom. Faith in the providence of God is a necessity of freedom because, without it, the anxiety of freedom tempts man to seek a self-sufficiency and self-mastery incompatible with his dependence upon forces which he does not control. Hope is a particular form of that faith. It deals with the future as a realm where infinite possibilities are realized and which must be a realm of terror if it is not under the providence of God; for in that case it would stand under either a blind fate or pure caprice. The knowledge of God is thus not a supernatural grace which is a "further gift" beyond man's essential nature. It is the requirement of his nature as free spirit.

Love is both an independent requirement of this same freedom and a derivative of faith. Love is a requirement of freedom because the community to which man is impelled by his social nature is not possible to him merely upon the basis of his gregarious impulse. In his freedom and uniqueness each man stands outside of, and transcends, the cohesions of nature and the uniformities of mind which bind life to life. Since men are separated from one another by the uniqueness and individuality of each spirit, however closely they may be bound together by ties of nature, they cannot relate themselves to one another in terms which will do justice to both the bonds of nature and the freedom of their spirit if they are not related in terms of love. In love spirit meets spirit in the depth of the innermost essence of each. The cohesions of nature are qualified and transmuted by this relationship, for the other self ceases to be merely an object, serviceable to the self because of affinities of nature and reason. It is recognized as not merely object but as itself a subject, as a unique centre of life and purpose. This "I" and "Thou" relationship is impossible without the presupposition of faith for two reasons: (1) Without freedom from anxiety man is so enmeshed in the vicious circle of egocentricity, so concerned about himself, that he cannot release himself for the adventure of love. (2) Without relation to God, the world of freedom in which spirit must meet spirit is so obscured that human beings constantly sink to the level of things in the human imagination. The injunction, "love thy neighbour as thyself," is therefore properly preceded both by the commandment, "love the Lord thy God," and by the injunction, "be not anxious."

These ultimate requirements of the Christian ethic are therefore not counsels of perfection or theological virtues of the sort which merely completes an otherwise incomplete natural goodness or virtue. Nor can they be subtracted from man without making his freedom a source of sinful infection. They are indeed counsels of perfection in the sense that sinful man lacks them and is incapable of achieving them. But they are basic and not supplementary requirements of his freedom.[2]

This analysis of the matter leads to the conclusion that sin neither destroys the structure by virtue of which man is man nor yet eliminates the sense of obligation toward the essential nature of man, which is the remnant of his perfection. This sense of obligation is, in fact, the claim which the essential nature of man makes upon him in his present sinful state. The virtue which corresponds to the true nature of man therefore appears to sinful man in the form of law. It is the "good that I would" but which "I do not." It is "the commandment which was ordained to life" but which "I found to be unto death" (Romans 7), of which St. Paul speaks. It is unto death

[2] *Cf.* Emil Brunner, *Man in Revolt*, Ch. 5, c. 1.

because the law states the requirements without helping man to fulfill them. In fact it heightens sin by arousing sinful egotism to a more conscious defiance of the essential nature of man (Romans 7:7). It may also arouse sinful pride by tempting man to assume that he keeps the law because he knows it.[3] It is not possible for man to understand himself merely from the standpoint of the law within him, *i.e.,* from the perspective of the good which he knows he ought to do. Fully to understand himself he must know that he violates the law which he regards as his norm; but neither can he be fully understood, if it is not recognized that this law is the claim of his essential nature upon him.[4]

[3]This is the point of the Pauline passage: "Behold, thou art called a Jew, and restest in the law, and makest thy boast of God, And knowest his will, and approvest the things which are more excellent, being instructed out of the law; and art confident that thou thyself art a guide of the blind, a light of them which are in darkness, an instructor of the foolish, a teacher of babes, which hast the form of knowledge and of the truth in the law. Thou therefore which teachest another, teachest thou not thyself? thou that preachest a man should not steal, dost thou steal?" Romans 2:17–21.

This challenge is remarkably relevant to the whole self-righteousness of modern culture which imagines that a man's acceptance of ideals of justice and peace proves that it is some one else and not he who is responsible for injustice and conflict.

[4]The utopian illusions and sentimental aberrations of modern liberal culture are really all derived from the basic error of negating the fact of original sin. This error, more fully discussed in Chapter 4, continually betrays modern men to equate the goodness of men with the virtue of their various schemes for social justice and international peace. When these schemes fail of realization or are realized only after tragic conflicts, modern men either turn from utopianism to disillusionment and despair, or they seek to place the onus of their failure upon some particular social group or upon some particular form of economic and social organization.

Obviously there are varying degrees of sin and guilt and some men and nations are more guilty than others of "disobedience to the heavenly vision." Also there are specific evils in history, arising from specific maladjustments in social and political organization. But these evils can be dealt with most adequately, if men do not give themselves to the illusion that some particular organization of society might be found in which men would no longer stand in contradiction to the law of their

Significantly Luther, who is so anxious to prove the destruction of the image of God in man, is just as emphatic in insisting that the law, and man's uneasy conscience, are the first point of contact between God and man. This conscience is the righteousness of the sinner (*justitia peccatoris*). Man's own heart accuses him (*cor accusator*). Without faith this accusation leads to despair and with faith it may lead to repentance.[5] Man's uneasy conscience is, in other words, an expression of the law which is written in his own heart. Man is most conscious of this law in terms of the contrast and tension between it and his sinful actions. There are in fact interpretations of conscience which practically limit its expression to the uneasiness which follows, rather than to any specific guidance which precedes, the act.[6] While such interpretations are too narrow, it is probably true that conscience is primarily known to man in terms of the disquiet, the sense of inner conflict which expresses itself in all moral life.

Following St. Paul, Christian thought has consistently maintained that the law must be regarded, not simply as something which is

---

own being. Furthermore, particular virulent forms and types of sin in particular men and nations can be checked most successfully if it is recognized that these types are but aggravations of a general human situation.

Both modern liberalism and modern Marxism are always facing the alternatives of moral futility or moral fanaticism. Liberalism in its pure form usually succumbs to the peril of futility. It will not act against evil until it is able to find a vantage point of guiltlessness from which to operate. This means that it cannot act at all. Sometimes it imagines that this inaction is the guiltlessness for which it has been seeking. A minority of liberals and most of the Marxists solve the problem by assuming that they have found a position of guiltlessness in action. Thereby they are betrayed into the error of fanaticism. The whole history of modern culture, particularly in its more recent efforts to defend itself against inferior and more demonic cultures, is a pathetic revelation of the weakness and confusion which result from these illusions about the character of man.

[5]*Cf.* M. A. H. Stromph, *Die Anthropologie Martin Luthers*, pp. 111–14.

[6]*Cf.* Rudolph Hoffmann, *Das Gewissen*, pp. 100 ff.

given man either by revelation, or for that matter by the authority of society, but as written in the heart.[7] This can only mean that the requirements of action, dictated by man's essential nature, are a part of his real self. They stand outside of the self in action; that is why they are "law," and appear in the guise of something imposed from without and are only the "form of knowledge and of truth" (Romans 2:20). The particular content of the voice of conscience is of course conditioned by all the relativities of history. Men may be mistaken in their interpretation of what life is essentially; and conscience may be, in its very content, a vehicle cf sin. Yet even in its content the universalities of conscience are at least as significant as its varieties and relativities.[8] One must conclude that the real structure of life, the dependence of man upon his fellowmen for instance, which requires both organic and loving relations between them, asserts itself, in spite of all errors, against the confusion which human egotism and pride introduces into the relations of men.[9]

If this analysis be correct it follows that if Protestantism was right in rejecting the Catholic doctrine that the Fall had not altered man's essential nature because it had only destroyed a *donum supernaturale,*

[7]*Cf.* Romans 2:14–15: "For when the Gentiles, which have not the law, do by nature the things contained in the law, these, having not the law, are a law unto themselves: Which shew the work of the law written in their hearts, their conscience also bearing witness, and their thoughts the mean while accusing or else excusing one another."

[8]In the words of David Hume: "The epithets, sociable, good-natured, humane, merciful, grateful, friendly, generous, beneficent, or their equivalents are known in all languages and universally express the highest merits which human nature is capable of attaining." *An Enquiry Concerning the Principles of Morals,* Sec. II, Part i.

[9]There are of course instances in which practices which are almost universally condemned are actually enjoined by the customs of a particular group; and become the content of conscience for the individuals in that group through the prestige and influence of the custom. In such cases the moral life may be said to approach a state of total depravity. It is significant, however, that no group custom enjoins lying, stealing or murder indiscriminately, since such a law would lead to complete chaos within the group. There is thus always a limit to the relativity of law in the conscience of men.

it was wrong in asserting that man's essential nature had been destroyed. The Catholic doctrine presumably saw an alteration only in the virtue and not in the structure of man. But its definition of that virtue, namely man's communion with God and intimate contact with him, contains by implication a part of the essential structure of man, namely his transcendent freedom, which can be tolerable and creative only when it has found its source, end and norm in the will of God. This structure of freedom is revealed in the very bondage of sin; for it is by this capacity for the eternal that man transmutes his finite self into infinite proportions. It is by this capacity that he is able both to sin and to have some knowledge of his sin.

The disavowal of the historical-literalistic illusion, which places the original perfection of man in a period before an historical Fall, thus clarifies and corrects both Catholic and Protestant thought. Against Protestant thought it becomes possible to maintain that the image of God is preserved in spite of man's sin. In distinction from Catholic thought it is possible to eliminate the unwarranted distinction between a completely lost original justice and an uncorrupted natural justice. What is called original justice in Catholic thought really represents the requirements of human freedom in its most ultimate sense. Natural justice represents the requirements of man as creature. Both are corrupted by sin: but both are still with man, not indeed as realizations but requirements.

If however "before the Fall" is not an historical period the questions are: (1) Where is the locus of this perfection as requirement upon man; and (2) what is its character and content?

III

THE LOCUS OF ORIGINAL RIGHTEOUSNESS

If there is no historical period to which we may assign the *justitia originalis,* the original perfection, is it possible to find a locus for it? The complexity of this problem may be gauged in terms of an analogical but simpler question: Where is the locus of health in the life of a diseased organism? Obviously the seat of infection may be in one particular organ of the organism, so that the other parts are comparatively healthy. Yet disease in any part of the organism affects the whole. The whole organism is thus diseased. Yet there is some health as long as there is life. The very pains of disease are a testimony of this hidden health; for pain reveals that the normal harmony of the organism has been disturbed and is therefore health's indictment of disease. It is not possible to assign a particular locus to the residual health in the diseased body.

In the same way it is not possible to exempt "reason" or any other human faculty from the disease of sin. Since sin is the self's undue pride and exaltation, any force in human life which tends to keep the self in a normal position of subordination to God and coordination with its fellows must be regarded as an element of health, without which life would become completely self-destructive. While it is not possible to give such elements of health a particular locus, it is possible to find a locus for the consciousness and the memory of an original perfection. We have previously noted that the self which knows itself guilty is the transcendent self or, to speak more precisely, the self in the moment of transcending itself. The self in the moment of transcending itself exercises the self's capacity for infinite regression and makes the previous concretion of will its object. It is in this moment of self-transcendence that the consciousness and memory of original perfection arise. For in this moment the self knows itself as merely a finite creature among many others and realizes that the undue claims which the anxious self in action makes, result in injustices to its fellows.

The consciousness and memory of an original perfection in the self-as-transcendent must not be regarded as the possession of perfection. The fact is that the self-as-transcendent always assumes, mistakenly, that its present ability to judge and criticize the undue and unjust claims of the self in a previous action is a guarantee of its virtue in a subsequent action. This is not the case, for when the self acts it always uses the previous transcendent perspective partly as a "rationalization" and "false front" for its interested action. The action is therefore always sinful, even though it is important to recognize that there may be infinite gradations of interested and disinterested action and of pretension and self-deception in covering these actions.

Perfection before the Fall is, in other words, perfection before the act; but it is important not to give too narrow a connotation to the concept of "act." The self may act even when the action is not overt. It acts whenever, as anxious self, it thinks or moves for its own protection in the welter of perils and passions which constitutes its world. Every thought, mood or action which proceeds from the self as anxious, finite, and insecure has some taint of sin upon it. But there is no consciousness of sin in such sinful action because the self is perfectly unified in its action. Without such inner unity it could not act at all. It is when, after the action, it takes a position outside rather than inside itself, that it becomes conscious of the inordinate character of its action.

The consciousness of original perfection is not in some universal self in distinction to an empirical self. There are obviously not simply two selves in conflict with each other. But in every moment of existence there is a tension between the self as it looks out upon the world from the perspective of its values and necessities and the self as it looks at both the world and itself, and is disquieted by the undue claims of the self in action. These two perspectives of the self are clearly revealed, for instance, in the Pauline process of self-searching. He declares on the one hand: "For we know that the law is spiritual; but I am carnal, sold under sin." Here the sinful self looks at a reality which seems to be outside the self. It is the law. But in almost the same breath St. Paul declares: "Now then it is no more I that do it, but sin that dwelleth in me" (Romans 7:14, 17). Here the self as ultimate subject looks at the sinful self and declares that it is not itself. It is "not I . . . but sin." *The "I," which from the perspective of self-transcendence, regards the sinful self not as self but as "sin," is the same "I" which from the perspective of sinful action regards the transcendent possibilities of the self as not the self but as "law." It is the same self; but these changing perspectives are obviously significant.*

The tendency of Augustinian thought, particularly as expressed in the Protestant Reformers, to deny these complexities in favour of a simpler emphasis upon the corruption of man, must be attributed not merely to the illusions of literalistic interpretations of the Fall, but also to the fear that any concessions to man's self-esteem would immediately aggravate the sin of pride. This is a justified fear, since the whole history of human self-righteousness proves that man always judges himself not from the standpoint of what he does but from the standpoint of his knowledge of what he ought to do. Assuming that he obeys "the law" because he knows it, he throws the onus of disobedience upon his fellowmen. That is why the strictures of St. Paul against the self-righteousness of the "good" people of his day have a relevance to the moral problems of our own day, though this relevance is not understood in liberal Christianity.[1] The greatest sin of moralistic Christianity is its tendency to encourage the assumption that men are as good as the ideals of justice and love which they entertain. This sin modern Christianity shares, of course, and also borrows from the general moralism of our culture. Nevertheless this confusion does not justify extravagant theories of total depravity, and such theories are not convincing refutations of the error in liberal moralism.

In placing the consciousness of "original righteousness" in a moment of the self which transcends history, though not outside of the self which is in history, it may be relevant to observe that this conforms perfectly to the myth of the Fall when interpreted symbolically. The myth does not record any actions of Adam which were

[1] The paradoxical relation between "original righteousness" and sin is perfectly expressed by Pascal in the words: "Vanity is so anchored in the heart of man that . . . those who write against it want to have the glory of having written well; and those who read it desire the glory of having read it. I who write this have perhaps this desire, and perhaps those who will read it." *Pensées*, p. 149.

sinless, though much is made in theology of the perfection he had before the Fall. Irenæus, with greater realism than most theologians, observes that the period was very brief, sin following almost immediately upon his creation. Adam was sinless before he acted and sinful in his first recorded action. His sinlessness, in other words, preceded his first significant action and his sinfulness came to light in that action. This is a symbol for the whole of human history. The original righteousness of man stands, as it were, outside of history. Yet it is in the man who is in history, and when sin comes it actually borrows from this original righteousness. For the pretension of sin is that its act is not in history but an act of impartiality, a deed of eternity.

IV

THE CONTENT OF JUSTITIA ORIGINALIS AS LAW

We have seen that the original righteousness or perfection is present with sinful man as "law" and we have tentatively defined this law as derived from man's essential nature and have distinguished between organic structure and freedom in man's essential nature. We have suggested that what is usually known as "natural law" in both Christian and Stoic thought is roughly synonymous with the requirements of man as creature and that the virtues, defined in Catholic thought as "theological virtues," that is the virtues faith, hope and love, are the requirements of his freedom and represent the *justitia originalis.* This righteousness, we have suggested, is not completely lost in the Fall but remains with sinful man as the knowledge of what he ought to be, as the law of his freedom.

(*a*) In making a more detailed analysis of the content of the law of original righteousness it is necessary to emphasize that the distinction between the natural law which states the requirements of man as creature and the *justitia originalis* which states the requirements of man's freedom can be only tentative and provisional. The primary mistake of Catholic theory is precisely the sharp and absolute distinction which it makes between the two. It speaks of an original righteousness which was lost in the Fall and a natural justice which remains essentially uncorrupted by the Fall. This distinction obscures the complex relation of human freedom to all of man's natural functions, and the consequent involvement of all "natural" or "rational" standards and norms in sin. There is therefore no uncorrupted natural law, just as there is no completely lost original justice. The freedom of man sets every standard of justice under higher possibilities, and the sin of man perennially insinuates contingent and relative elements into the supposedly absolute standards of human reason. Undue confidence in human reason, as the seat and source of natural law, makes this very concept of law into a vehicle of human sin. It gives the peculiar conditions and unique circumstances in which reason operates in a particular historical moment, the sanctity of universality. The confidence of medieval Catholicism in the ability of an unspoiled reason to arrive at definitive standards of natural justice thus became the very vehicle of the sinful pretensions of the age. The social ethics of Thomas Aquinas embody the peculiarities and the contingent factors of a feudal-agrarian economy into a system of fixed socio-ethical principles.

The relativizing effect of both freedom and sin upon all historical norms may be illustrated by a few specific examples. In Catholic natural law all social relations, including family relations, are precisely defined. *Inter alia* it is maintained that the natural law prohibits birth control and also that it enjoins the supremacy of the husband over the wife. The prohibition of birth control assumes that the sexual function in human life must be limited to its function in nature, that of procreation. But it is the very character of human life that all animal functions are touched by freedom and released into more complex relationships. This freedom is the basis of both creativity and sin. Freedom in relation to sex may occasion license and it may also provide for a creative relation between the sexual impulse and other more complex and refined spiritual impulses. In its teachings in regard to sex, Catholic theories of natural law might

actually be more plausibly expressed in terms of the Lutheran concept of "order of creation" or *"Schoepfungsordnung."* For the concept of "order of creation" limits the law to a natural fact, such as
natural bisexuality for instance, and does not introduce some spe-
cious universality of reason. It is not possible to escape the natural
fact that the primary purpose of bisexuality in nature is that of
procreation. But it is not easy to establish a universally valid "law
of reason" which will eternally set the bounds for the function of
sex in the historic development of human personality.

For the supremacy of the male over the female, all orthodox
Christian theory finds additional support in Pauline-Biblical thought
so that its assurance about its supposed absolute standard is made
doubly sure, having the support of both the Bible and the law of
reason. It is important to realize that no definition of the natural
law-between the sexes can be made without embodying something
of the sin of male arrogance into the standard. The relation between
the sexes is governed on the one hand by the natural fact of sex
differentiation and on the other by the spiritual fact of human freedom. The natural fact that the woman bears the child binds her to
the child and partially limits the freedom of her choice in the development of various potentialities of character not related to the
vocation of motherhood. A rationalistic feminism is undoubtedly
inclined to transgress inexorable bounds set by nature. On the other
hand any premature fixation of certain historical standards in regard
to the family will inevitably tend to reinforce male arrogance and to
retard justified efforts on the part of the female to achieve such freedom as is not incompatible with the primary function of motherhood. The freedom, which is the unique capacity of humankind,
makes it difficult to set precise standards for all time for any kind of
relationship, including the relation between the sexes. The sinfulness
of man, on the other hand, makes it inevitable that a dominant
class, group, and sex should seek to define a relationship, which
guarantees its dominance, as permanently normative. There are of
course certain permanent norms, such as monogamy, which, con-

trary to the relativism of such Protestant sceptics as Karl Barth, are maintained not purely by Scriptural authority but by the cumulative experience of the race. About these universalities, amidst the relativities of standards, a word must be spoken presently.

The limitations of Catholic natural-law theories are revealed with equal clarity when applied to the field of international relations. The Catholic theory of a "just war"[1] is a case in point. The Catholic theory is infinitely superior to the Lutheran relativism and moral scepticism which finally leaves the Christian without any standards by which he might judge the relative justice of his nation's cause. Nevertheless, it assumes that obvious distinctions between "justice" and "injustice," between "defence" and "aggression," are possible. Contemporary history reinforces the clear lessons of the whole of history upon this point. Not all wars are equally just and not all contestants are equally right. Distinctions must be made. But the judgments with which we make them are influenced by passions and interests, so that even the most obvious case of aggression can be made to appear a necessity of defence; and even a war which is judged by neutral opinion to be wholly defensive cannot be waged with completely good conscience because the situations out of which wars arise are charged with memories of previous acts of aggression on the part of those now in defence.[2] This does not mean that the

[1] The Spanish Jesuit Suarez defines a just war as follows: "In order that a war may be justly waged, certain conditions must be observed and these may be brought under three heads. First it must be waged by a legitimate power. Secondly its cause must be just and right. Thirdly just methods should be used, that is equity in the beginning of war, in the prosecution of it and in victory." *Tractatus de legibus,* I, 9.

[2] The present European war is a case in point. The aggression of Germany is justified by the German rulers as nothing but a correction of the "injustices of Versailles." These claims are certainly spurious to a considerable degree and there are standards by which they may be judged to be so. Yet there is no "universal reason" to which an appeal may be made to arbitrate the point. Judgments upon the points at issue are relativized by geographic and political circumstances. And even those who are most certain that the German aggression is something more than a mere correction of a previous injustice cannot escape an uneasy con-

moralists who would refrain from all war, because the issues of any particular war are always filled with ambiguities, are right. The very same war which fails to yield an absolutely clear case of "justice" may yet concern itself with the very life and death of civilizations and cultures. Men do have to make important decisions in history upon the basis of certain norms, even though they must recognize that all historic norms are touched with both finiteness and sin; and that their sinfulness consists precisely in the bogus claim of finality which is made for them. The perennial mistake of rationalists, whether Stoic, Catholic or modern, is to exempt reason from either finiteness or sin or both and to derive universal rational norms from this confidence in reason.

While it is important to reject this error it is just as important to disavow the opposite error of the moral relativists, who deny every validity of general norms. In secular theory this relativism is the fruit of an extreme naturalistic empiricism. In the history of religious thought Lutheran orthodoxy tends to regard reason as so completely involved in the corruption of sin that it has no confidence in any "natural law" norms.[3] This conflict between a too simple rationalism and a too complete relativism may be resolved by a more dialectical analysis of the function of reason. Reason is in fact in an equivocal position between the self-as-subject and the self-as-agent of action, between the self as transcending itself and the anxious self in action. It is the servant of both. Its universal judgments, its effort to relate all things to each other in a system of coherence, can be alternately the instrument by which the self-as-subject condemns the partial and prejudiced actions of the sinful self, and the vehicle of the sinful self by which it seeks to give the sanctity of a false universality to its

---

science about the injustices which were, in fact, involved in the peace which ended a previous war.

[3]W. Wiesner's chapter in the symposium *Christian Faith and the Common Life* (Oxford Conference) is an interesting example of a modern Lutheran's complete rejection of all rational or "natural law" norms of conduct.

particular needs and partial insights. An analysis of the complex facts which underlie the conception of "natural law," and of conscience in general, must do justice to both aspects of reason.[4]

(*b*) Thus far we have considered only the tendency of Catholic thought to derive too unqualified moral norms from a reason which is presumed to be limited but uncorrupted and pure as far as it goes. The discussion of this error is, however, only a negative approach to the problem of a *justitia originalis*, which Catholic theory regards as wholly lost in the Fall. A positive approach reveals that what is known as "natural law" and what is known as "original righteousness" are intimately related to each other, not only by reason of a common involvement in sin but by reason of the fact that human freedom places the requirements of "original justice" as ultimate possibilities over the requirements of the natural law. There is no justice, even in a sinful world, which can be regarded as finally normative. The higher possibilities of love, which is at once the fulfillment and the negation of justice, always hover over every system of justice.

The *justitia originalis* of Catholic theology is, as we have seen, the virtue of the soul's perfect communion with God, its perfect subordination to God's will and a consequent perfect co-ordination of all its impulses and functions with one another. This virtue is merely defined more fully when it is divided into the three virtues of "faith, hope and love" which, according to Catholic theory, are the "theo-

---

[4]Calvin's attitude toward reason stands between the Catholic and the Lutheran viewpoint. His position lacks consistency but it is probably more consistent with the facts than either the Catholic or the Lutheran position. He writes: "Reason, by which man distinguishes between good and evil, by which he understands and judges, being a natural talent, could not be wholly destroyed but is partly debilitated, partly vitiated, so that it exhibits nothing but deformity and ruin." *Institutes,* Book II, Ch. ii, par. 12.

It is hardly logical to claim that something which is only "partly vitiated" exhibits "nothing but deformity and ruin." But there is at least an approach in this inconsistency to the fact that reason is both a servant of sinful self-love and an organ of judgment upon it.

logical virtues" which divine grace supplies to sinful man, thereby completing a structure of virtue which the Fall had left incomplete. Whether these virtues are ever vouchsafed even to the redeemed man in as complete a form as Catholic theories of sanctification assume, is a question which we must consider later.[5] It is important at this point to establish that they are never as completely lost in the Fall as Catholic theory assumes. The original righteousness which sinful man has supposedly lost is in reality present with him as the ultimate requirement of his freedom. Because man is not merely creature but also free spirit, and because every moral norm stands under higher possibilities by reason of his freedom, there is no moral standard at which the human spirit can find rest short of the standard of "faith, hope and love."

This character of the theological virtues as "law" to sinful man is perfectly revealed in the "thou shalt" of the law of love: "Thou shalt love the Lord thy God with all thy heart, and all thy soul, and all thy mind. This is the first and great commandment. And the second is like unto it, Thou shalt love thy neighbour as thyself." Here something is commanded and demanded. That means law. But what is commanded is a state of heart and mind, a harmony between the soul and God ("Thou shalt love the Lord thy God"), a harmony within the soul ("with all thy heart, and all thy soul, and all thy mind"), and a harmony between the self and the neighbour ("thy neighbour as thyself") which, if attained, would exclude all commandment. Such a commandment can be understood as stating an ultimate condition of complete harmony between the soul and God, its neighbour and itself in a situation in which this harmony is not a reality. If it were a reality the "thou shalt" would be meaningless. If there were not some possibility of sensing the ultimate perfection in a state of sin the "thou shalt" would be irrelevant. It is significant that philosophical treatises on morals have universally misunderstood the "law of love" because they lacked the concept of sin as a basis for their analysis.

[5] See Vol. II, Ch. 4.

Whether it is possible for any man, either by nature or by grace, to fulfill this commandment and to heal the disharmony between himself and God, his neighbour and himself, is a question which we must postpone until we consider the Christian doctrine of redemption.[6] For the moment we are interested only in validating the law of love as a vision of health which even a sick man may envisage, as the original righteousness which man does not possess but which he knows he ought to possess, since the contradiction in which he stands, and the consequent compulsion and submission in his relations to God, the neighbour and himself, are obviously not an ideal state of health.

The relation of the law of love to law as such is perfectly comprehended in the story of Jesus' encounter with the rich young man. The young man had "kept all the commandments"; but the commandments, the "law" in the more restricted sense, did not satisfy him and his continued uneasiness prompted the question, "What lack I yet?" This question, "What lack I yet?" suggests that what lies in the uneasy conscience of the sinner is not so much a knowledge that the ultimate law of life is the law of love as the more negative realization that obedience to the ordinary rules of justice and equity is not enough.

Jesus defines the more ultimate possibility toward which the young man is yearning in the words: "If thou *wilt be perfect,* go and sell that thou hast and give to the poor." What is demanded is an action in which regard for the self is completely eliminated. All simple moralism, which assumes that the law of life needs only to be stated in order to be obeyed, is refuted by the response of the rich young ruler to this demand: "He went away sorrowful for he had great possessions." For the moment it would appear that only the extent of the young man's possessions made it impossible for him to obey the ultimate law, for Jesus observes: "Verily I say unto you that a rich man shall hardly enter into the kingdom of heaven." But the disciples quickly realize that the command runs counter to the

[6] See Vol. II, Chs. 5–6.

anxieties of all men about themselves and their possessions. Their question, "Who then can be saved?" quickly and justly extends the predicament of the rich young man to include all men, since all men are involved in the sin of establishing their own security by what they have and what they are.

The answer of Jesus to this despairing question implies a complete acceptance of the viewpoint of the disciples. Jesus admits that the ultimate possibility of human life is beyond the capacity of sinful man: "With man this is impossible." It is an ultimate possibility of divine grace: "But with God all things are possible." Modern liberal theology has made much of the difference between the attitude of Jesus toward human nature and that of St. Paul. But the thesis which is both implied and asserted in this story is the same as that which is the burden of Pauline soteriology. It is suggested that the contradiction between man's essential nature and his sinful condition is insoluble from the standpoint of man's own resources and can be solved only from the standpoint of God's resources.

The explicit and implicit views of human nature which this story yields, may therefore be summarized as follows: (*a*) Man as sinner is not unmindful of the ultimate requirements of his nature as free spirit. He knows that any particular historical concretion of law is not enough. (*b*) He is not fully conscious of the nature of these ultimate requirements, and (*c*) he is not ready to meet these requirements once they are defined. These three propositions give an accurate account of the typical relation of "original righteousness" to man as sinner (Matt. 22:37–39).

The specific content of this higher law, which is more than law, this law which transcends all law, this original righteousness which even sinful man has, not as a possession but in his sense of something lacking, has been tentatively defined, and this definition must now be further explicated. It contains three terms: (*a*) The perfect relation of the soul to God in which obedience is transcended by love, trust and confidence ("Thou shalt love the Lord thy God"); (*b*) the perfect internal harmony of the soul with itself in all of its desires and impulses: "With all thy heart and all thy soul and all thy mind"; and (c) the perfect harmony of life with life: "Thou shalt love thy neighbour as thyself."

(a) The first of these three requirements is the most basic one, just as unbelief or mistrust is the basic and primal sin. This basic requirement of the love of God is identical with the two terms in the Pauline triad, "faith" and "hope." Without faith in God's providence the freedom of man is intolerable. Hope is subordinate to and yet identical with faith. It is faith with regard to the future. The future is the symbol of the unpredictable possibilities of eternity which may appear in time. Without faith and hope these possibilities represent an intolerable threat to man's little universe of meaning. They may in any moment introduce uncalculated and incalculable elements into the little system of meaning by which men live and by which they seek to maintain their sense of domestic security. History is not rational. At least it does not conform to the systems of rational coherence which men construct periodically to comprehend its meaning. These systems are inevitably anchored in some specific anchor of meaning, which is itself subject to the vicissitudes of history. History can be meaningful, therefore, only in terms of a faith which comprehends its seeming irrationalities and views them as the expression of a divine wisdom, which transcends human understanding. Faith in the wisdom of God is thus a prerequisite of love because it is the condition without which man is anxious and is driven by his anxiety into vicious circles of self-sufficiency and pride. As we have previously noted, the admonition, "Be not anxious," has meaning only in conjunction with the faith expressed by Jesus: "Your heavenly father knoweth that ye have need of these things."

It is not to be supposed that the faith, hope and trust which eliminate anxiety are simple possibilities of human existence, not even for those who have some knowledge of God in Christ, that is for those in whom Christian revelation has penetrated through the confusion of sin. How little this commandment, "Be not anxious," is a simple possibility can be tested by any honest preacher who delivers a homily upon the text and searches his soul sufficiently to know how anxious he is to have the approbation of his congregation on his exposition of the admonition, not to be anxious. Freedom from anxiety, in other words, is an ultimate possibility which man as sinner denies in his action. Even the man of faith does so, inasfar as he is sinner. It belongs to the perfection before the Fall. The sinful self is anxious about itself and yet it knows that it ought not to be.

It might be argued that this knowledge, that faith and trust are a requirement of human freedom, is not a natural endowment of man, but becomes known to man only as Christian revelation discloses the full dimension of human freedom and the reality of God as the master of that freedom. In terms of Biblical symbolism this would mean that Adam's perfection before the Fall is not fully understood until the "second Adam" defines it. This thesis is, at least partially, correct. For the Christian faith is not only an answer to the human situation of self-contradiction; it is a fuller and clearer revelation of that contradiction. The revelation of God as redeemer accentuates a previous knowledge of God as judge, for the simple reason that the revelation of His redemptive love clarifies His character of holiness, in terms of which human sin is judged. The anthropological consequences of this paradox are that faith in God's ultimate resolution of the contradiction in which man stands clarifies man's knowledge of that contradiction. He sees that his anxiety is due to his unbelief.

Yet even when this is not clearly seen some echo of the commandment, "Be not anxious," comes to man in his anxiety. The serenity of faith is not his possession but he knows that it ought to be. It is instructive that the same Stoicism which elaborates a "natural law" and a doctrine of *"conscientia"* in which the "law" for man as creature is defined also has a doctrine of the "law" for man as free spirit. It is the Stoic doctrine of ἀπάθεια, which demands a state of indifference toward all vicissitudes of life which are beyond man's power. This doctrine may be regarded as a precise indication of what is possible within terms of natural theology for man to know about the commandment, "Be not anxious," and about the requirement of serenity as a condition of health for the freedom of man. It is significant, however, that it is not possible to achieve freedom from anxiety within the limits of Stoic pantheism without destroying creativity in history. The god of Stoicism is not himself free spirit and Creator. In consequence ἀπάθεια means, on the one hand, a self-sufficiency of the human spirit purchased at the price of withdrawing the soul into itself and cutting all its connections with the problems and obligations of history.[7] On the other hand, lacking a doctrine of Creation, and, therefore, having no distinction between God and the world and none between the world as created and the world in sin, Stoicism counsels freedom from anxiety in the false faith that all things are good.[8] Stoic freedom from anxiety is thus involved in both a self-sufficiency, which does not do justice to man's actual dependence upon the world about him, and also in a determinism which does not do justice to the evil in history.[9] These errors reveal the limits of a

[7]Epictetus expresses this idea in the words: "Of things some are in our power and others are not. In our power are opinion, pursuit, desire, aversion, and in one word whatever are our own actions. Not in our power are body, property, reputation, command, and, in one word, whatever are not our own actions. . . . If you suppose that only to be your own, which is your own; and what belongs to others, such as it really is; no one will compel you; no one will restrain you; you will find fault with no one; you will accuse no one, you will not do one thing against your will; no one will hurt you, you will not have an enemy, for you will suffer no harm." *The Enchiridion*, I.

[8]In the words of Marcus Aurelius: "If so be the gods have deliberated in particular of those things that should happen to me, I must stand to their deliberations, as discreet and wise. For that a god should be an imprudent god is hard to conceive.—But if so be they have not deliberated of me in particular, certainly they have on the whole in general, and those things which in consequence and coherence of this general deliberation happen to me in particular I am bound to embrace and accept." *Meditations*, VI, 39.

[9]Marcus Aurelius expresses both sides of the Stoic doctrine in one paragraph: "Thou must comfort thyself in the expectation of thy dissolu-

pantheistic rationalism, seeking to come to terms with the problem of man's freedom and dependence. This problem can be solved only in terms of the Christian conception of divine Providence. It is nevertheless important to recognize that Stoicism defines something of the trust and serenity which even sinful man knows to be his ultimate good. This is a part of the original perfection which man does not have but knows he ought to have.

(*b*) The second requirement of *justitia originalis* is expressed in the words, "with all thy heart and all thy soul and all thy mind," in the Biblical law of love. This requirement and ideal possibility is that of a complete inner accord within the soul. This inner accord is not a reality in sinful man, because there is compulsion and submission within the self just as between the self and God and the self and society. But even sinful man knows that only such an inner harmony would represent complete health. The sinful soul does nothing with all its heart and soul and might. The effect of sin is that it would do the good but does not do it, that "to will is present with me; but how to perform that which is good I know not" (Romans 7:18), which is to say that every action betrays a "defect of the will" (Augustine), an inability to carry out a right general intention in the specific instance.

Idealists have traditionally explained this inner contradiction as the tension between the intelligible and sensible self, or between the universal and the empirical self. This explanation always has a certain plausibility because there is an actual difference between the self as transcendent and the self as agent of action. But the idealistic explanation disregards the unity of the self and obscures the fact that there is only one will. This will stands in contradiction to itself because it cannot do the good which it wills. The will is deficient in the specific instance to carry out the transcendent purpose because the motive power of the will in the specific instance is partly furnished by the

---

tion and in the meantime not grieve at the delay but rest contented in these two things: First, that nothing shall happen unto thee which is not according to the nature of the universe. Secondly, that it is in thy power to refrain from doing anything contrary to thine own proper god and inward spirit." *Meditations*, V, 10.

fears and anxieties of the anxious self; and these fears drive in a different direction from the transcendent general intention.

The anxious self invariably makes itself its own centre and end; but since the self transcends itself in infinite regression only God and not itself can be its centre and end. Thus there is an inner contradiction even in acts of obedience toward God. The fact that the act is one of obedience rather than of love means that it is not done with "all thy heart and all thy soul and all thy might." The self, inasfar as it is centred in itself, withholds perfect trust and faith and must be coerced. Yet it can never persuade itself that it is its own adequate centre and security. Therefore there is always a suggestion and memory of an ideal possibility in which this inner disharmony has been overcome. This memory refutes every doctrine of total depravity. But the actuality of inner tension refutes every doctrine of an unspoiled human goodness.

Inasfar as the self is centred in itself, it can offer only coerced obedience. Inasfar as the self transcends itself it knows the inadequacy of such reluctant attitudes. Therefore acts of obedience which fall short of love produce an uneasiness of conscience, only different in degree and not in kind from the uneasiness created by disobedience. The ideal possibility is always that "they may love the things which thou commandest and desire that which thou dost promise."

The perfect harmony of the soul with itself is thus a derivative of its perfect communion with, and love of, God. Where the love of God transcends obedience, the soul is centred in its true source and end without reservation. There are obviously no actions of sinful men which perfectly conform to this ideal possibility. The sense that an obedience which is less than love is not normative even though it is universal, is the *justitia originalis*. It is the sense that there ought not be a sense of ought; it is the "thou shalt" which suggests that there are no "thou shalts" in perfection.

(c) The love of the neighbour, the perfect accord of life with life and will with will, is, in the same manner, a derivative of perfect faith and trust in God. Without such trust man is involved in the vicious circle of anxiety and self-sufficiency which inhibits him from genuine concern for the needs of the neighbour. Love between man and man is thus but one facet of the total *justitia originalis*. It is also the final form of that righteousness. Love is the final requirement of human relations, if the freedom of the persons who are involved in mutual relations be considered.

Human personality has a depth and uniqueness which escapes the ordinary processes of knowledge. Those processes always tend to reduce the fellowman to a thing or object. Human as well as divine personality is obscured when the self seeks to understand the other merely as object of observation. The creative initiative of the other, the unique depth of personality in the other, is veiled by an approach which touches the surface of his life but does not penetrate to the secret of his being. The uniqueness of each individuality can be known in love but not in terms of general knowledge in which the self seeks to subordinate uniqueness in order to fit the "other" into the general categories of reason.[10]

Real love between person and person is therefore a relationship in which spirit meets spirit in a dimension in which both the uniformities and the differences of nature, which bind men together and separate them, are transcended. This is no simple possibility. Each soul remains, in a sense, inscrutable to its fellows. It is a possibility only by way of the love of God. All human love between person and person is frustrated by inscrutable mysteries in the heart of each person and by opaque "walls of partition" between man and man. Inasfar as human love is a possibility, therefore, it is always partly a relation between the soul and soul via their common relation to God. Inasfar as it is not a possibility it points to God as the final realization of the possibility. Where the love of God does not under-

---

[10]For a profound discussion of this problem see Martin Buber's *I and Thou* and also Nicolas Berdyaev's *Solitude and Society*. Berdyaev's treatment of the subject to partially vitiated by the dualistic assumption that the tendency to reduce the "thou" of the other self to "it" is but one aspect of the "degraded" character of all knowledge of objects. All external knowledge is thus regarded as an aspect of the "fallen" world.

gird and complete the relation of man to man, the differences which nature creates and sin accentuates, differences of geography, race, time, place and history, separate men from one another; and the similarities of nature and of reason may indeed unite men but not on the level of spirit and freedom.

The law of love is thus a requirement of human freedom; and the freedom of the self and of the other both require it. The freedom of the self is such that no rule of justice, no particular method of arbitrating the interests of the other with those of the self, can leave the self with the feeling that it has done all that it could. In its freedom it constantly rises above these laws and rules and realizes that they are determined by contingent factors and that they fall short of the ultimate possibility of loving the neighbour "as thyself." A sense of justice may prompt men to organize legal systems of unemployment insurance through which a general sense of obligation toward the needy neighbour is expressed. But no such system can leave the self satisfied when it faces particular needs among those who are the beneficiaries of such minimal schemes of justice. The freedom and uniqueness of the other also raise moral requirements above any scheme of justice. The other has special needs and requirements which cannot be satisfied by general rules of equity. It is significant that even in communist theory, the basic equalitarianism of the theory is transcended in its final vision of utopia. In that utopia even "bourgeois equality" is left behind for a state of perfection in which every one "will give according to his ability and take according to his need."

Love is thus the end term of any system of morals. It is the moral requirement in which all schemes of justice are fulfilled and negated. They are fulfilled because the obligation of life to life is more fully met in love than is possible in any scheme of equity and justice. They are negated because love makes an end of the nicely calculated less and more of structures of justice. It does not carefully arbitrate between the needs of the self and of the other, since it meets the needs of the other without concern for the self.

v

THE TRANSCENDENT CHARACTER OF JUSTITIA ORIGINALIS

Against pessimistic theories of human nature which affirm the total depravity of man it is important to assert the continued presence in man of the *justitia originalis,* of the law of love, as law and requirement. It is equally important, in refutation of modern secular and Christian forms of utopianism, to recognize that the fulfillment of the law of love is no simple possibility. Love is the law of freedom; but man is not completely free; and such freedom as he has is corrupted by sin. All historic schemes and structures of justice must take the contingencies of nature and history and the fact of sin into consideration. Since man transcends race and nation, time and place, no scheme of justice which regulates the interests of China and America, for instance, can stop short of affirming the interests of the individual in China less than the needs of the individual in America. But there is no simple possibility of relating these interests to each other in terms of a perfect coherence of love so that the man in China or America would affirm the interests of the man in America or China as much as he affirms his own. The human imagination is too limited to see and understand the interests of the other as vividly as those of the self. Furthermore the realization of any such system of harmony would require more than individual action. It would require the organization of vast economic and political structures in defiance of, and transcendence over, the contingencies of geography, the fortuitous differences of natural resources, etc. There is, therefore, no historic structure of justice which can either fulfill the law of love or rest content in its inability to do so.

The fact of sin introduces an even more stubborn force of corruption into the inertia of nature and finiteness. The man who is limited by time and place does not merely fail to sense the needs of others who live beyond the limits of his time and place. He resists the claim of their necessities upon his conscience and makes demands of his own which are incompatible with their interests. In both Stoic and Catholic theory special consideration was given to the situation created by the fact of sin by distinguishing between an absolute and a relative natural law. The former represents the demands of conscience without compromise with the fact of sin. The latter stated the legal and moral necessities of a sinful world. Thus the absolute natural law demanded complete liberty and equality. The relative natural law, on the other hand, defined the necessary coercion of government, the inequalities of property and class, including slavery, and the necessities of conflict. The absolute natural law outlawed war while the relative natural law recognized it as a necessary method of achieving justice in a sinful world.

Just as Catholic rationalism makes too complete a distinction between natural law and the *justitia originalis,* it also tends to differentiate too completely between a relative and absolute natural law. Nevertheless these distinctions correspond to actual realities in the moral experience, which modern secular and Christian utopianism disregards. The distinctions are too absolute because it is never possible to define the limits of the force of sin or of the ideal possibilities which transcend sin. One cannot, by definition, determine where and when an inequality of nature or history must be accepted as ineluctable fate and where it must be defied. Nor can one determine in advance where and when tyranny and injustice must be resisted even if such resistance results in overt conflict. If the distinction between relative and absolute natural law is made too sharp (as it is in medieval theory) the inequality and conflict which the relative law allows is accepted too complacently. There are no precise distinctions either between relative and absolute natural law, as there are none between natural law and the law of love, for the simple reason that the freedom of spirit is so enmeshed in the necessities of nature, and the health and sickness of that freedom are so involved in each other, that it is not possible to make rules isolating certain aspects of nature and sin without having them disturbed by the claims of the law of love as the requirement of freedom.

Yet it is better to make these distinctions, however arbitrary, than to dispense with them entirely as modern utopians do. The Christian utopians think they can dispense with all structures and rules of justice simply by fulfilling the law of love. They do not realize that the law of love stands on the edge of history and not in history, that it represents an ultimate and not an immediate possibility. They think they might usher in the Kingdom of God if only they could persuade men not to resist tyranny and thus avoid conflict. They do not recognize to what degree justice in a sinful world is actually maintained by a tension of competitive forces, which is always in danger of degenerating into overt conflict, but without which there would be only the despotic peace of the subordination of the will of the weak to the will of the strong.

The secular utopians of the eighteenth century added the love which transcends all law to the liberty and equality of a transcendent and absolute natural law, and fondly imagined that "liberty, equality and fraternity" constituted the law of "nature" in the exact sense of the word. They thought that these ultimate possibilities of human freedom transcending all history were not only simple possibilities of history but that they were actualities of nature as given. The combined influence of religious and secular utopianism has brought confusion into the whole problem of justice in the modern bourgeois-liberal world and incidentally complicated the problem of defending the genuine values of this world against the peril of a barbarism which has grown out of the decadence of our civilization.

Since Christianity measures the stature of man in terms of a freedom which transcends the necessities of nature but also finds that freedom corrupted by sin, it obviously has no simple answer to the question, whether the original righteousness, the perfection before the Fall, which sinful man retains as law, can finally become a realized fact of history. This is the problem which we shall analyse in its various facets and implications in the second volume of this treatise. In such an analysis it will be important to reconsider the almost forgotten issues which were once raised by the Protestant

Reformation. For the general answer of pre-Reformation Christianity was that the *justitia originalis,* the law of love, was not a possibility for natural man but that it could be realized by the redeemed man in whom "grace" had healed the hurt of sin. The Reformation took the fact of sin as a perennial category of historic existence more seriously and maintained that there is no point in history where history is fulfilled and where man's self-contradiction is ended. It therefore defined divine "grace" not so much as a divine power in man which completes his incompletion but as a divine mercy toward man which brings his uneasy conscience to rest despite the continued self-contradiction of human effort upon every level of achievement. This central issue of the Reformation has been forgotten in modern elaborations of Protestant thought in which even the reservations of Catholic theories of sanctification and perfection have disappeared. In consequence modern liberal Protestant interpretations of human nature and human destiny stand in as obvious contradiction to the tragic facts of human history, particularly contemporary history, as the more secular interpretations by which modern culture has been chiefly informed.

The complete contrast between the repudiation of Catholic optimism by the Protestant Reformation and the repudiation of both Catholic and Reformation pessimism about human nature in modern Protestantism is but one of many indications of the unresolved problems of Christian anthropology. As between Reformation pessimism and modern Protestant and secular optimism about the nature of man, the more moderate Catholic theories seem wise and reserved by comparison. Yet the Catholic synthesis broke down under the combined pressure of Renaissance and Reformation. The Renaissance regarded human nature and human history as a realm of unmeasured possibilities and felt that medieval religion failed to do justice to human freedom and human destiny. The Renaissance was right in this; but it was wrong in imagining that the possibilities of good would gradually eliminate the possibilities of evil. A false idea of progress was implicit in the curious compound of Christian eschatology and classical rationalism which was the foundation of Renaissance spirituality.

The Reformation on the other hand was obsessed with the fact that no historical distinctions between good and evil could have significance beside the fact that all these distinctions were eliminated at the final level of divine judgment, before which no man would be justified; and that the tremendous possibilities for realizing good in history had no meaning beside the fact that human nature and human history remained in terms of self-contradiction upon the highest as well as the lowest levels of moral and social achievement.

Both Renaissance and Reformation explored complexities of human nature beyond the limits understood in the "medieval synthesis." But the discoveries of each stood in contradiction to each other. Some of the confusions of modern culture about human nature arise from this unresolved contradiction. Others are derived from the fact that the Renaissance triumphed over the Reformation so completely that the insights of the latter were preserved only in a few backwaters and eddies of modern culture.

In how far and by what means it may be possible to bring Renaissance and Reformation insights about human nature into terms of fruitful interrelation is one of the primary problems to which we will address ourselves in the second volume of this treatise.

INDEX OF SCRIPTURAL PASSAGES

GENESIS 1:26, 190, 270; 1:27, 229;
1:31, 167; 3:7, 238; 3:12, 96; 3:13,
204; 3:17–19, 174
JOB 7:13–14, 43; 7:16–21, 128; 42:3,
5, 6, 168
PSALMS 8:4, 3; 49, 139; 51:4, 257;
139, 128
ISAIAH 2:12, 17, 223; 3:14, 223; 14:12,
13, 15, 180; 26:5, 223; 28:1–5, 190;
29:19, 224; 33:1, 192; 40:6, 8, 167,
168; 40:15, 17, 167, 168, 215; 44:6,
137; 44:14–17, 138; 45, 138; 47, 204,
214; 47:3–7, 189; 47:10, 138; 49:25,
224
JEREMIAH 25:15, 214
EZEKIEL 28:2–9, 138; 29:3, 139; 30:8,
190
AMOS 4:1, 223; 5:18, 140; 6:4, 223;
7:16, 17, 214; 8:4, 223
ZEPHANIAH 2:15, 189
WISDOM 2:23–24, 174
SIRACH 10:14, 183
II ENOCH 24:4, 180

MATTHEW 6:25, 183 289; 6:27, 168;
6:32, 183, 289; 10:39, 251; 19:16–
23, 287; 22:37–39, 286, 288
LUKE 1:52 ff., 224; 12:19–20, 139, 191
JOHN 8:44, 204
ROMANS 1:18–23, 140; 1:19–20, 127,
132, 252; 1:21, 181, 241; 1:25, 204;
1:26–30, 230, 231; 2:1, 197 222;
2:14–15, 275; 2:17-21, 273; 2:20,
275; 3:22, 23, 219–220, 261; 5:12,
173, 241; 7:7–8, 218, 250, 273; 7:10,
272; 7:11, 204; 7:14, 17, 278; 7:18,
292; 7:19, 272; 10:2–3, 199; 13, 221
I CORINTHIANS 1:26, 224; 2:11, 152;
4:3–4, 129, 257; 5:3, 152; 5:10–11,
230; 15:56, 174
II CORINTHIANS 11:3, 204; 12:20, 230
GALATIANS 5:19–21, 230
EPHESIANS 2:1, 174; 5:3–5, 230
COLOSSIANS 3:5–8, 230
HEBREWS 1:10–12, 169; 3:13, 204
REVELATION 12:9, 204; 18:7, 189

INDEX OF PROPER NAMES

Adler, Alfred, 44, 192
Æschylus, 10, 12
Ambrose, bishop of Milan, 261
Aquinas, Thomas, 153–154, 176, 187,
232, 248, 267, 281
Aristotle, 6, 7, 9–10, 113, 152, 214-
215
Athanasius, 175, 248
Augustine, 152–159, 161, 165, 169–
170, 173, 186, 215–216, 230–231,
239, 241, 243, 247, 261–262, 267,
292

Baillie, John, 127
Barth, Karl, 158, 220, 269, 283
Bentham, Jeremy, 107
Berdyaev, Nikolai, 172, 294
Bergson, Henri, 37
Bosanquet, Bernard, 76–80

Bruno, Giordano, 19, 63–64, 218
Buber, Martin, 133
Butler, Bishop, 109

Calvin, John, 154, 158–159, 161, 187,
221, 242–244, 247, 262, 285
Carritt, E. F., 80
Chrysippus, 9
Chrysostom, 154
Clement, 144, 172, 229
Cœlestius, 247
Comte, August, 108–109, 195–196
Copernicus, 19

Dante, 217
Democritus, 9
Descartes, R., 20, 71, 72, 195–196
Dewey, John, 110, 111, 113–114
Duns Scotus, 172

Eckhardt, Meister, 58, 61–62
Engels, Friedrich, 44–48, 195
Epictetus, 291
Epicurus, 9, 98–99, 122

Fichte, J. G., 83, 89, 90, 120
Francke, August, 84
Freud; Sigmund, 34, 36, 42–44, 52–
  53, 121

Gentile, Giovanni, 79
Gilson, Etienne, 122
Godwin, W., 103
Gregory of Nyssa, 153, 172–173, 176,
  188, 229

Harnack, Adolf, 262
Hegel, G. W. F., 80, 93, 116–118,
  195–196, 263
Heidigger, J. J., 162, 183–184
Helvetius, 102, 106
Heraclitus, 8
Herder, J. G. von, 85, 87, 88
Hobbes, Thomas, 24, 25, 70, 71, 73,
  99, 100–101, 106, 121
Hocking, W. E., 117, 256
Holbach, P. H. T., 97–98, 106
Horney, Karen, 44, 192
Hume, David, 71–73, 107–108, 275

Irenæus, 173, 176, 261, 270, 280

James, William, 73
Jones, Rufus, 136
Justin Martyr, 172

Kant, Immanuel, 76–77, 118–120, 133
Kierkegaard, Soren, 44, 75, 81, 163,
  170–171, 182, 242–243, 245, 251–
  252, 254, 263
Kraemer, Henrik, 201

Laski, Harold, 205–206
Lavater, J. C., 85–86
Lawrence, D. H., 238
Leibnitz, G. W. von, 81, 115–117
Lenin, Nikolai, 46
Leon, Philip, 204, 212
Locke, John, 71–73, 101–102
Lombard, Peter, 243–244
Lovejoy, Arthur O., 88–89
Luther, Martin, 60, 84, 121, 160–
  161, 176, 183, 187, 200, 218, 232,
  244, 267, 270, 274

Machiavelli, Niccolo, 218
Mannheim, Karl, 196
Marcus Aurelius, 291
Martineau, James, 256
Marx, Karl, 35–36, 46, 93, 97
Mead, George, 56–57
Menninger, Karl, 234–235
Mercer, J. Edward, 135
Mill, James, 107
Mill, John Stuart, 107
Mirandola, Pico della, 21
Montaigne, M E. de, 19, 22, 64–65

Nicholas of Cusa, 61, 62, 63
Nietzsche, F. W., 8, 11, 24, 25, 34–
  36, 39, 41, 82, 83, 86, 88, 91, 121
Novalis, 85

Oman, John, 126
Origen, 153, 171, 229

Parmenides, 6
Pascal, Blaise, 187, 202, 243, 257,
  265, 279
Paul, 127, 129, 132–133, 139–140,
  152, 173–174, 181, 199–200, 204,
  218, 219–220, 221, 222, 224, 241,
  248–250, 252, 255, 257, 261, 272–
  273, 274–275, 278, 288
Pelagius, 245
Petrarch, 19
Philo, 172
Plato, 6–7, 30–31, 172
Plotinus, 78, 155

Rauschenbusch, Walter, 246
Ritschl, Albrecht, 178
Rousseau, J. J., 42, 83, 85, 94, 105,
  106, 121
Royce, James, 78, 79
Russell, Bertrand, 188, 189, 191, 193,
  253

Saint Simon, 108
Scheler, Max, 162, 164
Schelling, F. W. J. von, 254
Schiller, J. C. F. von, 27, 33
Schlegel, A. W. von, 85
Schleiermacher, F. D. E., 65, 84, 85,
  86, 87, 89, 246, 247
Schopenhauer, Arthur, 34, 38, 39
Seeley, J. R., 210
Seneca, 10
Sophocles, 10, 12

Spener, P. J., 84
Spinoza, Baruch, 114, 115
Stout, G. E., 74
Suarez, Francisco, 283
Swinburne, A. C., 3

Tennant, F. R., 247
Tertullian, 205

Vinci, Leonardo da, 19

Whitehead, Alfred, 112, 113
Wiesner, W., 284
Williams, N. P., 229, 230, 261
Wolff, Christian, 81

Zeno, 8, 10
Zinzendorf, N. L. von, 84

INDEX OF SUBJECTS

Absolute, 78, 79, 83
Anarchy, 38, 51, 59–61
Angst, 184
Anxiety, 43, 44, 168, 182–186, 192–
193, 250–252, 264, 271–272, 278,
290–291, 293
Aristotelian, 6, 152, 153, 154, 227,
232
Atonement, 142–148
Augustinian, 233, 279

Body, 7, 12, 13, 41, 54, 82, 116, 151–
152, 154, 167, 232
Bourgeois, 65–68

Capitalism, 20, 67, 102–103
Cartesian, 71
Catholicism, 59, 61, 201–202, 220–
221, 268–269, 275–276, 280–286,
297, 299
Christ, 28, 132, 142–146, 163–164,
266
Conscience—Easy, 93–122, 131; Uneasy, 17, 53, 143, 161, 196, 237,
256, 265–267, 274, 279, 293
Creation, 12, 28, 31, 32–33, 94, 131–
136

Death, 98–99, 167, 173–176
Devil, 180–181, 254
Donum superadditum, 154, 248, 271
Donum supernaturale, 270, 275
Dualism, 147, 173, 175

Enlightenment, 93, 96–99, 102–103,
298
Epicurean, 18, 49
Eros, 31–32
Eternity, 124–126, 144, 147–148, 253,
276

Evil, 2, 23–24, 96–104, 113, 114, 119,
120, 133, 134, 135, 167–169, 173,
254, 299–300

Faith, 183, 271, 289
Fall, 154, 160, 172, 174, 179–180, 238,
245, 248, 266–270, 275–276, 281
Fascism, 20, 23, 50–53, 82, 89, 104,
210, 212, 219, 249
Finite, 150, 167–177, 178–203
Forgiveness, 142–145
Form, 10–12, 17, 21, 26–53, 123, 135
Freedom, 14, 16, 17, 22, 24, 27, 28,
40–43, 55–56, 57–61, 74, 95–96,
99–106, 119–120, 124–126, 146–147,
162–166, 178–186, 197, 243–248,
250–264
Freudian, 24, 35, 36, 42, 43, 44, 52,
53, 238

God—as Creator, 131–136; as Judge,
62, 92, 129, 131–132, 136–144, 147–
148, 224–225, 290; as Mercy, 142–
144, 148; as Redeemer; 143, 290;
as Will, 28–29, 57–60; as Word,
130
Good, 119, 120, 134, 167, 299–300
Greek Classicism, 6, 7, 9, 12, 17, 21,
22, 61, 77, 116, 119, 186, 246
Grace; 299

Hedonism, 106–107
Hegelian, 32–33, 36, 45, 83, 251
Hellenistic Christianity, 147, 172–
173, 228–230, 232–233

Idealism, 12, 13, 18–20, 22–23, 27–29,
32, 75–81, 90–92, 112–120, 124,
170, 292
Ideology, 46, 48, 182, 194–197

Idolatry—of Church, 216, 218; of Reason, 13, 76, 165–166; of Sense, 233–240; of State, 209–212, 214, 216, 218
Incarnation, 144, 147
Individuality, 6–7, 14–17, 21–23, 54–71, 76–78, 81–92, 117–118, 123, 167, 170, 271–272, 294
Injustice, 110, 179, 252

Judgment, 16, 132
Justitia Originalis, 265–300

Kantian, 32, 119

Liberalism, 5, 53, 110, 145–146, 178, 274, 279, 299
Logos, 6, 28, 32, 114, 135
Love, 286–288, 292, 295–299
Lutheran, 220–222, 282–284

Man, as collective man, 83, 92, 118, 208–219, 249; contingency of, 86, 178, 185, 197–198, 212, 213, 251–252; as contradiction, 1, 17, 290, 293, 299–300; as creature, 16, 18, 19, 56, 58, 78, 92, 111, 146, 150, 166–167, 270–271, 276, 290–291; his deception, 203–207; as essential man, 7, 242, 267–270, 275–276; as evil, 7, 16–18, 23–24, 29, 60, 116, 119, 120, 150, 172; as good, 2, 18, 24, 93–94, 112; his guilt, 94, 200, 219–227, 235, 238, 257, 258; as image of God, 13, 18, 150–176, 266–270, 276; his insecurity, 188–198, 207, 212, 235–236, 249, 252, 256; involved in necessity, 16, 181, 197–198, 242–243; his pretenses, 1, 194, 196, 198, 205, 211, 212, 216, 218, 280; his responsibility, 241–264; as self-transcendent, 1, 2, 4, 14, 55, 68–69, 72, 75, 122, 124, 146, 150, 162–166, 175, 204, 206, 270, 276, 278–279, 293; his sensuality, 179, 185–188, 228–240; as sinner, 16–19, 23, 29, 92, 94, 121, 137, 140, 142, 168, 288, 292; his stature, 16, 18, 47, 96, 124–126, 161, 298; his total depravity, 248, 266–280, 296; as unique, 4, 6, 21–24, 55–56, 58, 62–64, 70, 71, 81, 128, 271, 294; his virtue, 2, 9, 93–96, 104–112,

117, 161, 286; his will, 15–16, 23, 58, 80, 85, 105, 119, 188, 242–246, 292; his will-to-power, 25, 41, 42, 44, 82, 86, 178, 189, 192–194, 211, 226, 227
Marxian, 20, 23, 33, 34–36, 43–48, 49–50, 51–53, 94, 103–104, 141, 195–197, 205–206, 274
Materialism, 9, 19, 44–52
Matter, 6, 47
Meaning, 164–166
Messianic, 141–144
Mind, 6, 7, 11, 12, 47, 56–57, 75, 77, 154, 179
Mysticism, 14–16, 37, 58, 61–63, 77–79, 125–126, 135–136, 157–158, 166

Naturalism, 4, 18–20, 22–24, 49, 69, 75, 81, 92, 99–102, 104–112, 134
Natural Law, 60, 141, 221, 278–298
Natural Theology, 160
Nature, 3–4, 17–19, 26–27, 32, 40–41, 54–56, 95–102, 104–110, 181, 295, 298
Neo-Platonism, 10, 14, 21, 157, 169
Nietzschean, 24, 49–50, 91–92
Nous, 6, 7, 14, 112–114, 133–135

Order of Creation, 282
Original Sin, 229, 232, 241–264

Paradox, 3, 18, 23, 37–38, 75, 77, 120, 161, 163, 166, 175
Pelagian, 245–248, 260
Perfection, 184–185, 268–269, 270, 290, 298–299
Pietism, 82–84
Platonism, 6–7, 23, 30–32, 144, 153, 171, 227, 229
Pride, 3, 11, 41, 42, 66, 80, 186–203, 208–219, 228, 256
Priesthood of believers, 60, 202
Progress, 24, 141
Prophetic, 137–142, 214–216, 223–227
Protestant, 5, 59–61, 148, 200–202, 218, 221, 268–269, 275–276, 279

Rationalism, 7, 13, 18–21, 31, 49, 51, 63, 64, 85, 89, 284
Reason, 1–2, 6–8, 27–28, 50–51, 75–76, 100, 106–116, 119, 123, 134, 155, 162, 165–166, 281, 295

Reformation, 5, 148–149, 160–161, 218, 279, 299–300

Renaissance, 5, 18, 21–23, 59, 61–65, 68, 70, 148, 218, 299–300

Repentance, 255–260

Resurrection, 63, 177

Revelation, 17, 126, 129, 130, 201, 289–290; general, 15, 28, 127, 130, 131–136, 143; special, 15, 28, 127, 130, 132, 142–143

Romanticism, 8, 20–21, 28–29, 33–34, 36–43, 50, 51–53, 81–92, 105, 121

Self—as object, 2, 4, 6, 14, 55, 72, 278, 284; as subject, 2, 14, 72, 272, 278, 284; in action, 75, 255, 258–260, 275, 277, 278; in contemplation, 75, 255, 258–260, 277, 278

Sex, 171–172, 228–232, 235–240, 281–282

Sin, 16–18, 76, 92–94, 116, 117, 120–121, 137–138, 140, 147–149, 168, 171–172, 174–177, 178–207, 249, 250, 266, 267, 269, 276, 278, 280, 281, 284, 292; collective sin, 208–227; inevitability of, 251–254, 262–263; responsibility in, 255–260, 262–263

Sorge, 183–184

Soul, 6–7, 13, 31–32, 55, 63, 73, 82, 116, 151–155, 158–159

Spirit, 3–4, 14–17, 27–29, 40–43, 47–48, 55–56, 57–58, 60–61, 63–64, 112, 114, 117, 151–152, 162, 251, 258–260

State, 79–81, 209–219

Stoicism, 6, 7, 8, 10, 19, 95, 215, 268, 280, 284, 290, 291, 297

Utopia, 273, 298

Vitality, 10–12, 17, 20–21, 26–53, 123, 135

War, 283–284